WAFC Speaker Series
95th Annual Convention
"Advancing the Food Industry
Through Education & Leadership"
Hilton Hawaiian Village
Honolulu, Hawaii
April 9-13, 2016

GABBY

A Story of Courage, Love, and Resilience

❧

Gabrielle Giffords
and Mark Kelly

with Jeffrey Zaslow

SCRIBNER

New York London Toronto Sydney New Delhi

SCRIBNER
A Division of Simon & Schuster, Inc.
1230 Avenue of the Americas
New York, NY 10020

First Scribner trade paperback edition October 2012

SCRIBNER and design are registered trademarks of The Gale Group, Inc.,
used under license by Simon & Schuster, Inc., the publisher of this work.

For information about special discounts for bulk purchases,
please contact Simon & Schuster Special Sales at 1-866-506-1949
or business@simonandschuster.com.

The Simon & Schuster Speakers Bureau can bring authors to your live event.
For more information or to book an event, contact the Simon & Schuster Speakers Bureau
at 1-866-248-3049 or visit our website at www.simonspeakers.com.

DESIGNED BY ERICH HOBBING

Manufactured in the United States of America

3   5   7   9   10   8   6   4   2

Library of Congress Control Number: 2011050578

ISBN 978-1-4516-6106-4
ISBN 978-1-4516-6107-1 (pbk)
ISBN 978-1-4516-6109-5 (ebook)

In memory of
Christina-Taylor Green, Dorothy Morris,
John Roll, Phyllis Schneck, Dorwan Stoddard,
and Gabriel Zimmerman

And in memory of Jeffrey Zaslow, 1958–2012

CONTENTS

GABBY

CHAPTER ONE

The Beach

I used to be able to tell just what my wife, Gabby, was thinking.

I could sense it in her body language—the way she leaned forward when she was intrigued by someone and wanted to soak up every word being said; the way she nodded politely when listening to some know-it-all who had the floor; the way she'd look at me, eyes sparkling, with that full-on smile of hers, when she wanted me to know she loved me. She was a woman who lived in the moment—every moment.

Gabby was a talker, too. She was so animated, using her hands as punctuation marks, and she'd speak with passion, clarity, and good humor, which made her someone you wanted to listen to. Usually, I didn't have to ask or wonder what she was thinking. She'd articulate every detail. Words mattered to her, whether she was speaking about immigration on the floor of the U.S. House of Representatives, or whether she was alone with me, talking about her yearning to have a child.

Gabby doesn't have all those words at her command anymore, at least not yet. A brain injury like hers is a kind of hurricane, blowing away some words and phrases, and leaving others almost within reach, but buried deep, under debris or in a different place. "It's awful," Gabby will say, and I have to agree with her.

But here's the thing: While Gabby struggles for words, coping with a constant frustration that the rest of us can't fathom, I still know what she's thinking much of the time. Yes, her words come haltingly or imperfectly or not at all, but I can still read her body language. I still know the nuances of that special smile of hers. She's still contagiously animated and usually upbeat, using her one good hand for emphasis.

And she still knows what I'm thinking, too.

There's a moment that Gabby and I are going to hold on to, a moment that speaks to our new life together and the way we remain connected. It was in late April 2011, not quite four months after Gabby was shot in the head by a would-be assassin. As an astronaut, I had just spent five days in quarantine, awaiting the last launch of space shuttle *Endeavour,* which I'd be commanding. It was around noon on the day before the scheduled liftoff, and my five crew members and I had been given permission to see our spouses for a couple of hours, one last time.

We'd be meeting with our wives on the back deck of this old, rundown two-story Florida beach house that NASA has maintained for decades. It is on the grounds of the Kennedy Space Center, and there's even a sign at the dirt road leading to it that simply says "The Beach House." The house used to have a bed that astronauts and their significant others would use for unofficial "romantic reunions." Now it's just a meeting place for NASA managers, and by tradition, a gathering spot where spouses say their farewells to departing astronauts, hoping they'll see them again. Twice in the space shuttle's thirty-year history, crews did not make it home from their missions. And so after a meal and some socializing as a group, couples usually break away and take private walks down the desolate beach, hand in hand.

The 2,000-square-foot house is the only structure on the oceanfront for more than twenty-five miles, since NASA controls a huge chunk of Florida's "space coast." Look in any direction and there's nothing but sand, seagulls, an occasional sea turtle, and the Atlantic Ocean. It's Florida pretty much the way it was centuries ago.

On our previous visit to this spot, the day before my shuttle mission in May 2008, Gabby and I were newlyweds, sitting in the sand, chatting about the mission, her upcoming election, and our future together. Gabby reminded me of how very "blessed" we both were; she often said that. She felt we needed to be very thankful for everything that we had. And we were.

The biggest problem on our minds was finding time to see each other, given our demanding careers in separate cities. It seemed complicated then, the jigsaw puzzle that was our lives, but in retrospect, it was so simple and easy. We couldn't have imagined that we'd return for a launch three years later and everything would be so different.

This time, Gabby entered the beach house being pushed in a wheelchair, wearing a helmet to protect the side of her head where part of her skull was missing. It had been removed during the surgery that saved her life after she was shot.

While the others at the house had come in pairs (each astronaut with a spouse), Gabby and I showed up with this whole crazy entourage—her mother, her chief of staff, a nurse, three U.S. Capitol Police officers, three Kennedy Space Center security officers, and a NASA colleague assigned to look after Gabby for the duration of my mission. The support Gabby now needed was considerable, and certainly not what my fellow crew members expected in their final moments with their wives. Instead of an intimate goodbye on a secluded beach, this became quite the circus. It was a bit embarrassing, but the men on my crew and their spouses were 100 percent supportive.

They understood. Gabby had just logged sixteen arduous and painful weeks sequestered in a Tucson hospital and then a Houston rehab center. She had worked incredibly hard, struggling to retrain her brain and fight off depression over her circumstances. For her doctors and security detail to give their blessings and allow her to travel, this was how her coming-out needed to be handled.

My crewmates and their wives greeted Gabby warmly, and she smiled at all of them, and said hello, though it was clear she was unable to make real small-talk. Some words and most sentences were still beyond her. Everyone was positive, but everyone noticed.

As I watched Gabby try to navigate the social niceties, I was very proud of her. She had learned since her injury that it could sap her energy and her spirits to be self-conscious about her deficiencies or her appearance. So she had found ways to communicate by employing upbeat hand motions and that terrific smile of hers—the same smile that had helped her connect with constituents, woo political opponents, and get my attention. She didn't need to rattle off sentences to charm a bunch of astronauts and their wives. She just had to tap into the person she's always been.

*　*　*

After we settled in at the beach house, I said to Gabby: "Want to go down to the ocean?"

"Yes," she said. "Yes, swim in the ocean."

Though Gabby grew up in Arizona, a daughter of the desert, she loves the ocean more than anyone I've ever known. She first saw the Pacific as a kid, traveling with her parents and sister through Mexico and Central America. They'd spend weeks at a time driving up and down the Pacific coast in a station wagon or camper. She loved to swim, to look for shells, to people-watch. Later, the Atlantic became equally alluring for her, including this stretch of beach, where we walked and swam together before my previous space flights. On those visits, Gabby had enjoyed swimming well offshore. And I admired how she engaged the other spouses so they all could shake off their nervousness over the risky missions ahead. She had just the right touch, embracing the duties that came with being the commander's wife, while also being completely down-to-earth and making everyone feel welcome.

But this time, of course, she was dependent on the kindness of others.

Her nurse took her into the bathroom and got her into her swimsuit. Though it was a warm day, she needed sweatpants and a jacket, since her injury leaves her cold so much of the time. Gabby helped dress herself the best she could, using her left hand, but she was limited. (Because she was shot in the left side of her brain, which partially controls the right side of the body, her right hand remained mostly useless and still, an appendage on her lap.)

When Gabby got out of the bathroom, those assisting her helped her into a special chair that emergency medical crews use when they have to carry people down stairs or out of the wilderness. It took three of them to lug her in that chair through the sand, step by step, a hundred yards toward the ocean. It was low tide, which made for a longer walk. I knew exactly what Gabby was thinking on this awkward journey down from the beach house. She was thinking what I was thinking; how desperately we both longed for the life we used to have together.

When the chair reached the water's edge, I thanked the men who carried Gabby for their efforts, and they lowered her to the ground. We unstrapped her, and after we helped her to her feet, she was able to navigate the hard, wet sand, taking a few steps, leading slowly with her left leg. That's when our support team moved back on the beach, trying to keep a respectful distance so Gabby and I could be alone.

In the days immediately after Gabby was injured, I had considered stepping down as commander of this shuttle flight. I was unsure of whether I'd be able to focus completely on the mission, and didn't know when Gabby would be leaving intensive care. But once she began improving and I returned to training, I found myself fantasizing about the possibility that Gabby would recover enough to join me on this beach on this day—the day before liftoff. That became a goal of ours. Now here we were.

It turned out to be a pretty amazing moment, a gift of serenity at a time when both of us were caught in the brightest of spotlights. The day before, millions of TV viewers had watched grainy, unauthorized footage of Gabby walking slowly and deliberately up a tarmac staircase and onto a plane in Houston to fly here for the launch. It had been taken by a cameraman in a distant, hovering news helicopter. Meanwhile, within twenty-four hours, 700,000 people were expected to descend on central Florida's east coast to see me and my crew blast off in the space shuttle. And yet, here at the water's edge, all of that attention felt very far away.

Gabby and I were focused only on each other, an intimacy heightened by all we'd been through, and by this isolated spot on the planet. Except for my crewmates and their wives walking a ways down the beach, stick figures in the distance, there was no sign of humanity to the south, the north, or off into the horizon. If we ignored our support team on the sand behind us, it felt like it was just the two of us. So neither of us turned around to look.

Inch by inch, I helped Gabby walk a dozen steps into the water, which splashed midway up our thighs. Given that hole in her skull, a fall could be deadly, so I remained alongside her, holding her arm and her waist, balancing her. I was being vigilant, but it was also nice to be so close to her.

Though the water was warm, an almost perfect 75 degrees, it was at first too cold for Gabby. Still, with the splash of each wave, she moved forward, determined to regain some small part of her former life.

What happened next was almost magical. As Gabby gazed out across the Atlantic with wide eyes and this huge, happy grin, I felt almost mesmerized just looking at her face. And that's when it hit me: For the first time since the shooting, Gabby looked absolutely joyous.

"Awesome!" she said. "Awesome."

The water started feeling warmer to her. The sky was clear and very blue. "You really love this, don't you, Gabby?" I said to her.

"Yes, yes," she answered. It almost brought a tear to my eye, seeing her so happy.

Gabby sat in her chair with her feet in the water. I sat in a chair next to her.

"You know what would be great?" I said. "In the future, we ought to buy a small house near the ocean, so you can swim."

"Yes," she said. "Great!"

"Maybe we'll get a little fishing boat. Or a sailboat. Maybe on a lagoon, somewhere where the water is warm."

"Yes!"

It felt good to tell her this, to talk about a plan that had nothing to do with a medical treatment or physical rehab or speech therapy.

"Waves," Gabby said. "Ocean!"

She then became quiet, preferring the soft sound of the waves to her halting voice.

I studied her face, which was luminous. In a lot of ways, she still looked like the beautiful, vivacious woman I'd fallen in love with. But there were differences. Her head was misshapen because of the missing piece of skull and the collection of excess cerebral-spinal fluid. She no longer had that full blond mane familiar to so many people from photos taken before she was shot. Her hair, which had been shaved for surgery, was very short, and had grown back in her natural dark-brown color. And she now had a full set of scars: one on her neck from her tracheotomy, one on the left side of her forehead, marking the spot where the bullet entered her brain, one over her right eye, which was also damaged in the attack, and a set of scars toward the top of her head that allowed her neurosurgeons the access they needed to save her life. Though she used to wear contact lenses, she now had to wear glasses. Because of her injuries, she'd lost about 50 percent of her vision in both eyes.

I took it all in. "You look great, Gabby," I said. And she did. Despite everything.

Gabby smiled at me. She knows I'm a sucker for that smile of hers. Then she looked back out toward the horizon and her smile widened as the waves lapped against her feet.

I knew what she was thinking: That in this brief moment, it felt as if everything was almost back to normal. That maybe, someday, she'd be whole again.

CHAPTER TWO

A New Year

"Spoon," Gabby said. "Spoon."

This was the word in her head and on her lips on the afternoon of February 13, five weeks after the shooting.

She was sitting in speech therapy holding a photo of a wooden chair and staring intently at it. She was trying, almost desperately, to describe what she was looking at.

"Spoon," she said again.

Angie Glenn, her speech therapist, a young woman of good humor and great patience, corrected her. "No, Gabby, not a spoon," she said. "It's something you sit in. You sit in a . . ."

"Spoon," Gabby said.

Angie tried again. "You sit in a . . ."

Gabby wished she could answer. That was clear by the intense look on her face, by the way she moved her left hand in a slight circle, as if the motion might bring her the word. But she couldn't come up with it.

Angie decided to move on. "A chair," she told Gabby. "You sit in a chair."

I had recently begun taping Gabby's therapy sessions here at The Institute for Rehabilitation and Research, TIRR Memorial Hermann, the rehabilitation hospital in Houston where Gabby had come to recover from her injuries. The video camera was on a tripod, and we often forgot it was there. I was making the tapes partly to chart Gabby's progress, and partly to have a record of all she went through, in case she ever wanted a road map of her journey. I'd end up recording dozens of painstaking therapy sessions just like this one.

On this day, the next photo in Angie's pile was of a lamp.

"Yes, yes, yes," Gabby said. She recognized it, but couldn't produce the word.

Angie offered a hint. "You turn on the . . ."

"Spoon," Gabby said. She knew as soon as she said it that she was wrong. She scrunched her face, closed her eyes, tried to think.

"You turn on the . . ." Angie said. "It's an 'L' word. You turn on the . . ."

Gabby stared at the picture on the table in front of her.

"Think of an 'L' word," Angie said. "What word do you say to Mark?"

This Gabby could answer very clearly. "I love you," she said.

"Right!" Angie said. "An 'L' word." She tapped the photo. "This is the same sound. You turn on the lllll . . ." Angie rolled the letter on her tongue, but Gabby couldn't follow through.

"Cheeseburger," she said, finally. She knew that wasn't it. She sighed, looked down at her lap, and readjusted herself in her wheelchair.

"Are you frustrated? Do you need a break?" Angie asked.

"Yes, yes," Gabby told her, relieved. That's about when I entered the room, bearing tulips, which I presented to Gabby with a light kiss. It was the eve of Valentine's Day.

I asked her, "What kind of flowers are these?"

"Chicken," she told me. That was another word she was inexplicably stuck on in those early days.

I gave her a clue. "It's your favorite flower." She looked at the tulips, then at me. She didn't answer.

I wasn't always comfortable pushing Gabby and testing her. I knew this was all terribly hard for her, and that she often felt like she was disappointing us. But her doctors had told us that engaging and challenging her would help her brain repair itself. We had to help her think.

Angie offered Gabby something to mull. "These aren't roses, they're . . ."

"Tulicks!" Gabby said triumphantly. She'd gotten it. Almost.

"Tulips," Angie corrected. "Yes, Gabby, tulips. Mark brought you tulips."

"Tulips," Gabby said.

Angie returned to the photo of the lamp. "You turn on the . . ."

"Lice," Gabby said. She'd gotten close. Angie helped her: "Light."

"Light," said Gabby. Then they both looked over at the flowers, which were attached to a balloon with the words "I love you" on it.

"Tu-lips," Gabby said. As Valentine's Day approached, I was happy to hear her deliver those two syllables, and Gabby was happy to have said them. Both of us were learning to appreciate small victories.

*　*　*

Five weeks earlier, when 2011 began, the new year was shaping up to be a very meaningful one for Gabby and for me. We were both excited by the prospects and the possibilities. Maybe it would be the best year of our lives. Gabby would be returning to Congress for a third term, I'd be returning to space for a fourth time, and we also had high hopes that Gabby would finally become a mother.

She had just won a close reelection to the U.S. House in a campaign that had been draining and disturbing. She was troubled by the hostile political rhetoric, and we both worried that the angry discourse might even descend into violence. But now that the election was over, Gabby was her usual optimistic self. She looked forward to redoubling her commitment to serving her constituents in southeastern Arizona, including those who didn't like her or her positions. "I represent them, too," she liked to say.

As for me, I was at a turning point in my career as an astronaut and naval officer. NASA's space shuttle program was winding down—I'd be commanding the second-to-last mission—and the next step for U.S. space exploration was uncertain. NASA and its contractors had begun laying off thousands of workers, a dispiriting acknowledgment that it would be years before the government again launched astronauts from U.S. soil. Given my age, almost forty-seven, and the fact that the need for astronauts was dimming, I knew I'd likely be going into space for the last time. It was bittersweet, of course, but I was committed to ensuring that my last mission was executed as flawlessly as possible. In simple layman's terms, I didn't want to screw up. Yes, I looked forward to savoring one last view from on high. But I also wanted to again prove to myself that I was worthy of the promises of space exploration.

Gabby, the hardest worker I knew, understood such ambitions and ideals, and what it would take in 2011 to see them through.

Meanwhile, on the personal front, Gabby and I hoped that 2011 would be the year we finally could have a child together. Gabby knew it would have been tough to be pregnant or give birth during an election year. Her schedule was too crazy. She didn't get enough sleep. We wouldn't have enough time together. So our strategy had been to wait until the election was over.

Gabby, who turned forty in 2010, was in great health and her doctors assumed she could get pregnant naturally. The problem wasn't her, it was me. I was a divorced father of two teenaged daughters when I married Gabby in 2007, and surgery to reverse my vasectomy hadn't worked. So Gabby and I enrolled in a program where my sperm was harvested directly from me and mixed with eggs that were harvested from Gabby, who'd been taking fertility drugs. Our doctor at Walter Reed Army Medical Center said our chances for success were better than 40 percent.

We hoped Gabby would be pregnant by Valentine's Day. We couldn't have fathomed that instead she'd be in a hospital, trying to say the names of simple objects.

And yet, when Gabby and I look back at the week before she was shot, we see certain moments that foreshadowed the life we're now living.

Gabby and I had gone to Rome for four days just before New Year's, touring the country with Gabby's parents, Gloria and Spencer. They're terrific traveling companions; they love art and food and meeting people from other cultures. Gloria, as a gifted painter and longtime art conservator and historian, was like our own private tour guide for the trip. It was a short but lovely vacation. We saw the Pope at midnight mass. We toured museums. We ate at great restaurants.

Spencer, who has had degenerative disc injuries in his back, was mostly in a wheelchair in those days, and it usually fell to me to push him wherever we were going in Rome. That wasn't easy. He weighs about 250 pounds and the streets and sidewalks weren't exactly smooth. At one point we visited a spot near the Coliseum where the Romans used to hold chariot races, and Gabby got a kick out of watching me push her father around. "It's like my dad is the chariot and you're fill-ing in for the horses," she said, laughing.

After Gabby's injury, when I'd push her in her wheelchair, I'd sometimes think of that trip to Italy, and I was grateful that Gabby is less than half her father's weight. "Remember how I had to push your dad up those hills in Rome?" I'd say to her. "In comparison, pushing you is a breeze."

Gabby and I have a lot of nice memories of Rome, including just relaxing in bed together in our room in the small hotel. It was pretty romantic. The window was open, with the sounds of Italy rising from the streets below, and we found ourselves talking about what our mar-riage would look like in the year ahead, and in the years after that.

"Our lives are so full now," I said at one point. "Just finding time to be together takes all this scheduling. Adding a baby to the mix is going to increase the magnitude of everything."

But Gabby was undaunted by the prospect of motherhood. "We'll figure it out," she said. "We'll find solutions. I'm not worried. I'm excited."

That's how Gabby had run her entire life. I'd learned not to doubt her ability to do anything, or to overcome any challenge. Given my age and the fact that I already had two wonderful children, I could have gone either way on the question of having a baby. But that day in bed with Gabby, seeing again how she yearned to be a mother, I was envel-oped by her faith and confidence that everything would work out. She had waited a long time to find me, and to build her career. "Having a baby is really important to me," she said, and that made it important to me.

One night in Rome, Gabby and I broke away from her parents and had dinner with an official from the European Space Agency and the physicist heading a major project on my space shuttle mission. We were on the top floor of this terrific restaurant, and talk turned to poli-tics in both Italy and the States. Gabby and I explained how heated her election had been.

"It's gotten so nasty," I said. "It's almost like people are going to get violent."

Gabby agreed with me, though she always had a way of putting a positive spin on a negative discussion. "Yeah, things have gone a bit over the line," she said. "We'll just have to figure out a way to pull it back a little."

We flew home to the States and spent New Year's Eve in Charleston, South Carolina, at the annual retreat known as Renaissance Weekend. When people hear about this event, they always think that you're dressing up like a knight and eating giant turkey legs. But it's actually just a relaxed, nonpartisan gathering where people from different walks of life, many of them very accomplished, gather to discuss issues and have fun together. This year, Gabby sang in the Renaissance Weekend choir, which puts together smart, funny lyrics about current events.

A lot of people bring their children, and Gabby and I came with my daughters, Claudia and Claire, then fifteen and thirteen. The girls love these annual weekends, too. They get to spend time with Olympic athletes, Nobel laureates, scientists, professors. Over the years, we've met Ted Sorensen, a speechwriter for John F. Kennedy; Thurgood Marshall, Jr., son of the Supreme Court justice; Li Lu, a student leader of the 1989 Tiananmen Square protests; and the diplomat Joseph Wilson and his wife, Valerie Plame, the covert CIA agent whose identity was famously leaked by political opponents in 2003.

For a guy like me, the son of cops, it's a crowd I certainly wasn't hanging out with as a kid. But I feel fortunate that I can offer such experiences to my girls. It's a perk of being an astronaut married to a rising young politician; we get invited places. Over the years, we've made some close friends at Renaissance Weekend—such as the NPR host Scott Simon and his wife, Caroline—who'd end up being there for us in unexpected ways in the wake of Gabby's injury.

The New Year's Eve celebration at this year's retreat was fairly low-key, and near midnight, Gabby and I found ourselves sitting at a table, thinking about the twelve months we'd just been through. Her reelection campaign had been so wearying and hard. "The coming year will be better," I told her, and she agreed.

"Absolutely," she said. "A lot of good things are going to happen."

On Sunday, January 2, Claudia and Claire flew home to Houston to go back to school, and Gabby and I drove north together, toward Washington, D.C., where, on Wednesday, she'd be sworn in for her third term. I took three days off from work so I could be with her.

The weather was pretty rotten on our drive, a lot of rain, but we were grateful just to be alone together. Given our crazy schedules, there are many days each year when we're apart. Granted, ours was not the usual marriage, but it was working for us because we valued the time we did have for each other. People would say we acted like perpetual newly-weds, which sounds pretty saccharine, but that's how we felt.

Sure, maybe we'd argue more if we lived in the same city. Maybe we'd get on each other's nerves more. Maybe a baby would add an unavoidable level of tension. We understood that. But on the other hand, maybe our bonds became stronger because we logged an hour or two every night on the phone. A lot of married couples share house-holds, but don't carve out any time to talk. Our relationship had forced us to focus on each other night after night. We had to listen. We had to respond. And you know what? I kind of had a thing for Gabby's voice. She was so intelligent, so eager to hash out ideas. Talking to her was the favorite part of my day.

That was especially true when we were actually together. On this drive to Washington, our conversation turned to the next career steps for each of us. Gabby was weighing the idea of running for the U.S. Senate in 2012, if the incumbent, Jon Kyl, a Republican, chose to retire. She was also considering passing on that race, and instead, wait-ing until 2014 to run for governor of Arizona.

Gabby was troubled by some of the policies of Governor Jan Brewer, especially her signing of Arizona SB 1070, the act that required local law enforcement officers to determine the immigration status of people they suspected could be in the country illegally. The bill encouraged racial profiling and shifted attention away from the real problem: the federal government's failure in its duty to secure our borders and fix our broken immigration system. Gabby's 9,000-square-mile congres-sional district borders Mexico for 114 miles, and she has devoted much of her public life to finding ways to better secure the border. Still, she felt that SB 1070, which stirred anger and protests nationwide, had damaged her state's reputation, hurting business and tourism.

A part of Gabby felt a calling to run for governor, to do what she could to improve policies—especially in education and budget man-agement—that she considered destructive. She had other worries, too, about her state's housing crisis, its vulnerability to the economic downturn, and the deep problems in the health care system, including the inadequacies of mental-health policies.

Gabby was a raging optimist, but she was also a pragmatist, and as we drove north, I saw both sides of her. She knew it would be hard for her, a Democrat from Tucson, to win statewide office. Arizona is a red state, with passionate conservatives wielding a lot of influence, and those Democrats who are able to succeed usually come from Phoenix, where their voters and campaign contributors are more plentiful. (The last time a Tucsonan had won a statewide election was in 1976, when Dennis DeConcini was elected to fill a vacant seat in the U.S. Senate.)

"I don't know that I could win the governor's race or a Senate seat," Gabby told me. "But someone has to do something for the sake of Arizona. Maybe I'm the someone. Maybe I have a duty to run."

Later on the drive, talk turned to my future. Gabby was always the biggest dreamer. Nothing was going to hold her back, and she didn't want anything holding me back, either. The Navy had loaned me to NASA for the astronaut program, and Gabby thought that when I left NASA, I ought to aim high. Maybe I could be an admiral.

"Gabby, I've been at NASA, and essentially out of the Navy, for fifteen years," I reminded her. "I don't know if the Navy would want me as an admiral." Gabby was undeterred. She didn't just think I should come to Washington to seek a spot on the Joint Chiefs of Staff. She thought I ought to be *chairman* of the Joint Chiefs. "That's not a very realistic idea," I told her, shaking my head at her audacity.

"Well, you'd be great," Gabby told me. "And you'd enjoy yourself, too."

Being married to Gabby was like hanging out with a full-time motivator. It was hard to be lazy or unenthusiastic when she was making plans for your life.

On Monday night, after we pulled into Washington, we had dinner with Senator Kirsten Gillibrand of New York and her husband, Jonathan. Gabby had gotten very close with Kirsten and a few other women on the Hill, including Representative Debbie Wasserman Schultz of Florida. There aren't a lot of young women in Congress, and when they find and like each other, the bond is pretty powerful.

Not all women share a passion for talking about government regulations or the differences in various congressional districts. When Gabby would meet legislators like Kirsten or Debbie, women who seemed sort of like her, she had to pick their brains, learn their secrets, and share her own.

Over that dinner in D.C., Gabby asked Kirsten how she handled having two young kids and a political career. Since Kirsten became a senator, Jonathan had taken a larger role in caring for the kids, and Gabby was intrigued by the ways in which the couple made everything seem doable. In 2008, when Kirsten was in the House, she became just the sixth woman to give birth while serving in Congress. In the year ahead, Gabby hoped to join her on that short list.

The next morning, Tuesday, January 4, we headed over to Walter Reed to meet with Mark Payson, the physician overseeing Gabby's fertility treatments. I'd already donated sperm, which had been frozen, and on January 20, Dr. Payson planned to remove eggs from Gabby, fertilize them for a couple days in a dish containing my thawed sperm, after which he'd be implanting them back into her.

Very few people knew that we were trying to have a baby. Most of Gabby's colleagues and staffers had no idea. We'd kept it to ourselves. But this was not the first time we'd been through this process. Once, when Gabby was going her usual thousand miles an hour for her job, she lost track of exactly when she was supposed to take the medication. After she learned the mix-up meant she would have to start all over again, she was tearful but resolute. "It's OK," she said. "On the next try, I'll be more careful."

Another time, she was in Tucson for meetings and to see constituents, and a snowstorm on the East Coast kept her from making it back to see her doctor in Washington. By the time she landed in D.C., her cycle was off. Another disappointment. She'd have to try again.

The next attempt, in August 2010, was just three months before the toughest election of Gabby's career. Although there were no mix-ups in her medication, and no blizzards to delay her, doctors worried that the campaign stresses and Gabby's lack of sleep would affect her chances. She went ahead with the surgery, but doctors weren't able to extract as many eggs as we hoped.

Now, for this 2011 attempt, our third, Gabby was determined to get everything right. She asked Dr. Payson to carefully go over all the medicines and procedures. "So when do I take this," she asked, "and when do I take that?" She was focused like a laser beam, the way she'd get at congressional hearings about border issues or solar energy or space exploration. She wanted to understand everything. She also made sure that, for this round, she was getting lots of sleep and exercise.

She made an appointment with Dr. Payson for six days later, Monday, January 10, at 7:00. She planned to fly home to Tucson on Friday, and then back to Washington on Sunday, so she could be sure to make it to the appointment. We were a little nervous, but the anticipation was exciting. If everything worked out, she'd soon be pregnant.

* * *

Wednesday, January 5, was a special and memorable day on a lot of fronts. Gabby was sworn in for her third term, and those of us who loved her were there to proudly cheer her on. But January 5 was also the day Gabby made a decision that would change her life forever, a decision made with the best of intentions and an open heart, but with ramifications that would impact the lives of other people in terrible ways. January 8, 2011, was the day six people were shot to death in Tucson, and thirteen people, including Gabby, were wounded. But we also can't help but think back to January 5, the day the dominoes of that tragedy were set in motion.

That morning began with an open house in Gabby's office in the Longworth House Office Building. Her staffers invited everyone in their Rolodexes, and as a tribute to Gabby, almost everyone wanted to come. About three hundred people showed up—Gabby's friends, constituents, colleagues, all sorts of people she'd met over the years in Washington. Her parents were there and so were mine.

The open house is a nice tradition before the swearing-in ceremony, and Gabby really loved saying hello to people, thanking them if they played a role in helping get her reelected.

"So great to see you," she'd say, again and again, and she meant it. She'd remember names, children's names, hometowns, and the particular issue that might be on someone's mind.

A guy from Raytheon, the defense contractor, stopped by. Raytheon is the biggest private employer in Tucson, and Gabby bantered with him about the new SM-6 air-defense missile. "So I hear you're going to deliver it on time and on budget, right?" she said. She had a friendly way of putting people at ease while also letting them know she was watching things closely. She kidded with a lobbyist from the United Services Automobile Association, which insures military families. "I hope you guys are taking good care of those veterans," she said. As the line inched forward, she saw a constituent from Arizona she'd met during the campaign. "Hey, thanks for making the trip to Washington," she said. "So what do you need? You want someone to take you over to the White House? Maybe I can do it later in the week."

On days like this, watching the ease with which she hugged everyone, Gabby reminded me of Bill Clinton on the campaign stump. Like him, she had great personal skills, and an ability to look people in the eye and listen to their concerns. I know people are suspicious of politicians and their motives. And yes, Gabby wanted to be liked and to win elections. But she also completely cared about her constituents and the issues that moved or upset them. As my mother liked to say, "Gabby is pure of heart, always thinking of the betterment of everyone else." That's a pretty good endorsement from a mother-in-law, I'd say. Too bad we couldn't put it on Gabby's campaign posters.

I don't want to give the impression that we all thought of her as Saint Gabby. But if you had seen her that day in her office, you'd know what I mean. The line of well-wishers stretched out into the hallway, and snaked through the outer office and into Gabby's private office. She gave each visitor her full attention. It was as if she were the bride at a wedding reception, except she was in a knit suit rather than a bridal gown.

I stood with her for a while, like a fidgety groom, saying hello to people, but then I got bored and started wandering around the office, looking at the pictures on the walls. Gabby, on the other hand, would have stood there hugging and talking until springtime if that's what it took to see everyone.

Gabby's mom, Gloria, is a great photographer as well as an artist, and she took photos of everyone passing through the office. Gabby's staffers have since mailed a lot of those photos on to the people in them. No one realized it at the time, of course, but it was as if everyone was getting one last keepsake of themselves with Gabby as she was before her injury.

The open house went three hours, an hour longer than scheduled, because of the mob of visitors and the attention Gabby paid to everyone. That put her behind for the rest of the day.

Next on her agenda, she had to cast a vote for the next Speaker of the House. Because the Republicans had won the majority of seats in the 2010 elections, it didn't really matter who Gabby voted for: the GOP's John Boehner was going to win. But Gabby knew her vote would have ideological ramifications in her district and among her peers. That meant it wasn't a decision she could take lightly.

Arizona's 8th District has more registered Republicans than Democrats, and a great many independents. Gabby, a moderate herself, had to be politically astute and constantly mindful of how non-Democrats among her constituents would view her every decision. Though she considered Nancy Pelosi to be a friend and valued party leader, she knew a vote for Nancy wouldn't play well with the conservatives back home, many of whom had vilified Nancy when she served as Speaker. Gabby would need to make a political decision, and that meant not supporting Nancy, who had supported her throughout her congressional career.

Gabby and her chief of staff, Pia Carusone, had spent days talking through the question of the vote for Speaker. Just thirty years old, Pia is precociously smart and terrifically wise about the inner workings of elected office. Like Gabby, she views government service as a high calling. But both of them understood that to survive in Washington, and to win elections back home, they had to accept and indulge political realities.

None of us knew Gabby's decision until we were sitting in the visitor's gallery, watching her cast her vote. I think she got a kick out of keeping us in suspense. In the end, she was one of just two representatives to vote for Georgia's John Lewis, the legendary civil rights leader. I smiled. That wasn't even a name we'd talked about. But it was a smart way to go: Gabby had found a way to avoid controversy by using her vote to honor a man who deserved recognition.

It continued to be a very hectic day, rushing around with my parents and Gabby's parents in tow. Gabby and I took turns pushing her dad in his wheelchair, in and out of elevators and down the halls of Congress. Then, when late afternoon came, it was hard for me and Gabby because it was time to say goodbye.

I needed to be back in Houston for work first thing Thursday morning. So Gabby walked me out to the street, where her operations director, Jennifer Cox, was waiting to drive me to the airport. We hugged, and I said, "I'm proud of you. Enjoy the new term." Of course, I didn't know that would be my last time seeing her whole and healthy. But it was sad just the same, like all of our many goodbyes.

As that Wednesday wound down, and our parents headed for home, Gabby found herself back in her office with Pia, thinking about the weekend.

"So what's on the agenda when I'm in Tucson on Saturday?" she asked.

Pia said that there was a memorial service in the early afternoon for a campaign supporter who had just died. The morning was free.

"I have to wear a suit anyway for the memorial service," Gabby said. "Why don't we do a Congress on Your Corner?" Gabby had already held a couple dozen of these events in her career, and she thought they were an important part of her responsibilities. She felt constituents deserved the chance to ask her questions, to air grievances, and to meet the people on her staff who might be able to help them.

Pia tried to dissuade her. Gabby had been going nonstop all during the 2010 campaign, and in the months since. "Why don't you take Saturday for yourself?" Pia said. "Give yourself a break. And it might be too late to set things up, anyway."

"No, let's do it," Gabby told her. "I want to start off the new term strongly. And there's so much going on in Washington. Let's hear what people think of everything."

Normally the Congress on Your Corner events—dubbed COYCs by Gabby's staffers—take two weeks to organize. Now here was Gabby, asking to set this one up on just two and a half days' notice. Pia knew that it was tough to tame Gabby's enthusiasm for encounters with constituents. COYCs were always scheduled for ninety minutes to two hours, but usually lasted four hours. That was Gabby. It was hard to stop her.

And so Pia relented. "Let me e-mail Ron and Gabe and see if we can pull it together," she said.

Ron Barber had been Gabby's district-office director since 2006. Born in England, he had retired from Arizona state government after a long career helping to run programs for people with developmental disabilities and mental illness. Now, at age sixty-five, he served as a much-appreciated voice of wisdom and experience for Gabby.

Gabriel Zimmerman, thirty, was director of community outreach for Gabby in Tucson, and she always said he brightened the office there with his positive energy. When enraged constituents were calling on the phone, or when Gabby's staffers felt overwhelmed with tedious duties and wondered whether it was time to find another line of work, Gabe was like a twenty-first-century Jimmy Stewart character—tall, handsome, and filled with idealism. "We're so lucky to have this job," he'd say to his colleagues. "We're lucky to serve constituents, to serve the country. Hey, we get to help people. How many jobs are there where you really get to do that? It's great, isn't it?"

Rather than complain about having to quickly organize a COYC for this upcoming Saturday, upsetting his weekend plans, Gabe was enthusiastic, as usual. He promised to get on it right away. "It'll be easy," he said. "I can do it in my sleep. No problems." Other staffers in Tucson also rose to action.

Ron and Gabe huddled and came up with a location to host the event—a Safeway supermarket in northwest Tucson. They liked that spot because the surrounding neighborhoods had a diverse group of constituents. Coincidentally, this was the same location as Gabby's first COYC event in January 2007. The two staffers began to update her policy-paper handouts for the event.

Gabby knew she'd need to get to that memorial service on Saturday, and she liked that the Safeway wasn't far away. In her two previous appearances at that supermarket, staffers there had been cordial and accommodating. "It's a nice venue," Gabby said.

After the COYC decision was made, she went to the ceremonial swearing-in photo opportunity with John Boehner. Many Democrats declined to have their photo taken with the opposition leader—where would they display it?—but Gabby respected the office of Speaker, no matter which party held the position.

She stood there in line with all the Republican representatives, and when it was her turn, she flashed that giant smile of hers. That photo would turn out to be the one most widely used by the media in the days immediately after the shooting.

That Wednesday night, Gabby had dinner with Pia and Rodd McLeod, her campaign manager. They both thought she seemed slightly melancholy. Almost all the other members of Congress were celebrating the new term by having dinner with their spouses and children. But I was in Houston, as were my girls, and Gabby wasn't yet a mother, of course. Her staffers felt a little sorry for her: She was stuck having her celebratory meal with them.

That was the life of a hard-charging congresswoman with a high-flying husband. We've missed a good many moments when it would have been nice to be together.

* * *

On Thursday, January 6, Gabby and I were very busy with our respective jobs. I had a meeting with my flight directors, and then attended a class on ammonia decontamination. Two of my crew members were going to be doing a space walk on our mission to the International Space Station, and there was a likelihood they'd be sprayed with ammonia emanating from vents in the station. We had to learn the risks of that and how to decontaminate them when they came back inside.

Gabby was busy, too. Her day was filled with meetings about solar energy, missile systems, border security, and local economic issues. At one point, she went down to the House floor to participate in a Republican-led opening-week reading of the Constitution; she delivered lines from the First Amendment, which was a thrill for her. She began contemplating a letter she'd draft to Nancy Pelosi explaining why she hadn't voted for her. She was also interviewed by several Arizona radio shows, asking about the new term. She had prepared her sound bites: "My top priorities this session, like last session, are border security, economic security, national security, and energy security. On each of these issues, we cannot succumb to partisan bickering. The challenges—and the cost of failure—are too great."

Later that day, she and eighteen cosponsors introduced legislation that would cut her own salary and the $174,000 annual salaries of her colleagues in Congress by 5 percent. Gabby, who had authored the bill, issued a press release which stated: "If approved, it would be the first time in 78 years that members of Congress have taken a pay cut."

Then, in the afternoon, Gabby got an OK from the Franking Commission of the Committee on House Administration, which needs to approve all mass communications from members of Congress. The commission's approval allowed Gabby to record a script for an automated "robo call" that would go out to the phone lines of constituents selected for their zip codes. They all lived in neighborhoods in the vicinity of the Safeway that would be hosting the COYC event.

Gabby was, as always, very cheerful as she recorded her message: "Hi, this is your congresswoman, Gabrielle Giffords, inviting you to a one-on-one meeting. I am hosting Congress on Your Corner this Saturday at the Safeway located at 7110 North Oracle. That's the southeast corner of Oracle and Ina. I'll be there with my staff from ten to eleven thirty a.m. to meet with you and answer any of your questions about what is going on in Congress. For more information, please call 881-3588. Again, this is Congresswoman Gabrielle Giffords and I hope to meet with you in person this Saturday!"

The robo call went out to the homes of about twenty thousand constituents, including the residence of a very troubled young man who had attended an event with Gabby in the past. None of us, of course, could have anticipated the ramifications of Gabby's decision to host a COYC event and to record that robo call. We couldn't have imagined that it would be the modern-day equivalent of publishing the route of John F. Kennedy's motorcade in 1963.

At the time, for Gabby and her staffers, it was all in a day's work.

* * *

Gabby returned to Tucson on Friday evening. Her close friend Raoul Erickson picked her up at the airport, and though it was cold, they suited up and went on a ten-mile bike ride on a trail not far from Gabby's condominium. They had dinner together, too, at one of their regular haunts, Char's Thai on Fifth Street, where as usual, they asked for their favorite waitress, a friendly fifty-five-year-old woman named Toi.

"Toi died today," they were told. The news made for a somber meal. "It feels like a funeral," Gabby said to Raoul at one point. She thought she'd end up remembering this weekend because of the unexpected death of an admired waitress.

On Saturday morning, Gabby called me while driving her green Toyota 4Runner over to the Safeway. I was at home in Houston, and it was a quick conversation. "I'm on my way to the Congress on Your Corner," she said. "I'll call you when it's over."

"OK, sweetie," I answered. As always, we both said "I love you."

A few minutes after we'd hung up, Gabby got a text from Pam Simon, the sixty-three-year-old outreach coordinator in her Tucson office. "It's chilly out here. Be sure to dress warm," wrote Pam, who had already gone inside the nearby Walgreens to buy mittens.

Gabby replied: "Too late. I'm on my way." She was wearing a light red jacket and a black skirt.

Five of her staffers were at the Safeway waiting for her, including Gabe, who had made good on his promise to pull off the event without a hitch. Helped by two interns, the staffers had brought several blue-cushioned folding chairs and a folding table from the office, along with an American flag, an Arizona flag, and a banner that read "Gabrielle Giffords, United States Congress."

At about 9:55, Gabby pulled into the parking lot, and before leaving her car, she took out her iPad and typed a message: "My 1st Congress on Your Corner starts now. Please stop by to let me know what is on your mind or tweet me later."

Though the Founding Fathers never tweeted, and though they never saw a woman in Congress, their idealism lived on in Gabby. As this new year began, Gabby was right where she wanted to be, on this corner, the intersection of Oracle and Ina, in her hometown of Tucson, meeting her fellow citizens to hear about their needs. Despite everything, she believed in the possibilities of elected office, and she accepted the risks embedded in the constitutional guarantees of freedom. She thought that it was her job to go out in public, to listen to people, and to help them if she could. I missed her on days like this, but I admired her. I had learned early on that I would be sharing my wife with the world.

On this Saturday morning at Safeway, fifteen constituents, including a nine-year-old girl, were already in line as Gabby made her way toward the front.

"Nice to see you," Gabby said. "Thanks so much for coming."

CHAPTER THREE

The Things We Have
in Common

From the moment we met, Gabby and I were good at talking to each other frankly. We both come from families of straight shooters. Our parents, my brother, Gabby's sister—they all say it as they see it. There's not much tiptoeing. If you're annoying, you hear about it. If you're complaining, you're reminded to quiet down; things could be worse.

But all of us changed a little after Gabby was injured. We all saw the great pain she was in, and the awful frustration she felt, living without language. The natural impulse was to feel sorry for her, of course, to think about all she had lost. But early on, I made a decision to try hard to resist that, and I asked others to do the same. I'd warn people to leave their long faces at the door when visiting Gabby at the rehab hospital in Houston. I even posted rules, one of which was "No crying."

I also tried to cheer up Gabby when she was down. The woman I'd fallen in love with years earlier was the most positive person I'd ever met, and I wanted her to hold on tight to that piece of herself. To help her, I realized, I'd have to talk her through it.

During our courtship and marriage, I'd say Gabby did 60 or 70 percent of the talking when we were together. She had a lot to say. Now I was handling 95 percent of every conversation. But rather than give her upbeat pep talks over and over, sometimes it helped if I just told her about stories in the news or about life outside the hospital. I'd also give her the details of my day, good or bad. Though words failed her, Gabby still could understand pretty much everything I said.

One evening in early April, three months after she was injured, I got to the hospital after a couple days in Florida, where I was training for the shuttle mission. I immediately saw that Gabby was depressed. The reason: She'd been having difficulty making it to the bathroom in time after she'd gotten into bed for the night. There had been close calls.

Getting her off the mattress was something of an ordeal then. The nurse had to help her sit up, a slow process given that Gabby could hardly move her right side. Then the nurse had to find Gabby's helmet and carefully strap it on her head. Gabby couldn't go anywhere without a helmet, even if she was just getting into or out of her wheelchair, because if she fell, she might hit the part of her head where her skull had been removed. A fall could be deadly.

All of this maneuvering meant that it was a while before Gabby would finally get on her way. So, just as a precaution, the nurses had been putting her in adult pull-ups before she went to bed.

"Last night, Gabby didn't make it to the bathroom in time, and she's upset about it," one of the nurses told me when I arrived.

I walked over to Gabby and sat down. "Awful. Awful," she said. She was agitated. She felt humiliated.

I understood that she didn't like having to wear those pull-ups, and being so dependent on others. Anyone in a hospital setting loses a measure of dignity, and Gabby was in for a long stay. It was clear that this latest trip to the bathroom was an episode that spooked her. She knew she had waited too long to alert the nurse that she needed to go, and she feared it would happen again.

I didn't want Gabby to sit around feeling depressed. So I told her a story about my long, tough day of training at the Kennedy Space Center. My story was partly for entertainment value, and partly because, well, I thought I could offer her perspective.

My crew and I had been inside space shuttle *Endeavour* for what we call TCDT: Terminal Countdown Test. "This is where we practice the launch count," I explained to Gabby. "We're on the launchpad, in the space shuttle, and the test takes us all the way up to the moment when the engines start."

When we get suited up to fly into space—or when we do this countdown test—we spend nearly six hours in what NASA calls "launch and entry suits." Those are the big, orange pressure suits we wear when we walk out to the launchpad. We leave for the pad about three hours before launch and we don't get out of the suits until two and a half hours after we're in space.

"That's a long time to hold it in," I said to Gabby.

"Yes," she said. "Long time."

"So we wear pull-ups," I told her, "just like the ones you have to wear at night. Huggies."

Gabby was listening intently. We've always had a lot in common, the two of us. Now we could add something else to the list.

"Anyway," I said, "the test lasts for six hours, and we can't change out of those pull-ups. I don't like to dehydrate myself, so I'll normally stuff four maxi-pads in there as well."

"Yes," Gabby said.

"But this time, for some reason, I wasn't thinking and I only grabbed three maxi-pads. That was a bad plan."

I explained to Gabby that when we're on our backs for those hours, with our feet up—the position astronauts are in for launch—the fluids shift in our bodies and our kidneys start working overtime. It wasn't long before I was filling the Huggies. And I quickly realized that the awkward positioning of the maxi-pads, combined with my mistake of being one maxi-pad short, was not helping the situation. I could feel the urine soaking into my long johns on my legs, and then heading up my back.

There was so much that over the next two hours it defied gravity, working its way up my right leg, which of course was higher than the rest of my body. It traveled uphill, and even soaked the top of my right sock.

"By the time I desuited a couple hours later, I had ten pounds of wet diapers and maxi-pads to dispose of," I told Gabby. "I had urine-soaked long johns. And I had a wet right sock." I paused. "There you have it. That was my day."

My wife looked at me empathetically.

"So, Gabby," I said, "stop complaining."

* * *

Gabby and I met in a roundabout way, thanks to my twin brother, Scott.

Scott is also an astronaut, which made us a curiosity at NASA, and led to mild interest by the media. We'd given a number of interviews over the years, answering questions about what it's like to be "twin astronauts." We'd also get a lot of invitations to give speeches or to meet NASA supporters. The astronaut office receives about eight thousand requests each year for astronaut appearances, and there are only seventy-five of us. So we're lucky if we can accommodate a tenth of what we're asked to do.

Most invitations are pretty basic: Can you come speak to a school assembly or to a civic luncheon? But once in a while, an invitation comes in that is more exotic. Astronauts keep their eyes open for those.

In the summer of 2003, a request arrived from the National Committee on United States–China Relations. It was an organization that invited professionals and rising leaders from both countries to spend time together, sharing cultures and ideas. The group of about fifty participants, all under age forty, would meet for one week in China, and the following year, would gather again in the United States. Perhaps the bonds created at this Young Leaders Forum would lead to a strengthening of ties between the countries.

The organizers thought it would be good to add an American astronaut to the mix. It sounded like an all-expenses-paid vacation, and Scott, no dummy, signed up for it. But then, a few days later, he looked at his schedule and realized his wife was set to give birth the very week of the trip to China. "Want to go in my place?" he asked me.

To the organizers, one twin astronaut was as good as another, so they took me. At age thirty-nine, Scott and I had just made the cut.

Because there's no direct flight to China from Houston, I had to first fly to Vancouver, British Columbia, where I was told I'd meet up with two other participants from the trip. One was a young high-tech executive from California. The other was a thirty-three-year-old state senator from Arizona named Gabrielle Giffords.

The three of us were being put up that night at the same Holiday Inn in Vancouver, and we had exchanged e-mails a few days earlier, planning to meet for dinner. When I got there, however, I learned the executive from California had missed his flight. It would just be me and this state senator from Arizona.

I was married at the time, and for me, this dinner would be just another professional encounter, like hundreds I'd had before. I certainly didn't see or consider anything romantic. But I was impressed with Gabby immediately. I couldn't help but notice the obvious. She was beautiful, ambitious, incredibly smart, accomplished, and a lot of fun to talk to.

At the time, my first wife and I were struggling in our marriage. We already had filed for divorce once and then reconciled, but we were preparing to file again. I didn't get into any of that with Gabby. We were both very circumspect. We ate, we talked about our jobs and the trip ahead, and then we said good night.

The next day, as we boarded the plane for China, Gabby spotted me, the only familiar face in the crowd, and said, "Why don't we sit together?" That sounded like a good way to pass twelve hours, so I agreed. We talked the whole way to China. Again, it was very professional. I was a married guy with two daughters. She was dating someone and told me a little about him. We remained friendly while in China, but our schedules were so full there, we didn't get to spend a whole lot of time interacting.

After we all returned to the States, a year passed without any contact between us. But then, in 2004, it was time for the group to meet up again in the United States, and Gabby being Gabby, she volunteered to host the entire gathering in Arizona. She wanted to show off her state—the Grand Canyon, the Red Rocks of Sedona, the charms of Tucson. It was a lot of work, but the civic booster in her embraced all of it.

My life had changed since I'd last seen Gabby. I arrived at the reunion as a divorced man. In fact, the divorce had been finalized just two days earlier.

Though Gabby and I were glad to see each other again, I still didn't have romance on my mind. For one thing, I thought she was way out of my league. Given all that she had going for her, I doubted that she'd want to get involved with a newly divorced guy who had two kids and lived almost a thousand miles away in Houston.

But we did enjoy spending time together during that reunion in Arizona. Gabby brought the Chinese-American group to a local ranch for a cattle roundup, and after we all assembled, the ranch owner made a very generous offer. "If any of you can lasso three cows in a row," he announced, "I'll give you my ranch."

Gabby always reveled in a challenge, and she figured I must have a similar personality, being an astronaut. When we were broken into teams of six, she wanted to be on my team. She figured we'd win.

As the rancher surmised, this group of smart, proud, self-confident Chinese and American go-getters turned out to be ill-suited for cow-lassoing. Only one person got the hang of it: me. None of the participants could lasso even one cow, but for some reason, I was able to lasso two of them. I just missed on the third—the rope was on the cow's head and slipped off—so I didn't get the deed to the ranch. But I did impress Gabby. "So you can fly space shuttles. You can lasso cows. What else can you do?" she asked.

I didn't want to tell her I was running out of amazing feats. She'd figure that out soon enough.

We spent more time together at this gathering than we had in China. One day, Gabby and I skipped the aerial tour of the Grand Canyon and went hiking instead. For the first time, we talked in more detail about our personal lives. Gabby told me about the men she had dated. Some were very wealthy or had big jobs, but she didn't think there was the right chemistry or she saw no future. "It's tough to be single," she told me.

I talked about my daughters, Claudia and Claire, then ages nine and seven, and about how my ex-wife and I were figuring out the best way to share custody. Gabby was easy to talk to, and she was a great listener.

When I got back to Houston, what I saw as a growing friendship continued. We'd trade e-mails. We talked a little bit on the phone. I went on a few dates with women in Texas and Gabby gave me advice so I wouldn't seem like an oaf. "Call her the next day to thank her," she said, "even if you didn't have such a great time."

I thought I'd made a friend. Truly, I didn't think Gabby wanted to get romantically involved with me. But she was beginning to see the possibilities. The distance, my divorce, her busy career, my busy career—she was hesitant, but willing to give us a try.

Gabby talked about me to her mother. Gloria liked to say that Gabby was on a lifelong quest for "a glamorous guy who will understand and adore her." That was a tall order. So far, as her mother saw it, Gabby had been coming up blank, dating men who were mostly self-involved and not fully comfortable with her smarts and ambitions. "I've always known my life would be pretty irregular," Gabby told her mom. "I need a guy who will support me and my career, but who is strong enough to stand on his own."

As she gave her mother a few details about me, she pulled out a photo taken in China of the entire young leadership group. "So which one do you think is Mark?" Gabby asked.

Gloria studied all the faces in the photo. She thought a Navy pilot in the astronaut corps would be tall, blond, well-built, and movie-star handsome. Not expecting a bald, regular guy like me, Gloria couldn't pick me out of the lineup. When Gabby pointed me out, her mother said, "Hmmm, OK."

With her mother's lukewarm endorsement, Gabby took the lead. In November 2004, she called me in Houston and asked me out on our first date, though it didn't exactly sound like a date to me. "I've got to go to the Arizona State Prison in Florence," Gabby said. "I need to visit Death Row. Want to come with me?"

She was working on legislation in the Arizona Senate regarding capital punishment and, always diligent, figured she'd better get an up-close look at the issue before she weighed in on it. That was Gabby. Her idea of a date included a foray into public policy.

As for me, the son of cops, this trip sounded like an adventure. Not everyone gets the chance to visit a maximum-security prison and possibly sit in the chair in the gas chamber. It would also be nice to see Gabby again.

Because I was training then as a pilot on the space shuttle, I was required to log a considerable amount of time flying the Northrop T-38 Talon, the supersonic jet trainer. I needed a lot of hours in the air, so I could take it up pretty much anytime I wanted and fly it anywhere. "I'll fly the T-38 over to Tucson and meet you," I told Gabby.

I reserved a room at the officers' quarters at the Davis-Monthan Air Force Base in Tucson. But then four days before the trip, Gabby called and said it wasn't a good time to come. Her dad wasn't feeling well. I'd later learn that her dad's health was secondary. In truth, she was getting cold feet. Did she really want to start a long-distance relationship with a divorced father?

I told Gabby I'd already reserved the jet and the room at the Air Force base. "I'll come anyway so I can get the training hours," I said. "I'm sorry I won't see you."

A couple days later, Gabby reconsidered. She called and told me her dad would be OK. She wanted to take me to the prison. I flew in as planned and she picked me up at the air base.

It was a forty-five-minute drive to the prison, and at first we talked mostly about the criminal-justice system. She had been a supporter of the death penalty, but her feelings about it were shifting, and she eventually changed her position. She had been reading a book about death penalty cases in the United States, and how mistakes were made in some of them.

"Innocent people have been executed," she told me. "And besides that, I've come to believe that the state shouldn't kill its citizens." I told her I agreed with her. (Our conversation in the car that day would return to my mind after Gabby was shot, when the U.S. Attorney's Office asked for our views on the issue of capital punishment. As a victim, Gabby will get to weigh in as the government decides whether to seek the death penalty in her case. As the spouse of a victim, I'm entitled to have my voice heard, too.)

Later on our drive to the prison, we got to talking about Gabby's dating history. She said she was always attracted to successful people, but it was hard for her to find anyone she really liked. She had dated one man who was a Republican politician, which made for ideological differences. He later tried to run against her for the congressional seat she held, but lost in the Republican primary.

She dated a doctor with offices all over Tucson. There wasn't enough chemistry. She dated another man who had recently sold his computer company for tens of millions of dollars. He picked her up in limos and wined and dined her, but then he spent two weeks skiing in Italy and neglected to even call her. Gabby didn't want a man who could disappear for two weeks without thinking of her. When he returned, she gave him the brush-off.

"It's not been easy finding someone," Gabby told me. "Not every guy wants to date a thirty-four-year-old career woman."

"Well, I'd date you," I said. I don't know what made me say that. I think I was confused about whether this death-row visit was an actual date. It certainly wasn't dinner and a movie.

When we got to the prison, the warden was happy to give Gabby a tour, hoping it would help her make decisions as a state senator. We were given full access, and I noticed that Gabby was pretty fearless, propelled by curiosity and a need to understand the societal and governmental issues that informed this place. For both of us, it was quite an education. We had to wear shields over our faces as we entered one of the cell blocks. We were told some inmates would throw feces or other things from their cells. We also were given "stab vests" for our protection.

Gabby had a lot of questions, though sometimes I found the conversations to be surreal.

In one maximum-security wing, she met with an inmate in his cell. "So why are you in here?" Gabby asked him. He was a giant man. He looked like he could be the twin brother of Michael Clarke Duncan, the six-foot-five, 315-pound actor from *The Green Mile* and *Armageddon*.

"I'm in here for murder," the inmate said. He had the deepest, scariest voice I'd ever heard. He sounded like a tuba.

"Who did you kill?" Gabby asked.

The man corrected her. "You mean, who was I *accused* of killing?"

"Yeah, that's what I meant," Gabby said, not missing a beat.

"Well, I was *accused* of killing my girlfriend," the inmate told her. "But I'll be getting out of here."

"Oh," Gabby said. "When are you being released?"

"Six years from now, in 2015," he said. I did the math in my head. It was 2004. We were actually eleven years away from 2015. But I wasn't going to give him the bad news, and neither was Gabby.

Gabby then asked him what he liked best about this prison. He said he liked having a television in his cell.

"Well, thank you for your time," Gabby said. "It was nice visiting with you." She was cheerful and friendly to voters and nonvoters alike. (Convicted felons can't cast ballots.)

The warden told us that the televisions in cells were actually more of an accommodation for the guards than the prisoners. "A large percentage of these prisoners can't read," the warden said. "Without TV, they're bored and completely unruly."

As our visit continued, I was so impressed with Gabby. She wasn't there on a lark. She truly wanted to learn about the justice system, incarceration rates, and what elected officials could do to improve the prison system in Arizona.

We stopped by the plant where the inmates made furniture and license plates. We talked to guards and other prisoners, including a sex offender who told Gabby about the lack of good treatment options in the system. "I'm glad you shared your story with me," Gabby said. "It's helpful for me to know this when we're voting on which programs to fund."

And then we got to Death Row, where Gabby asked detailed, intelligent questions and I behaved like a tourist, asking to step inside the gas chamber. I sat down and pulled the door closed. I just wanted to sense what that might feel like. Gabby had no need to do that.

"Do the men who visit always want to sit in the gas chamber?" Gabby asked.

"No, not usually," the warden said.

I wasn't sure what Gabby thought of me, sitting there in the gas chamber, in contemplation, a slight grin on my face. But she liked me enough to suggest we go out to dinner after our prison tour. Dinner, at El Charro Café in Tucson, turned out to be great.

When the evening ended, rather than a kiss good night, Gabby gave me a quick hug. I returned to the officers' quarters at the air base, Gabby drove back to her house, and we both just knew. This was the start of something.

* * *

I began coming to Arizona every other weekend to see Gabby. At the time, she was living in a house no bigger than a three-car garage. "If it was any smaller," I'd say to her, "some little girl would break in and start setting up dolls in here!"

"Well, I like this place," Gabby said. It was all she needed.

I'd often fly into Tucson in the T-38. That tiny house of hers was in line with the flight path of the air base, and sometimes I'd call her to suggest that she step outside, because I was going to fly directly over her. She got a kick out of that.

"I could even see the word 'NASA' on his plane!" she later told her mother.

"Very nice," Gloria said. "In my time, we'd date boys based on how hot their cars were, not by how supersonic their jets were."

Gabby's mom seemed as impressed by my flyover as she'd been by my photo from the trip to China. But Gabby told her that she was falling fast for me, and Gloria noticed that Gabby's face lit up as she spoke. "I look forward to meeting your astronaut," Gloria said, figuring that once we met, she'd decide for herself if I was just another suitor or if I was "the one."

To other people, Gabby said it was "a huge relief" that she had found me, after years of wondering if the right man for her would ever materialize. Gabby felt that she and I were very much alike. We'd both chosen careers in public service, we shared a curiosity about everything, we were both devoted to our families, and we found the same things to be funny. It had been a while since a woman really laughed at my jokes, and I definitely could make Gabby laugh.

Gabby told me she was in love after three or four visits. I took a little longer. Maybe because of my marital history, a part of me was too scared to fully commit myself. I had two young kids and a one-of-a-kind job in Houston. If Gabby and I were to marry, how would it work? Where would we live?

Gabby came up with all sorts of possible scenarios. She and I spent a lot of time on the phone and on e-mail, talking them through. She wasn't yet thinking about running for Congress, because Jim Kolbe, the popular, long-term representative from her district, had given no indication he'd be retiring soon. But Gabby saw many other options.

Maybe she'd move to Houston and live on a houseboat near my home, so we could figure out our feelings. Maybe she'd come to the University of Texas for law school after she finished her term in the Arizona senate. Maybe she'd stay in Arizona and we'd just turn the long-distance love affair into a long-distance marriage. "There are a lot of ways to make it work," she told me.

There was one issue, though, that was a likely deal-breaker for Gabby.

"Would you be willing to have more children?" she had asked me, very directly, on our second real date.

It was a big question, and though she asked it somewhat hypothetically, I could see she wasn't just asking about me. She was asking about us.

I thought for a moment. "I wouldn't be opposed to having more children," I said. I knew that was what she wanted to hear. But I was also making a declaration to myself, an acknowledgment of my feelings for Gabby.

*   *   *

In 2005, Jim Kolbe surprised the Arizona political world by announcing that he wouldn't seek another term in Congress. After Gabby decided to run for his seat, I became the tagalong guy, hanging out at her stump speeches. ("People are excited to meet Mark," Gabby would say, "even though he doesn't wear his space suit.") In political circles, I was labeled "the astronaut boyfriend." Then, when I went on my July 2006 mission on space shuttle *Discovery,* Gabby came to the launch. Around NASA, she was called "the girlfriend running for Congress."

One morning during that mission, Gabby was given the opportunity to choose my crew's wake-up song, and she selected "Beautiful Day" by one of her favorite bands, U2. I didn't know it, but she was hoping that, after almost two years of dating, I'd surprise her by calling down from space and asking her to marry me. "I want the whole world to know about us," she told her mom. The mission lasted twelve days, and day after day, Gabby waited for me to make my move. But, as she complained to her mother, I just kept circling the planet, oblivious.

I knew she wanted to get engaged, but I had no idea she wanted a big public proposal. Maybe she had given me hints and I was too dense to pick up on them. When I came home, after traveling 5.28 million miles and orbiting the Earth 202 times, she was glad to see me, but not as glad as she would have been if I'd had a ring with me.

One day not long after I'd returned, Gabby called. "We need to talk," she said.

From the tone of her voice, I knew the exact topic. She got right to the point.

"Look," she said. "I'm thirty-six years old and we've been dating two years. This relationship of ours will go either one way or the other, and I'm not waiting around."

I felt a need to reveal myself. "I've got a plan."

"A plan?" she said. "What does that mean, a plan?"

I couldn't keep the secret any longer. I figured she wanted to know, so I'd tell her. "I've already bought a ring."

She didn't seem at all happy to hear the news. "Why did you tell me that?" she said. "Now you've ruined it!"

At least I didn't tell her when I'd be giving it to her.

About a month later, in September 2006, Gabby had to be in New York for a couple of fund-raisers. The same day, I was invited to give a speech at the U.S. Merchant Marine Academy, my alma mater, in Kings Point, New York. I asked Gabby to join me at the academy between her appearances.

We stood in the academy's main square, alongside the famous fountain that surrounds a flagpole. This was the spot where I used to come before big tests when I was a student. By tradition, students toss coins there for good luck. There's a little conch shell in the fountain, which sits at the base of a sculpture of Athena, the Greek goddess of wisdom. We'd always aim to land our coin in that shell, which supposedly brings extra luck.

"OK, watch this," I said to Gabby. "There's something I want to show you."

I tossed a coin about fifteen feet toward the conch shell—and it went in! "That means we're destined to have good luck," I told Gabby. She smiled at my skill. Hey, I could lasso two and a half cows. I could toss a coin exactly where it needed to go. Did I have anything else in my bag of tricks?

I did.

I had already called Gabby's father to ask for her hand in marriage. Now the moment had come. I didn't get down on one knee. I thought that would be too corny for a thirty-six-year-old woman and her forty-two-year-old boyfriend. But I did speak from the heart.

"Gabby," I said. "You're the most amazing person I've ever met, and I want to spend the rest of my life with you. Will you marry me?"

"Yes," she said, "absolutely." She was a little teary as I handed her a one-carat, round-diamond engagement ring. She slipped it on her finger.

I thought this was a nicer way to propose than me being up in space, popping the question and then hoping I'd make it back OK to live out our lives together. This way, Gabby and I could share a brief, private kiss behind the fountain, and then rush off together to New York City for her event. We didn't really know anyone at the fund-raiser, and as we mingled, we kept our engagement as our own little secret. That was romantic, too.

Gabby would have that engagement ring for four and a half years. Because she was wearing it the day she was shot, it ended up in the possession of the FBI, held for inspection with every other piece of potential evidence that had been at the crime scene.

When I finally got back Gabby's ring a week after the shooting, I had to scrape little specks of her blood off it. I held it in my hand, remembering not just the day Gabby and I got engaged, but also the ways in which we first discovered each other. They remain warm memories for both of us.

* * *

A few months after Gabby was shot, I was going through an old file of paperwork and happened to come upon a three-page letter she wrote to me at the end of 2004. It was a keepsake from our courtship, and I smiled as I began reading it.

When Gabby wrote the letter, she was about to go on a long-planned trip to India with a friend, and she felt bad that she'd be missing New Year's Eve with me. We wouldn't be seeing each other until January 9. To make up for her absence, she sent me a bunch of wrapped gifts in a box labeled "The Hippest Astronaut's 8-Day Entertainment Kit." She had a separate present—a book, a CD, a toy—for each of the first eight days of 2005, and her letter described why she had chosen every gift.

For January 1, she included her horoscope (Gemini) and mine (Pisces). She was especially taken with the prediction in her horoscope—that she'd be having "a year of mind-wobbling, heart-opening adventures in love."

For January 3, she sent me a CD by the Latin artist known as Juanes. "My dirty little secret is that I love Latin Pop," Gabby wrote. "I promise not to make you listen to it too much but if you don't dig track 9, with Nelly Furtado, we will have to have a serious discussion."

For January 5, she sent an astronaut action figure. "The truth is that I love toys! Your profession lends itself to cool action figures. Who ever heard of a political super hero?" That day's gift included an album by Gila Bend, a band popular in Tucson. Gabby wrote, "If you hate this CD, lie!"

I can't recall what gift Gabby gave me to be opened on January 8, the last day of her gift-giving extravaganza. Her accompanying letter mentioned toasting my new home, so it might have been a bottle of champagne. Most of what she wrote focused not on the gift but on her desire to be with me again. She promised to call me as soon as she arrived back in the States, ending her message: "I'm looking forward to talking to you."

It felt good to read Gabby's letter again. It was so enthusiastic and flirtatious. I could hear her voice as I read it. The last line, though, that's what really got me. Because Gabby was shot on January 8, 2011, I was totally struck by those words she had left for me on January 8, 2005: "I'm looking forward to talking to you."

It was like a message from Gabby as she was, telling me not to worry, that we'll get through everything. She'll be talking to me again.

CHAPTER FOUR

"Tomorrow"

From the time Gabby was a little girl, she always had an irrepressibly upbeat personality and a clear, beautiful singing voice. She was a kid who sang with a smile. And so, in 1981, when she was a fifth grader at Tanque Verde Elementary School in Tucson, she became the obvious choice to play the title role in the school's production of *Annie*.

I've been told that eleven-year-old Gabby embraced the part as if it were her destiny. She delivered her lines with heart and enthusiasm, and to make sure she had chemistry with her costar, she brought along her own dog, a half-shepherd, half-Airedale terrier, to play the role of Sandy.

Adults who saw her in that show said Gabby had star quality, and some even got teary-eyed watching her. When she sang about the sun coming out tomorrow, no one needed to check the weather forecast. They believed her. (Of course, it helped that this was the desert. The sun always came out.)

Months after the show, on one of her family's many trips south of the border, they went to Mexico City to see a performance of *Annie* in Spanish. Their seats were near the stage, and Gabby stood up and sang along with the Mexican Annie, belting out the lyrics in her own mix of English and Spanish: "Mañana, mañana, I love ya, mañana!"

Gloria leaned over and whispered to Gabby's dad, Spencer: "Tell Gabby to sit down or they're going to throw us out!" But actually, Gloria was secretly enjoying her daughter's performance. She thought to herself: "Unlike that songbird onstage, at least Gabby can carry a tune and keep up with the conductor."

As Gabby got older, "Tomorrow" became a connection between her and her mom. Whenever Gabby would be frustrated or disappointed, her mother would sing to her: "Oh, the sun will come out, tomorrow . . ." And then Gabby would respond: "Bet your bottom dollar that tomorrow, there'll be sun . . ." They'd sing in unison: "Tomorrow! Tomorrow! I love ya, tomorrow. You're always a DAY A-WAY!"

It may sound corny, this mother-daughter ritual, but it connected them. And in the early days after Gabby was shot, when she was still in a medically induced coma, Gloria would sit by her bed, softly singing that song to her.

Gabby was silent, of course, her eyes closed tight, but as night became daybreak, and tomorrow arrived, Gloria wanted that song in Gabby's ears. It was remarkable, actually, for me to watch this as a son-in-law.

I got to see how fierce a mother's devotion can be. I saw how optimism is a form of therapy and hope is a form of love. And when Gloria wasn't singing to Gabby—or advocating on her behalf to doctors, nurses, orderlies, custodians—she was tapping out e-mails on her BlackBerry, letting friends and relatives know that she had great faith that Gabby would recover.

"I am convinced that inside that small, still form in this hospital bed in Tucson," she wrote in one e-mail, "attached to and surrounded by blinking machines, my daughter Gabby is struggling to find a lifeline that will pull her back up to the surface. On my watch, 'Tomorrow' is one of the songs I sing to her."

Weeks later, after Gabby arrived at TIRR Memorial Hermann, the rehab hospital in Houston, she began attending regular music-therapy sessions. The therapist explained to us that singing aloud could possibly help Gabby regain her ability to speak in sentences. The reason: When Gabby was shot, the bullet went through the left hemisphere of her brain, where speech tends to be processed and formed. But "music centers" are found in various spots in the brain, right and left, meaning Gabby still had access to her ability to sing.

Through therapy, she reconnected to familiar tunes—"Happy Birthday," "Twinkle, Twinkle, Little Star," "American Pie"—first by mouthing the words, and then, eventually, by actually singing aloud. We were told the repetition of these songs would help create new pathways in Gabby's brain, strengthening her vocabulary. In those months, she could speak only one word at a time, and often it was the wrong word. But in time she could sing whole verses correctly, almost without hesitation. And one of her favorite songs, of course, was "Tomorrow."

One day in early April, three months after Gabby was injured, she sang "Tomorrow" for her speech therapist Meagan Morrow. Gloria was there and joined in on the chorus.

"That's beautiful," Meagan said. "And I bet I know why that song is a favorite of yours. Maybe you identify with the hard life in the song. It's about a little girl's hard life in an orphanage."

"No, no!" Gabby said.

Gloria added her own "no" almost instantaneously. Then she explained. "Gabby and I have always thought the message in that song is one of hope and perseverance," Gloria said. "That's why we love it and find it so meaningful."

Gabby nodded in agreement. "Hope," she said.

* * *

I spend a great deal of time with Gloria now. We're the two top decision-makers in Gabby's life. I'm still the son-in-law and she's still the mother-in-law, but since the shooting, our relationship has grown into a respectful, loving, sometimes stressful partnership. We're constantly interacting, discussing, weighing treatment options, and trying to figure out what's best for Gabby. We'll agree, we'll disagree, and sometimes we'll go to our separate corners and revisit a discussion in the morning. I was the only astronaut on the International Space Station whose in-box was filled with Earth-to-space e-mails from his mother-in-law.

Gloria says she is sometimes uncomfortable being so present in Gabby's life, and in mine. As an adult, Gabby had been a self-sufficient world traveler, someone who loved her parents and saw them whenever she could, but never needed a great deal from them. "She was always so busy," Gloria says. "She had a full life. I didn't know the names of all her friends or her staffers. Days could go by and I wouldn't know what she was up to or which city she was in. Gabby was living her life and I was living mine."

But now, at age seventy-three, Gloria has returned to motherhood in the most intimate ways. She spends much of every day and night at Gabby's side. She monitors the food Gabby eats, the drugs she takes, her bathroom visits, her shower schedule, her mail, her pain, and the stitches on her skull. Everything.

I watch in admiration and appreciation. During the first four months of Gabby's recovery I was training intensely for my space shuttle mission, and then I was in space for sixteen days. "Whenever you can't be at the hospital, I will be your eyes and ears here," Gloria promised me early on. "I'll watch for the subtle things. I'll tell you everything."

She kept her word. Those e-mails I get from Gloria start at daybreak and continue lighting up my BlackBerry until well after midnight. And even when the rest of us have doubts, she remains a raging optimist. A month after the shooting, Gloria wrote an upbeat e-mail to friends. She said Gabby had gone from "a kind of limp noodle" to someone who was "alert, sits up straight with good posture, and works very hard. Little Miss Overachiever is healing very fast." Someone leaked that e-mail to the media, and a reporter called Gloria, asking her how she'd sum up Gabby's progress. "Yippee!" Gloria said. "And you can quote me on that!"

I see how Gabby has gotten her strength from both her parents. Gloria and Spencer gave her the foundation, the life experiences, and an offbeat view of the world that helped shape her.

On the Mother's Day before she was injured, Gabby wrote a message on her campaign blog: "Today I am thinking about my mom, Gloria. I am very much her daughter, and I am grateful for all her love and support. My mom truly is my greatest inspiration. Both my mom and dad instill in me their values of hard work, treating others with dignity and respect, and giving back, which have made me the person I am today."

Gloria, nicknamed Jinx, is well known in Arizona art circles as a painter, mostly in oils, and as an art conservator and historian with a great interest in the religious art and architecture of Mexico. She teaches, she collects, she writes art books, and she takes a stand on issues. She believes, for instance, that artists and artisans have a responsibility to consider the effects of aging and the environment when they create their works. She has studied the varnishes artists use, and how sculptures should be crafted to stand the tests of time. As she sees it: "Competent artists are obligated to produce products of structural integrity."

That statement speaks to how Gloria looks at life and how she raised Gabby and her older sister, Melissa. We all have obligations to our jobs, our families, our communities, and those obligations extend far beyond this moment. In her commitment to public service, Gabby recognized that she had to make good decisions not just for today, or for this election cycle, but for future generations. Gloria taught Gabby that, like a well-made piece of art, her efforts needed to stand the test of time.

Born in Nebraska and raised as a Christian Scientist, Gloria spent parts of her childhood in Arizona and Kansas. When she was twenty years old, in 1958, she got engaged to the son of a farmer her mother knew in Nebraska. "I was raised to go to college to find a husband—the MRS degree," Gloria says. "This young man was handsome, I was cute, we dated, and then we planned our wedding."

On the day of the ceremony, 120 guests were waiting inside the church when Gloria pulled up to the front curb. She was sitting with her mother in the backseat of her uncle's car, looking perfectly lovely in her wedding dress, and in that instant, she came to a realization. "I'm sorry," Gloria announced. "I can't get out of the car. I don't want to marry him."

Her mother and uncle were shocked, but saw that she meant it. "We put the pedal to the metal and drove off," Gloria says. They stopped at a gas station, where Gloria found a pay phone and called the church. Someone tracked down her fiancé. "I can't do it," Gloria told him. "I'm so sorry. I just don't see a future together."

"But everyone is here, standing around, waiting," the young man said.

Gloria apologized profusely, wished him well, and never saw him again. Her family covered the cost of the reception that never happened. It was a mortifying experience for Gloria, and she felt awful for her fiancé. Still, she doesn't regret her decision.

Not settling into an ill-conceived marriage at age twenty would help

Gloria become a mother who encouraged her two daughters to dream bigger dreams. She let them know that marriage was a wonderful option, but it didn't have to happen right away, or at all. It was important that Gabby and her sister, Melissa, make something of their lives, and that they be of service to others. Gabby became a career woman and then a public servant in part because her mother showed her the way.

Gloria never shared her runaway bride story with her daughters when they were young. And she told me why: "If you tell children a story like that, you empower them with a lot of goofiness. A girl might think it was OK to do what I did, when it was actually immature, foolish, impetuous, and immoral."

After moving on from the canceled wedding, Gloria ended up in Tucson, where she studied at the University of Arizona, earning both a bachelor's and a master's in fine arts. It was there, in 1963, that she met Spencer, a twenty-eight-year-old local tire dealer. He made her laugh. She made him think. They got married the next year. (For both Spencer and Gloria, their marriage was a fresh start. He had been married briefly to a woman in Mexico and had a son there.)

Spencer's roots in Tucson went back to 1942, when he was seven years old and his family moved there from New York. His father, born Akiba Hornstein, had contracted the Spanish flu in World War I and was told that if he didn't find a dry climate, he'd die. The move to Tucson at age forty-two helped save his life.

Akiba's family tree included a long line of rabbis. In elementary school, a teacher couldn't pronounce "Akiba" and decided to call him "Gifford." When he and his two brothers started a business in New York in the 1930s selling home-heating oil burners and fuel, they named it Giffords Oil after him. Every day, customers on the phone wanted to talk to the boss: "Let me talk to Mr. Giffords!" He got tired of saying, "It's Gifford Hornstein. You can talk to me." So he decided to change his last name as well. By the time he got to Tucson, Akiba had made things easy for himself by morphing into Gif Giffords.

Gif was a natural salesman and a bit of a huckster who yearned to be a philosopher. For a while, he peddled costume jewelry and hearing aids, and also became a real-estate broker. Then, in 1949, he discovered his calling in the tire business, founding El Campo Tire and Service Centers. Spencer began working there as a teen, pumping gas.

In the 1950s, Gif took to airing commercials for his store on local TV, and each spot would begin with Gif's signature line: "It's a good, good evening!" After that catchphrase, he'd deliver homilies or offbeat philosophy.

In one commercial he announced, "You are who you are!" and then in sixty seconds told "the story of the scorpion": A scorpion was clinging to a piece of wood in a river, and a man came along and rescued it by putting it on the riverbank. Without saying thanks, the scorpion stung the man. "Why did you do that?" the man asked. "I just saved your life." The scorpion answered: "You are who you are. I'm a scorpion and I sting."

Gif filmed his commercials while standing in front of a banner for El Campo Tire, with a giant tire displayed behind his head. "My father never mentioned tires or why anyone should buy them from him," says Spencer, who found the commercials embarrassing. "It was excruciating for me to be the son of a TV preacher."

The commercials, however, were very effective. Gif wasn't just selling tires, he was selling fulfillment, and everyone in town knew him. Years later, people would tell Gabby that they appreciated the wisdom in those commercials. Some even said, "Your grandfather changed my life."

Spencer took charge of the company in 1959 and, with savvy business sense, expanded the operation to twelve locations. Meanwhile, Gif eased into retirement. For years, people would stop him on the street to ask him about his philosophy—or their tire pressure. He liked being a mini-celebrity.

To passersby, Gif radiated friendliness and optimism. "It's a good, good evening," he'd tell them. It was too bad that he was a remote and often uninterested grandfather to Melissa and Gabby. He could be jovial with them, but mostly he paid little attention to their lives. As they got older, they learned to have no expectations of a meaningful relationship with him or their paternal grandmother, though they were lucky to be close to their maternal grandmother. (Spencer's parents remained aloof in part because they disapproved of his marriage to a non-Jewish woman.)

And yet, whether it was genetics or coincidence, Gif's positive out-look seemed present in Gabby. From the time she was a kid, she liked thinking it would be a good, good evening, and that tomorrow morn-ing might be even better.

* * *

Spencer and Gloria raised Gabby and Melissa in the Tanque Verde Valley, east of Tucson. The site of the Native-American Hohokom culture dating back to the tenth century, it's a landscape far differ-ent from the one I knew growing up in New Jersey. Tanque Verde is bordered by the Rincon Mountains to the east and the Santa Catalina Mountains to the north, and it's the very definition of a desert. Its riv-erbeds are dry much of the year, and its average high temperature on summer days is 99 degrees. The Giffords would become fixtures in the community there, like the cacti. For eleven years, Spencer served on the Tanque Verde school board. Gloria was busy helping to preserve historic art and missions, and supporting local galleries in Tucson.

Spencer was overwhelmed at work, and he didn't always have a lot of time for Gabby and Melissa. But there was one parenting rule that was important to him, and he stuck to it: He made sure to be home for dinner every night, to join Gloria and the girls in discussions about schoolwork, current events, politics, art, music, whatever was on their minds. Gabby enjoyed listening to her father, who could be a lovable curmudgeon. He spoke without much of a filter; what he thought was what he said. Though he resisted the impulse to star in El Campo's TV commercials—he left the hawking of tires to others—if he had become the face of the operation, he may have been more memorable than Gif in spouting his views of the world.

Spencer and Gloria were not your usual suburban couple. When I saw the movie *Meet the Fockers,* the characters played by Barbra Strei-sand and Dustin Hoffman reminded me a little of my in-laws. They could be exuberant eccentrics. Conformity never mattered to them.

When Gloria would pick Gabby up from school, she'd sometimes show up wearing a costume—a vampire's cape or some goofy out-fit she had found around the house. For Gabby, it was horrifying to see her mother stepping out of the car-pool line in a turn-of-the-cen-tury bandleader's uniform, complete with an old, dented black top hat made of beaver hair. All the other kids' eyes widened at the sight of her, and they all had the same thought: "That's one weird mother." But in Gloria's mind, she was doing Gabby a favor. "Let this be the most embarrassing thing you ever have to endure in life," she'd say.

Gabby wished she had taken the bus. But looking back as an adult, Gabby realized that surviving her mother's costume antics actually made her tougher and more immune to criticism. If you can live through this kind of childhood mortification, the embarrassments of adulthood are easier to handle.

Gloria and Spencer also had other techniques for toughening up their daughters.

When summer came, they'd load the kids in the car, drive them to the middle of Mexico, and drop them off at a camp where none of the other kids knew English. This was Mexican summer camp. Gloria and Spencer figured it would be a good way for the girls to learn Spanish. This total-immersion experience might have been daunting for other kids, but Melissa and Gabby mostly enjoyed themselves. They liked hanging out with kids from other countries, and even came back with a smattering of French, which pleased Gloria and Spencer.

While Gabby and Melissa were struggling with their Spanish, Gloria and Spencer would disappear into Central America. Later in the summer, they'd pick the girls up and, on the drive back to Arizona, they'd stop in tiny towns collecting artwork, meeting the locals, and tasting another culture.

They'd also learn about poverty.

Gloria and Spencer taught altruism by example. Each year, they sponsored scholarships at a school in Belize, the only Central American country where English is the official language. In 1975, they invited one recipient, a bright boy named Francis, to come live with them in Tucson for a year. (Francis would go on to become a veterinarian and school vice principal, and Gabby still considers him her brother. His connection to Gabby would make national news in Belize after she was shot.)

In part because of her upbringing, Gabby was a kid, and then an adult, who developed a deep concern for other people. But as Melissa sees it, the example set by their parents doesn't fully explain Gabby's sense of compassion. There was also something inside Gabby, something Melissa decided was pretty rare.

"Most human beings care about a relatively small group of people," Melissa says when she's asked about her sister. "They care about their family, their friends, their neighbors, some of the people they work with. Maybe that adds up to fifty people. Gabby's number is way past fifty. Her number is in the hundreds of thousands—or the millions. I started realizing it when we were kids. That makes her different from the rest of us."

Gabby had a kind of empathy that would sometimes backfire on her. When she was in eleventh grade, she traveled to Spain to be an exchange student, and she was hosted by a wealthy family with children her age. The family had servants who took care of all the chores around the house, and that made Gabby uncomfortable. She was always trying to help them out, which upset her hosts.

"Stop doing the dishes," they told her. "Stop making the bed. Stop helping the maid."

As they saw it, she was setting a bad example for their children. It was a class issue. The help was there to help.

But Gabby ignored the family's admonishments, and kept doing the dishes and offering to help the maid. A month into her stay, her hosts came into her room. "Make your suitcase," they said.

She wondered what that meant. They said it again. "Make your suitcase."

She realized they were kicking her out. In disbelief, she started packing. Because not everything would fit in her suitcase—she'd bought gifts for her family back home—her hosts gave her a large cardboard box that cartons of tampons had come in. They dropped her off at the train station with her suitcase and that giant tampon box. Near tears, she called her parents collect.

The exchange program was able to find her somewhere to stay that night, and eventually she was placed with another, far more welcoming family. But Gabby had learned the old lesson that no good deed goes unpunished. Things don't always go well for people who are too nice.

* * *

Gabby wasn't completely selfless, of course. Mixed with her urge to help people was a sense of political savvy that Gloria and Spencer noticed early on. From a young age, Gabby was both a charmer and a negotiator. One day in first grade, she accidentally damaged a library book. "You'll need to get me a dollar so we can pay the library to make the repair," Gloria told her. She obviously intended Gabby to use her allowance money. Instead, Gabby went straight to Spencer.

"Hey, Dad," she said. "Mom says she needs a buck."

Spencer dutifully reached into his wallet to give her the money. He didn't ask any questions.

When Gloria discovered what Gabby had done, she wasn't happy. But she also noticed how carefully Gabby had worded her request. Though Gabby certainly was conniving, she hadn't lied. Gloria had indeed said she needed a dollar. If Gabby wasn't stuck in first grade, she could have gotten a gig as a politician's speechwriter.

"Gabby was always so agreeable, so cute, and she was cunning in this charming way," Gloria says. Melissa says that throughout her childhood, she watched Gabby's ability to win over people and felt a mix of awe and envy.

Melissa, now a preschool teacher, is two years, two months, and two days older than Gabby. The sisters always have been very different. "When I was young, I was a nerd, playing Dungeons and Dragons," Melissa says. "Gabby was highly social and gregarious. We had a lot of sibling rivalry, and we came to identify each other as opposites. For a while, she was a preppy. Later, I was a Goth. She was into horses and pop music and musical theater, so I wasn't. I was into books."

Melissa admits that she was jealous of Gabby's social life. "I didn't have a lot of friends, and when a friend of mine would be at the house, and Gabby played with us, it bothered me. I'd think: 'You have so many of your own friends. Let me have my one friend, OK?'"

Gabby could be boy-crazy, too. In middle school, she and a friend made a list of the cutest boys in descending order. She was thrilled when number 3 accompanied her to a school dance. She was always very feminine, too, and very clothes conscious. Her morning would begin with a call to her best friend. "What are you wearing?" she'd ask. Gabby developed a fondness for leather jackets, vests, and long sweaters in the winter.

Though Gabby was mostly a Goody Two-shoes, she had her moments of quiet rebellion. After she entered her teens, there were nights when she'd dutifully kiss her parents good night, head into her bedroom, and close the door. Then she'd climb out her bedroom window—luckily it was on the ground floor—to meet a boyfriend. One night, someone Gloria knew saw Gabby and a girlfriend walking through the desert on their way to a convenience store, no doubt to meet boys. Gloria was informed, and from then on she kept better tabs on Gabby's sweet-talking good-night routine.

In addition to boys, Gabby had a great appreciation for horses. She paid for her saddle and riding lessons by mucking out stalls, and when she was a teen, Spencer and Gloria helped her buy a horse, named Dink. Later she'd have another horse, Gus, which she nicknamed Buck-Stretcher, the slogan of El Campo Tire. She'd end up taking Buckstretcher with her to college. ("I learned a lot cleaning out those stalls," Gabby would later say on the campaign stump. "It was good training, all of that manure-shoveling, for when I entered politics.")

Looking back, Melissa says, "I think the reason my parents got Gabby that horse was so she'd be too tired and too busy to go after boys." Gloria doesn't dispute that. She says that plan worked "most of the time."

But not always. When Gabby was fourteen, she and some other girls who rode together went to a weeklong horse show in Flagstaff. A young woman who worked at the stables served as their chaperone. One night, Gabby called Gloria. "Hey, Mom, I'm having a problem with my contact lenses," she said.

Gloria recalls hearing loud music and what sounded like women whooping it up in the background. "Gabby, where are you?" Gloria asked.

"We're in a bar," Gabby said.

"A bar?" Gloria said. "And what's all that screaming?"

"Well, it's a male strip show," Gabby told her. The chaperone had taken her and the other fourteen-year-old girls to see a performance of male exotic dancers. (This is how Gloria recalls the story. Gabby insists there were no strippers.)

In any case, the next day Gloria drove to Flagstaff and gave Gabby's trainer what she calls the "stern eyeball." "Listen," Gloria said, "the reason I got this girl this horse was so that it would be a substitute for boys. I know this is the Wild West, but I don't want my daughter to be a wild woman at age fourteen."

Gloria didn't have to worry. Gabby would become a serious, accomplished student at Tucson's University High School, a public school for gifted students. She wowed many of her teachers, who found her to be winningly engaging and self-confident. They saw her as a very bright, optimistic young woman who was excited to find ways to make her contribution to the world.

Gabby has often talked to me about how her upbringing and her Tucson roots shaped her and strengthened her. When she was young, she knew she wanted to make a difference, but she wasn't exactly sure what path she'd take in life. She didn't ever say she wanted to grow up to be a congresswoman. And yet I now see that, starting in childhood, all these steps along the way combined with fate and happenstance— and a commitment to her family—to bring her to where she is today.

When Gabby left Tucson for college in 1988, she never would have imagined that, just nine years later, she'd be back in town running the family tire business, following in the footsteps of her grandfather Gif Giffords by starring in her own El Campo commercials.

She couldn't have guessed that those commercials would make her a recognized face in southeastern Arizona, helping to spark her political career. Or that her political career would almost cost her her life, leading her to a rehabilitation hospital in Houston. Or that in rehab she'd be sitting with her devoted mother, singing "Tomorrow," her childhood song of hope, as a way of reconnecting the damaged pathways in her brain.

CHAPTER FIVE

A Family of Risk-Takers

It was the ninety-third day of my brother's second mission to the International Space Station. He had flown there as an American astronaut aboard a Russian Soyuz spacecraft, and was serving as commander of the ISS.

As morning broke in the United States, Scott was hard at work, attempting a vital repair job that he didn't want to entrust to any of his crew members. This was something best left to the commander.

"There are two pieces of equipment in space that are the most important," Scott likes to say, "and both of them are toilets."

And so for two hours on that Saturday, Scott had been trying to fix a broken toilet, which is a difficult and complicated task in space, considering how complex a space toilet is. If he couldn't get it working, and the other toilet failed, too, he and his crew would be left using bags to relieve themselves, and then they'd have to store the bags. It would not be pleasant. Scott knew that much depended on his efforts.

While he was working, he got a call from the CAPCOM, the "capsule communicator" in Houston. That's the person on the ground, usually a fellow astronaut, whose job it is to remain in constant touch with the crew of a manned space flight.

"Scott, we're going to privatize the space-to-ground channel," the CAPCOM said. "Peggy wants to talk to you."

Peggy Whitson is chief of the astronaut office at the Johnson Space Center in Houston. The arranging of a private line meant that Peggy wanted to make sure her conversation with Scott couldn't be monitored by the public, the media, or anyone else within the space program. Such a procedure almost always indicates that an astronaut is about to get very bad personal news. Suddenly the toilet issue seemed unimportant to Scott.

He floated into another module on the space station and awaited Peggy's call. It took five minutes to set up the private line, in which time Scott traveled 1,460 miles through space, while the thoughts in his mind seemed to be moving even faster. Had one of his kids been in a car accident? Had someone in our immediate family died?

Peggy was finally patched through. "I have bad news for you," she said. "Your sister-in-law, Gabby, has been shot."

It was forty minutes after the shooting had begun in Tucson. Peggy told Scott what she knew, which wasn't much. NASA, meanwhile, had already cut off the system that allows astronauts to watch an intermittent, blurry satellite feed from CNN. It was decided that Scott was better off getting information directly from the astronaut office rather than from speculation in the media.

"I'd appreciate it if you could keep me informed with everything the news is reporting," Scott said, and when the call ended, he sat in that module by himself for a moment, feeling very alone and helpless. There was nothing he could do for Gabby, of course, but he also was unable to be of assistance to me. After Gabby, he is my closest confidant on the planet, the person whose judgment I value most. But he wasn't on the planet, and he wasn't scheduled to return for another sixty-six days.

Scott called me and we spoke briefly. I gave him the few facts I had, but there were so many issues I was dealing with that there was no time to talk. Shortly after we hung up, Scott got another call from NASA on the privatized line. "This isn't confirmed," he was told, "but many news organizations are reporting that Gabby has died."

Scott tried to call me again. I was already in the air, heading to Tucson, with my cell phone off. But Scott was able to get in touch with Tilman Fertitta, our mutual close friend. Tilman is a well-known businessman in Houston whose company owns restaurant chains such as Bubba Gump Shrimp Co. and Rainforest Cafe, and casinos, including the Golden Nugget in both Las Vegas and Atlantic City. Through our long odyssey in the wake of Gabby's injury, Tilman would turn out to be a generous friend in a time of need.

Tilman had stepped in to help as soon as we got word of the shoot-ing. First he offered his private plane to take me from Houston to Tuc-son. And then, knowing how besieged I was, he became a reassuring voice to Scott up in space. "Gabby isn't dead," Tilman told him. "It's a bunch of bullshit! I've talked to Mark. The media's got it wrong." Eventually, Scott was able to get through to me, and I confirmed that, yes, Gabby was alive and in surgery.

All my life, Scott has been everything to me: my nemesis, my fist-fighting opponent, the most irritating presence in my life—and my best friend. He and I no longer go at it like we did when we were kids, but we're never touchy-feely either. Over the next sixty-six days, while he remained in space, I had many urges to talk to him, to hear his voice.

I talked to him about decisions that needed to be made regarding Gabby's medical care. He listened, but he couldn't really help me decide. "I'm not a doctor," he said.

I talked to him about the swirling political issues. The whole coun-try was debating whether heated campaign rhetoric had played a role in the massacre in Tucson. Did I need to make a statement about that? Scott listened but couldn't give definitive answers. "I'm not a political analyst," he said.

However, when I talked to him about whether I should continue as commander of my upcoming space shuttle mission, that's when Scott spoke up. He isn't a doctor. He isn't a politician. But he is an astronaut. He knew the job that needed to be done. And he knew me.

There was speculation in the media, and frankly, within NASA, too, that I'd be too distracted by Gabby's injury to perform at my best. Though news reports focused on how I was struggling with the deci-sion, in truth, NASA officials weren't sure they even wanted to keep me on the job. They said they needed to watch me in training first, to monitor my ability to concentrate and perform. Their uncertainty about their faith in me only added to the stresses of those early days. Gabby was in a medically induced coma and I was in NASA-induced limbo.

From the start, Scott urged me not to step down. Like everyone else who knew Gabby, he told me that she absolutely would want me to remain on the mission. "You're a military pilot," he said. "You're trained to put aside personal issues, to focus on your mission. And the more people scrutinize you, the better you're going to be. I have no doubts."

Scott finally headed home from space on March 16, traveling with two crewmates aboard a Russian Soyuz capsule. The conditions that day at the landing site in arctic Kazakhstan were terribly cold and windy, but the capsule landed safely, on its side, in knee-deep snow. A medical tent was supposed to be erected, but conditions were too treacherous. Instead, Scott and his crewmates were taken away in helicopters to the city of Kostanay and then directly back to Houston.

I was waiting for him at the bottom of the steps as he came off the plane. We never hug or shake hands. Never. It's always been that way, since we were kids. But on this day, for the first time, we reached toward each other and shook hands. It was a spontaneous act of affection, though I know it sounds pretty limited compared with the embracing that goes on in a lot of families.

My brother had to undergo the usual battery of postflight medical tests. He had muscle pain, not uncommon after a long-duration flight, and he wasn't walking normally yet. All of us who've been in space know that, at least for a few days after we return, we'll likely be banging into walls when we try to turn a corner. We lose our ability to judge when it's time to turn left or right.

Given his deficiencies, Scott wasn't allowed to drive yet. So the next day, his girlfriend, Amiko, a NASA colleague of ours, drove him to the rehab hospital to see Gabby.

Gabby was in a therapy session, out of her room, when they arrived. I was waiting for them, and offered a heads-up about what to expect. "You have to be patient," I said, "and give Gabby time to respond. And she can't follow when two people talk at once, so don't do that." I explained that Gabby understood most everything, but wouldn't necessarily be able to answer them. "You know what it's like when you're trying to remember a word and you can't come up with it, and it's so frustrating? That's what it's like for Gabby every minute of every day."

Scott looks like me, only six minutes younger, and many people can't tell us apart. But when Gabby was wheeled in, she had no trouble. "Scott!" she said to him, not me.

He kissed the top of her head and sat down beside her. At first, he was shocked by Gabby's appearance. Her head was misshapen, her hair was short and a darker color, her right arm was so still. He was almost startled. But as he spent time with Gabby, he saw that her personality remained: her smile, her laugh, her trademark attentiveness.

He showed her the turquoise rubber bracelet he'd been wearing. I'd sent it up with the crew of space shuttle *Discovery* when they visited the space station a month earlier. The bracelet, worn by Gabby's staffers, family, and friends, has a heart, a peace sign, and the word "Gabby" on it. "I wore this in space," Scott said.

"Yay!" Gabby said, and pumped her left fist.

I watched my brother and my wife interacting. Here were the two people I am closest to in the world. Both were safe, and we were finally all together. It felt good, but I wasn't the type to get mushy.

When Scott stood to walk across the room, struggling on his land legs after 159 days in space, I gave him a little dig. "Hey, you're pretty wobbly," I said. "Gabby is doing a better job of walking than you are!"

If I have a choice between complimenting my wife or my brother, it's always going to be her. Always.

* * *

My brother likes to say that Gabby is way too good for me. If you look at my background and Gabby's, he's got a point. On paper, we're not exactly a natural fit.

Unlike Gabby, who had her own horse when she was young, I grew up on a lower rung of the socioeconomic ladder. I didn't have a horse when I was a boy in West Orange, New Jersey. I had rocks, which my brother and I would sometimes launch like missiles in the direction of other kids who had their own rocks.

While Gabby was the type who got excellent grades, I was a late bloomer on the academic front and on a lot of other fronts, too. And even though both my mother and father were cops, some people considered Scott and me to be borderline juvenile delinquents.

In February 1964, when we were born, my mother, Patricia, was just twenty years old and my dad, Richard, was twenty-three. They had met by happenstance. My dad had been in the army, stationed in Fort Bragg, North Carolina, jumping out of planes as part of the 82nd

Airborne. One day in 1961, he bummed a ride back home to New Jersey, and when he got there, he decided to attend a dance put on by local firefighters. That's where he met my mom. She was very pretty and vivacious, and my father was lucky that she gave him her number.

After they got married, my mother had hoped to have a lot of kids, but a series of miscarriages limited her to the two of us. That was enough. We were more than a handful.

From the time we were two years old, Scott and I were fighting with each other daily, sometimes for hours, often destroying things in the house. We'd go at it, fists flying, and we'd accidentally kick in a door or damage the paneling. Then we'd make peace and, starting in our pre-teens, we'd repair everything together before our parents came home and noticed. "I smell paint!" my father would say when he arrived.

He bought us boxing gloves and a heavy bag when we were six years old and started teaching us how to box. Then he had second thoughts. "If I give them one more lesson they're going to know enough to kill each other," he said to my mother, who had already nixed karate lessons for the same reason.

Scott and I were always climbing, too. We'd be outside a restaurant with my parents and if they blinked, we'd go missing. Eventually, they learned to look up. We were usually on the roof, having climbed up the gutters.

My mother says that, starting when we were eighteen months old, Scott and I would talk in this gibberish twin language that only we understood. We were probably plotting something. Later, when we were about five years old, my mother thought we had somehow taught each other Spanish. She was impressed, but we weren't savants. We were just singing the "Frito Bandito" song.

From the time we could walk, we were neighborhood roamers. One morning before we were two years old, my mother woke up and noticed that we had wet oil stains on the bottom of our footed pajamas. It was a mystery until a neighbor came to the door to tell her we'd been seen that morning hanging around the gas station up the street. While our parents were sleeping, we had unlocked the back door and escaped. They had to install new locks on the doors that were above our reach.

Looking back, I feel like I had a pretty unconventional childhood. In the summers, when the bug-spray truck passed through, my parents would let me and Scott run through the mist of chemicals. People then didn't know any better, especially in my neighborhood.

While Gabby was growing up as a child of the desert, I was more of an urban menace, palling around with a motley crew of characters.

When I was young, I figured the whole world looked like our neighborhood: a third Jewish, a third Italian, and a third Irish, like us. We lived just twenty minutes from Manhattan, and some of our playmates were the sons of mobsters. Their fathers would get in trouble—my father even arrested some of them—and the children could be troublemakers, too. That's why my mom insisted that our friends hang out at our house, playing pool in the basement. She wanted to keep an eye on all of us.

The kids in our neighborhood were the types who'd throw things at passing cars just for the laughs. One Halloween, we threw a scarecrow dummy in front of a car. The driver was at first hysterical, thinking she'd killed a pedestrian. It wasn't until we pulled the scarecrow out from under her car that she was able to breathe again. We're lucky she didn't have a heart attack. When Scott and I did completely stupid things like that, and someone called the police, we'd get off with a warning because the cops worked with our parents.

Warnings didn't have much impact, however. Our group of friends was incorrigible. When we were young, the Good Humor guy would drive his ice cream truck down our street on summer afternoons. Eventually, though, after being pelted with half-eaten ice cream, he wised up and never returned. We'd hear the tinkling music from his truck on the block before ours and the block after ours, but he knew better than to venture down our stretch of Greenwood Avenue.

* * *

I'm lucky I lived through my childhood, because I was the most injury-prone kid in West Orange.

My brother and I shared a crib, and I broke my jaw falling out of it. My brother claims he pushed me. Sounds likely. Other injuries were due to my own stupidity or bullheadedness.

When Scott and I were in kindergarten, my mother asked us to put a letter in the mailbox across the street. "Make sure you cross at the corner," she told us. We were usually pretty obstinate, but on this particular day, my brother decided to listen to her. He walked toward the corner. Me, I walked straight across the street, between two parked cars, and got nailed by a passing motorist. I went flying through the air and woke up in the hospital, throwing up from a bad concussion.

When I was twelve, my friend Tommy dropped a jar of worms while we were fishing. I stepped on it and got worm guts, glass, and dirt in my foot. I was in the hospital for a week with blood poisoning.

Another time, Tommy's cousin shot me in the foot with a pellet gun. The doctor recommended just leaving the pellet in there, but my mother wanted it out. So this surgeon started cutting where the hole was and he wound up taking my foot halfway off trying to find the damn pellet. I ended up with nerve damage. When I woke up after surgery I heard the doctor saying, "I don't know if he'll be able to walk right anymore."

In ninth grade, I broke my knuckles in a fight. That taught me a lesson: Don't punch someone as hard as you can, because it's going to break your knuckles.

There are more injuries to recount, but I'll stop here.

I guess I had a habit of coming out swinging in part because I was the son of a hard-charging, hard-drinking, hardworking Jersey detective. Every year or so, my dad would come home with a cast on his right hand. Working the narcotics unit, he had to use his fists a lot, he'd say. I assumed there were a few bar fights thrown in there, too.

Neither my mom nor my dad went to college, but they both had PhDs in street smarts, and Scott and I were proud of them. As the sons of career police officers, we grew up knowing what it meant to serve the public and to put your life on the line. We also saw how crazy a calling police work could be.

When we were five years old, my father would take us to this particular playground and push us on the swings. We didn't know it, but he picked that playground so he could stake out a nearby house. He needed evidence to obtain a search warrant and we were his cover. "Just keep swinging, boys," he'd say, with one eye on us and the other on the house.

My dad was a cop who had his own special tool kit. He'd be interrogating some nitwit, and he'd have the guy put his right hand on the police-station photocopier. "This is our lie-detector machine," he'd say sternly, and the sort of degenerates he dealt with wouldn't know any better. My father would ask a leading question, and if he didn't like the answer, he'd hit the "print" button. "The machine says you're lying!" he'd bark. Such creativity often led to confessions, and helped my father rise to the rank of captain.

My father could be equally audacious on the home front. Gabby's father toughened up his daughters by sending them to that Mexican summer camp where no one knew English. That was easy! My father toughened up Scott and me by sending us into shark-infested waters.

We did a lot of boating as boys, and one day when we were about fifteen years old, we were out with my father in New Jersey's Barnegat Bay. We ran aground on a sandbar, and making things worse, sharks had begun surrounding the boat. "You boys get in the water and pull us off the sandbar," my dad ordered.

"But, Dad, what about the sharks?" we asked, almost in unison.

My father took out his gun—he was a cop, after all—and said, "If they come too close, I've got you covered. Now get in the water!" Maybe the sharks heard my father and knew he was aiming for them. They left us alone and we freed the boat.

Suffice it to say that flying in space is not necessarily the riskiest thing we've ever done.

My mother, meanwhile, has her own history of putting herself in peril. In the mid-1970s, she became the first female police officer in West Orange and one of the first in the state. She was always pretty fearless. One night, she got dispatched to a home where a man in his twenties had killed his parents and was holding his sister hostage. When my mom arrived with a partner at 3 a.m., the young man was shooting out the window. My mother took cover on a dirt patch outside the house, only it wasn't just dirt. "Oh my God, I'm in dog shit," my mother said to herself, "and if I stick my head up, I could be shot." She stayed sprawled for two hours atop that stinking pile, her gun poised, until reinforcements came and the gunman surrendered.

My mother tells people: "The boys don't fear being astronauts, because they were born into a family of risk-takers. It's in our blood."

Her father was a New York City fireboat captain. Her sister is a retired FBI agent. Her brother is a retired cop.

In 1982, my mother was seriously injured on the job. It happened on a night she was in a squad car alone, patrolling behind a strip mall. She saw two men with a large garbage bag and asked them what they were doing. They scuffled with her as she tried to grab the bag—she never learned what was in it—and then they knocked her down and ran off. She ended up falling fifteen feet into a creek behind the store, ruining her back and knees. She was up to her armpits in water and couldn't get herself out. She ended up retiring on disability, and she still copes with daily pain from that incident.

My dad warned us not to be police officers. He described his job as being "a human garbageman." "The job sucks everything out of you," he told us. "If you want to be cops I'll break your legs."

We assumed he didn't mean it, because he seemed to like his job. And, at least when we were very young, a career in law enforcement felt like an option. We talked about being astronauts, like a lot of kids do, but we certainly didn't think we'd make it. Astronauts were usually academic all-stars, which Scott and I most definitely were not.

My parents weren't on top of us to do our schoolwork. They didn't give us the suburban mantra: "Study hard and you'll be a success." But they did have a blue-collar work ethic that spoke to their aspirations for Scott and me. "You both have the ability to do anything in this world if you try hard enough," they'd say. They knew we were both bright underachievers. Unlike some of our teachers, they liked to think that nothing was beyond our potential.

Sometimes they had to fight to make their point.

At our fourth-grade parent-teacher conference, our teacher told my parents that both Scott and I had learning disabilities. My father was having none of it. "You're out of your mind, lady!" he said to her. "We'll be back tomorrow with a real expert, and we're not going to sit in these little chairs, either."

His expert was his mother-in-law. My grandmother happened to be a learning-disabilities specialist, and she had tested us. She explained to the teacher that we were rambunctious boys with very high IQs. My father had the last word. "I think someone should be testing the teacher!"

Through junior high, my grades, like my brother's, were mostly embarrassing—Cs and Ds—and my father got tired of our academic indifference. Eventually he came up with a plan, and he started with me. "I've set up a deal for you," he said. "I'm going to get you into the welders' union. I've got a contact there."

A part of him was being realistic. Given how lackadaisically I approached my studies, maybe college wasn't for me. But my father was also picking his moment to make a strategic play. He figured that deep down, I had ambitions beyond being a welder. He was right. After that conversation with my dad, I truly had an epiphany. I thought, "Jeez, I'd better get myself together!"

I had always assumed that my parents viewed me as someone bright enough to go to college. Now here they were, telling me that maybe I wasn't. It was hurtful.

Until then, my school day had been spent looking out the window or staring at the clock, waiting for class to be over. But after my dad's lecture, I decided to start paying attention. I would tell myself, "I'm going to sit in this class and try to understand whatever it is the teacher is saying. I'm going to read whatever she puts on the board. I'm going to understand all of it."

The way I remember it, that's all it took. Starting in ninth grade, and for all the years that followed, I was nearly a straight-A student.

As my parents see it, my transformation, and Scott's, too, was not as abrupt as we remember it. In their own way, they'd been trying to show us the light, usually by example.

My mother decided she wanted to become a cop in 1975, when she was thirty-two. She'd been a waitress and a secretary but wanted a greater challenge. Thanks to a class-action suit, the state of New Jersey had just changed the weight and height requirements for police officers, which meant women could qualify. My mother was determined to be the first woman in our community to be hired.

Scott and I, then eleven years old, watched her train two hours a day for the physical. Her exercises were posted on the refrigerator. To pass the test, she'd have to scale a seven-foot-four-inch wall in nine seconds. My father built a wall out of plywood in our backyard, and without telling her, he made it seven feet, five inches tall. She spent two months trying to get over it, but never could. Then she figured out the secret: She had to run, hit the board with her left foot, use the momentum to grab the top of the wall, and then flip over it. She was able to scale the thing in just four seconds.

As part of the test, she'd also need to drag a 125-pound dummy seventy-five feet in twelve seconds. She used Scott as her dummy, which made sense to me, and dragged him around the backyard.

When she finally took the test, she passed easily, coming in fifty-sixth out of more than three hundred applicants, almost all of them men.

Scott and I had accompanied her to the test. We saw her actually jump in the air and kick up her heels when she passed. We saw her wipe away tears.

My mother knows that Scott and I think she didn't push us enough. She didn't make us study for hours every night. But she believes, and she's surely right, that we developed our ambition and our drive in part by watching her.

"You knew how badly I wanted to be a police officer, and that I'd been told I'd never get the job," she says. "You saw how hard I worked at it day after day. You saw my determination. Maybe watching me helped you."

For his part, my father thinks he may have told us things that, somewhere along the way, sank in. He recalls standing on the beach with me and Scott when we were maybe twelve years old. We were all looking into the water. "These friends you're hanging out with, a lot of them will never leave West Orange," my dad said. "They're not looking beyond the horizon. But you two, you need to remember that there's something over that horizon. Go look for it. Go find it. Go do it!"

I don't think we were really listening, but the way our lives turned out, we must have heard him.

* * *

Unlike Gabby, who was born as an overachiever, my brother and I had a late start. But once we got the urge to succeed, we took off.

At Mountain High School in West Orange, both of us wanted to run for student congress president our senior year. Rather than duke it out like we used to, we took a mature approach, flipping a coin. I won the coin toss and the election, and Scott served as vice president.

He and I did everything together. We were both captains of the swim team, and we were both pole-vaulters and scuba divers. We served together as emergency medical technicians on the local ambulance corps, working from 8 p.m. to 6 a.m. on many school nights. We have a lot of shared memories of pulling passengers out of car wrecks and helping elderly people who'd fallen and broken bones. Once, the two of us had to carry a three-hundred-pound woman down several flights of stairs, giving her CPR every time we stopped on a landing. I can still see the grimace on Scott's face as we carried that woman on the stretcher.

After our ambulance runs ended at dawn, we'd usually shower and go to school—but not always. Sometimes we just had to crash. I missed sixty days of classes my senior year and still worked hard enough to get mostly As.

The shooting in Tucson led me to have a few flashbacks from my teen years as an EMT. Scott and I worked some tough neighborhoods. I put on my first bulletproof vest at age seventeen. I remember one night we picked up a young African-American man in Newark who had seven bullet holes in him, including a gunshot wound to the head. He was alive when we delivered him to the hospital emergency room, but I never found out what became of him. After Gabby was shot, I found myself thinking about that young man. I wonder how he is doing today, if he's still alive.

I'm lucky I have Scott to talk to about all of these memories.

* * *

Once Scott and I became astronauts—the only twins and the only siblings to fly in space—people often asked us about the role our upbringing played in shaping our lives and careers. Later, after Gabby and I got married, people often asked us about how our upbringings shaped our marriage.

Well, here's an answer.

Gabby and I have come to realize that though our backgrounds appear so different on the surface, we have much in common. We both come from families that are colorful in their own ways. That's obvious. And we both come from parents who stressed to us the importance of public service. For my mom and dad, dangerous police work was their way of making a difference. For their part, Gabby's parents spent a lifetime being charitable and serving their community, instilling in Gabby the idea that she had it within her to change the world.

There's another thing, too. I think both Gabby and I were raised to be risk-takers. Going into space is one kind of risk. But setting up a table in a public square as an elected official is a risk, too.

Sometimes, risk-taking yields inspiration and hope. You take a risk—as a cop, an astronaut, a congresswoman—and good might come of it. You might get new perspectives you can share with other people.

After Scott returned from space, on that first day when he saw Gabby, he told her a story. "You know," he said, "I had such a unique vantage point from up there. I'd look out the window, and I'd see a lot of beauty."

He explained to Gabby that in the wake of her injury, he had tweeted a photo from space of the Tucson area as a tribute to her. He said that people in Arizona and beyond were very touched by that. He talked about how inviting and peaceful the Earth looks from space, how there are no borders between countries. Gabby listened and nodded.

I was grateful that my brother came bearing this message. It was as if he wanted to reassure Gabby that, although she was a victim of violence, he saw the possibilities of a more peaceful planet.

CHAPTER SIX

"Fly Away Home"

During the five months when Gabby was in the hospital and then in the rehab facility, her doctors and nurses joked that the elevator door would open and they never knew who might be asking for directions to Gabby's room. It could be a senator, a former cabinet member, the president of the United States, or someone less assuming—a colorful old friend from Tucson who had come to reminisce and make Gabby laugh.

Especially at the beginning, we limited visitors. Like many brain-injury victims, Gabby was often exhausted and in pain. Those of us closest to her appreciated that people wanted to see her, but we noticed that being around too many visitors felt overwhelming to Gabby. Her natural inclination to be perky and engaging sapped her strength.

We also had to consider well-wishers' motivations. We'd hear from lawmakers, Democrats and Republicans, asking to stop by, and we'd have to think: How close to Gabby is this person? Honestly, there was a concern, too, that someone from Washington might use a visit to assess Gabby's competence and her ability to remain in office. That's only natural in the cutthroat world of politics. Competitors want inside information they can pass along, or that will help them raise funds or recapture congressional districts. Especially in the early months after Gabby was injured, we thought she was entitled to privacy as she tried to heal. That's why we didn't release photos of her, we didn't go into great detail describing her recovery to the media, and we didn't encourage a parade of politicians—even allies and friends—to walk through her hospital room.

We also learned to closely study the list of would-be visitors. Some were people Gabby hardly knew or had met once or twice. Others were merely curiosity-seekers. Several times, doctors from out of state introduced themselves at the front desk and said they'd come to see Gabby. They flashed their credentials. When the security detail discovered that they had never treated Gabby and didn't know her, they weren't permitted to go to her room. We were taken aback that medical professionals would behave this way.

Other strangers stopped by, too. Though they likely meant well, they were turned away. Because Gabby was the victim of an assassination attempt, the U.S. Capitol Police guarded her room in shifts, twenty-four hours a day. The gunman in Tucson had been captured, yes, but there were concerns that a deranged copycat might seek to finish the job. Those of us who loved Gabby had to be cautious and alert. The security issues were stressful for all of us.

In late January, after Gabby first arrived at TIRR Memorial Hermann, the rehab hospital, former president George H. W. Bush wanted to come by and welcome her to town. It was very kind of him to call, but things hadn't been easy for Gabby early on, so I asked him to wait.

"Well, why don't you come by our house and bring your daughters?" he said. "Barbara and I would like to say hello."

He was reaching out as both the eighty-six-year-old elder statesman who lives in town, and as someone who seemed genuinely concerned about Gabby and her loved ones. The girls and I took him up on his invitation and stopped by the Bush house in Houston's Tanglewood neighborhood.

We stayed for two hours, talking about Gabby's career, her recovery, my upcoming shuttle mission, and the girls' life in Texas. It turned out to be a lot of fun. At one point, Mrs. Bush asked Claudia where she was thinking about going to college. "Maybe Pepperdine," Claudia said.

"Well, how about Yale?" President Bush said. "I went to Yale. That's a good school."

That's when Barbara said, "You know, our son George went to Yale, too, and then he went to Harvard. I don't know why people say he's the stupidest president ever!"

"Yeah, I never got that either," I said, and we all laughed, especially Mrs. Bush.

President Bush and I were both naval aviators, and I told him that I had served during the first war with Iraq in 1991. "I was one of your guys over there in Desert Storm," I said.

He asked for details, including what ship I'd flown from—it was the USS *Midway*—and then he told me, very soberly, "Thank you for your service."

The visit to the Bushes' house was surreal in some ways, especially when I thought about the chain of events that brought me and my kids there. I flew thirty-nine combat missions in the Persian Gulf, but it wouldn't have occurred to me during the war that twenty years later I'd be hanging out at the president's house, receiving a personalized thank-you. Or that I'd be there because my wife was seriously injured in the line of duty during an attack on U.S. soil, also while serving her country. It would have been hard to fathom any of it.

In early March, about two months after Gabby was shot, I thought it would be an OK time to finally invite the Bushes over to see her. I'd told Gabby they were coming, but she wasn't clearly focused on everything then. When the Bushes arrived, Gabby was feeling pretty beat. She was in a chair, not her bed, but she had her head in her hand and was dozing off. The president walked in and she opened her eyes and looked up, not recognizing him at first. Then he came closer and she sat up straight.

"Wow!" Gabby said.

I could see the wheels turning through the haze in her head. It was almost as if she were thinking, "What happened to my life? I open my eyes and out of nowhere a former president is standing in front of me." She looked around the room, perhaps wondering if Jimmy Carter would be coming out of the closet.

President Bush sat next to Gabby for fifteen minutes, holding her left hand. It was very touching to watch. "You've been so strong," he told her. "I'm really proud of you. And I'm praying for your recovery."

"Chicken," Gabby replied. "Chicken."

This was one of those early days, when that was still the most frequent word on Gabby's lips. No matter what she was trying to say, that was the word that came out. "Chicken."

"Why does she keep saying that?" Mrs. Bush asked.

"We don't know," I told her. "Doctors can't really explain why patients get stuck on certain words."

Gabby was struggling with aphasia, an impairment of the ability to remember words, to speak, and to write. But she was also coping with perseveration, the repetition of words and phrases, which is common among people with brain injuries.

When the visit ended, I didn't think the Bushes would speed home and call Republican headquarters with insights into Gabby's condition. The former president is now beyond politics, beyond partisanship. I could see that. He was just a veteran of public service who knew the risks of the job and wanted to show his concern.

Gabby was appreciative when she was visited by public figures such as the Bushes, but because she wasn't communicating well, I'd sometimes see frustration and embarrassment on her face. She was a woman who used to be able to get dressed fast and look great, a woman who socialized easily and winningly. I knew it was hard for her to feel so deficient and exposed.

She was more comfortable during visits with old friends, especially Raoul Erickson. He's a forty-three-year-old free spirit who runs a business in Tucson designing and repairing electronic equipment. Extremely bright and unafraid to be unorthodox, he always reminded me of a younger version of Doc Brown from *Back to the Future*. Gabby had gotten to know him fifteen years earlier when he'd shown up at El Campo Tire to fix the company's computer system. A siblinglike friendship blossomed from there.

Raoul is the ultimate go-to friend. As Gabby's mom puts it, if you need a rattlesnake relocated, your car pulled out of a ditch, or Wi-Fi installed in your house, he's the guy you call, and he shows up eager and able to help. He's there if you want to have fun, too. It was Raoul who'd gone on that long bike ride with Gabby the evening before she was shot.

The first time Raoul flew down from Tucson to visit Gabby in Houston, she was thrilled to see him. "Christmas, best ever!" she said cheerily. It was likely that she meant to say something along the lines of: "It's great that you're here, Raoul!" But those unintended words about Christmas were what came out of her mouth. It didn't really matter. Her exuberance while greeting him was clear.

Being with Raoul, Gabby could connect with her best memories of Tucson—her active and athletic life there, her career before Congress, her most-cherished haunts. Gabby and Raoul didn't have to reminisce or even trade any words. They could just be together, and Gabby felt more like herself. I saw that.

I was very grateful that Raoul was willing to spend so much time with Gabby, especially because I was caught up in training for my mission. When he visited, he often ate meals with Gabby in her room at TIRR. Gabby's right hand remained in her lap, totally still, as she held her fork with her left. Like Gabby, Raoul is right-handed, but he decided to leave his right hand in his lap, too. Eating with his left hand was a show of solidarity that Gabby appreciated. When she first noticed, she acknowledged his empathetic gesture by touching his left hand with hers and smiling at him. Then the two new lefties continued eating in silence.

Before her injury, Gabby was diligent about trying to avoid all processed food. Raoul had turned her on to eating natural products, and with his encouragement, she was always reading the labels on food packaging. That continued even after she was injured, though I'm not sure she could make sense of the ingredients she was reading about, or that she was able to decipher the fine print with her damaged eyes. She'd frequently have to cover or close one eye to read those labels, or she'd alternate from one eye to the other.

Raoul saw that Gabby didn't like a lot of the hospital food—she'd make that clear by pushing it away—so he'd smuggle in things he knew she'd eat, such as Greek yogurt, fresh fruit, vegetables, and salads.

Raoul had an intuitive sense about Gabby, and he recognized that when she was feeling depressed, she often didn't have much of an appetite. "Eating is part of the healing process," Raoul told her. "You've got to eat. You'll heal faster and get out of here faster. And you've got to stay positive. That's really important."

In her own chosen words, Gabby kept telling Raoul—and the rest of us, too—that she wanted to leave the hospital. "Fly away home," she'd say. "Fly away!"

The imagery of that, as if Gabby could rise from her wheelchair and fly off like a bird, was so poignant to us. When Raoul was on duty, his answer was often the same: "Well, let's be positive and you'll fly out of here faster."

They'd continue sitting together, Gabby picking at her food, and a few minutes later, she'd reflect on his advice. "Positive," she'd say, almost to him but more to herself. It was as if she were trying to shrug off her sadness and her urge to cry. A few more bites of food. "Positive. Positive."

* * *

Even when Gabby wasn't greeting visitors at the hospital, it was as if she had unexpected company. Letters and e-mails came in every day from well-wishers: strangers, constituents, die-hard Democrats, die-hard Republicans, people who'd recovered from brain injuries, and well-meaning people offering therapeutic advice. A boy in Arizona sold his toys for $2.85 and sent it along so Gabby would have lunch money. A woman from Florida sent Gabby her very own "Astronaut Barbie," which included the tag line "First stilettos on the moon!" The woman wrote: "The adage is 'the sky is the limit,' but certainly not in your case."

Gabby also heard from almost everyone she'd ever known earlier in her life. Her mom, Gloria, would sit with her reading these letters from friends and acquaintances, stopping to interject her own comments or flashes of memory. Gabby seemed to enjoy the reminiscing, even though she couldn't articulate her own recollections.

A lot of the letter-writers described their impressions of her back when she was younger. It was as if they felt a need to remind her about the kind of person she was, and the traits they admired in her before she was injured. She heard from a long-lost cousin, now teaching in China, and from her long-ago Brownie troop leader. A friend from college recalled Gabby's "tenacity, wit and strength as a listener," and how people viewed her as a one-of-a-kind woman on campus, "always rehabilitating old Vespa scooters and motorcycles." Gabby was pretty handy as a mechanic.

Bob Gardner, a former El Campo Tire employee now living in Virginia, described his initial thought when he heard that Gabby, the boss's twenty-six-year-old daughter, would be taking over the business: "To me, that meant a spoiled, snot-nosed kid would be going through the motions of running the company, asking questions, getting in the way of everyone while we did the real work." He wrote of how shocked and impressed he was when Gabby insisted on learning every position in the company "including busting tires, loading trucks and running the front counter."

In Bob's letter to Gabby, he also recalled the first day he met her: "I walked into the main office and was startled to find a petite, young, beautiful woman in sweats and tennis shoes, sitting on the counter. You were fully engaged in reading 'Modern Tire' as I stammered 'hello.' You jumped to your feet and cheerfully introduced yourself, 'Hi, I'm Gabby!' You quickly made me feel comfortable as you explained your background and asked about mine. We spent a half-hour getting to know each other. You made me feel like you were truly interested in me and my future with the company."

As Gloria read the letter, Gabby remembered Bob. "Yes, yes, yes!"

She didn't say it, but she surely knew it. Bob was the manager of El Campo's store on North Oracle, the street where she would hold her ill-fated Congress on Your Corner event.

Like many letters from Gabby's old friends and acquaintances, Bob's ended with optimism: "I'm sorry you have to go through these hard times, but I feel assured that your recovery will be quick and complete, and it won't be long before you are back where you belong, in Washington, D.C., and Tucson, representing the people who love you."

Day after day, Gabby listened as her mother read letter after letter. It was as if people from her past were coming to life in her hospital room, encouraging her to reclaim herself. Gabby grinned at the good memories. But at times, I'd also see sadness on her face. She'd close her eyes.

"Fly away home," she'd say. "Fly away."

* * *

Looking back, Gabby's life has been defined by a series of unexpected detours. She always felt that her quirky, nonlinear path through early adulthood made her stronger, more curious, more self-possessed, and more aware of the needs and yearnings of different people in a variety of cultures. She was all at once an intellectual, a businesswoman, a tire-changer, a community advocate, a lone horseback rider, a cowgirl, an art-and-music aficionado, a biker chick, and a fledgling politician. She took steps toward becoming a sociologist, an anthropologist, a divinity student, and a farmer.

When Gabby and I were dating and I began learning her life story, I realized she was like no one I had ever met. She was ten different women combined. She had been engaged by everything!

It wasn't that she was striving to be a renaissance woman. It was that all her varied interests couldn't be contained. She described it as "a kind of lunacy," but also thought her journey suited her perfectly.

After high school, Gabby attended tiny Scripps College in Clare-mont, California, and she'd later tell me that her education there was a great gift, largely because it was an all-female institution. "Boys in classrooms dominate the conversations, especially in math and sci-ence," she said. She felt that she nurtured her self-confidence and pol-ished her ability to speak up by asserting herself in those all-girl classes. She wondered if she would have ended up running for Congress had she spent her college years sitting quietly in classrooms, waiting for the boys to finish talking. At Scripps she could be silly, serious, opinion-ated, whatever. She could figure out who she was.

Gabby loved the words of Ellen Browning Scripps, who founded the college in 1926. The school's mission was to develop in students "the ability to think clearly and independently, and to live confidently, courageously and hopefully."

An ambivalent math student in high school, Gabby discovered a passion for calculus at Scripps. Though she was interested in many subjects, she finally settled on a double major in Latin American stud-ies and sociology. Meanwhile, outside the classroom, she began to real-ize how crucial it was for her to sort out her own feelings about public policy and public service.

While I was a twenty-six-year-old combat pilot in the thick of Oper-ation Desert Storm, following orders, Gabby was a twenty-year-old student at Scripps, standing on the fringes of peace demonstrations and angry student rallies. She wasn't a knee-jerk pacifist, shouting slo-gans. She wanted to better understand why we'd gone to war, so she'd stay up late into the night watching coverage of the fighting, or reading about the politics and Iraqi actions that led to it.

Gabby was no pushover. She came from the Wild West, remember, and walked the campus in cowboy boots. Behind her sweet smile was a tough broad, especially if someone messed with her. She'd speak her mind.

She once took a course about minority women in literature. She was the only white student in the class, and the African-American instructor wasn't very welcoming to her. "This course is for women of color," she said to Gabby.

Gabby answered, "I *am* a woman of color. I'm just a lighter color."

Gabby was also more fearless than the average student at Scripps. When she wasn't riding Buckstretcher, the horse she'd brought to college, she'd tool around campus on her Vespa. Then it was stolen, and the thief had the audacity to advertise it for sale. Gabby found out where the scooter was being stored, used a chain-cutter to free it, and stole it back. If the thief had come by to confront her, she'd have just kept cutting. She understood a thing or two about frontier justice.

After graduating from Scripps in 1993, Gabby drove off in her Ford pickup with one of her motorcycles, a German model from 1946, strapped into the bed. As soon as she reached Tucson, she enrolled in summer school at the University of Arizona, studying economics.

I once asked her why she did that. "I thought that maybe I could become a really smart farmer and solve world hunger," she said. "I was thinking big."

That overly ambitious urge passed, and she instead applied for a Fulbright scholarship to study the eighty thousand "Old Colony" Mennonites in the Mexican state of Chihuahua. She was accepted and received a grant for a one-year academic adventure.

Gabby immersed herself in the Mennonite community, living with them in their homes, without electricity or indoor plumbing, and asking countless questions about their conservative views and their commitment to nonviolence. She compiled data on their fertility and mortality rates, and took a special interest in those who strayed from the faith, which she jokingly referred to as "Mennonites gone bad." When she was with them, Gabby wore their traditional clothing. In her long-sleeved Mennonite dress, with a brimmed hat and a tight scarf, she looked like someone from the 1800s.

Gabby later ended up at Cornell University, earning a master's degree in regional planning. Her interest in the field was rooted in her love of Tucson. She had watched the surge in the city's population and commercial development over the years, and saw the dangers of mismanaged growth. In 1996, that master's degree helped her land a well-paying job in New York at Price Waterhouse, the top-tier accounting firm, where she consulted on the demographic impact of regional development. She was excited that her responsibilities included traveling to eleven Latin American countries.

Not long after she started that job, Gabby was called into her boss's office. She'd been dressing in appropriate attire: mid-1990s power suits. Colleagues, however, were taking exception to her footwear. "This is Price Waterhouse and this is New York City," the boss said. "You've got to stop wearing cowboy boots to work." Fearing she'd lose the job, Gabby left the boots in her closet and tried to embrace East Coast urban life.

A part of her was hugely excited to be in New York. She'd later reminisce about her arrival there by saying: "It seemed like the beginning of a grand and glittering adventure in the big city: posh apartments, pointy-toed shoes, and maybe even my first martini."

She wrote those words in 2009, during her second term in Congress, when she was asked to give the commencement speech at the Scripps College graduation. Gabby gave a lot of thought to that speech. She wanted the young graduates to know that the life we live isn't always the life we plan, and to see the beauty in that. She was always telling me that she wanted to find ways to empower young women, and to that end, she wrote the commencement speech very carefully.

She told the graduates what happened to her when she was a few months into her new job in New York City: The phone rang and it was her father calling, saying he needed her to come home as soon as possible to take over the family tire stores. She'd have to resign from Price Waterhouse.

"This was completely unexpected and not at all in my cosmopolitan plans," Gabby explained in her speech. "But inevitably, there comes a point in all of our lives where our role as the child begins to reverse with our parents. Our protectors now need protection. For some of us it comes while we are established in life, and for others it may come while we are young. But whenever that call comes, we pick up the phone and we respond. In my case, it meant packing up my heels and putting on my cowboy boots, getting back into the same old Ford pickup truck and heading back west."

She explained that her return to the family tire business in Tucson was the first step in a progression. "I learned the tire business from the ground up and also started to manage the company's philanthropic aims, the part that tried to give back to the community that had been so generous to us through the years.

"I started to see things about southern Arizona that were not perfect and needed to change. So I ran for office determined to make that change and put right the things that were wrong, to represent those who didn't have a voice. And I realized then and there what my heart was saying: that for me, the highest calling in my own life was service to others. I have not looked back since."

She told the young women at the graduation a little about her journey, her long list of possible careers, her enthusiasm for offbeat adventures. She hoped her story would encourage them to be restless and creative, to step outside the lines. "You are blessed to be living in a country that gives its citizens the freedom to bump around the scenery a bit, to try new things and make mistakes and stretch your talents and make adjustments and to find every rich and satisfying thing, and it will still be OK in the end.

"Remember what the authors of the Declaration of Independence said about the inalienable rights of each person, which are 'life, liberty, and the pursuit of happiness.' Think of that! These words are one of the deepest expressions of who we are as Americans. This is the mission statement of the United States. I hope you will choose to make it your mission statement as well.

"Pursue your passion, and everything will fall into place. This is not being romantic. This is the highest order of pragmatism."

The tire business was certainly not Gabby's first passion. And yet she embraced her job at El Campo with a commitment rooted in her passion to serve her family. She didn't know it at the time, but her decision to help her father would put the rest of her life in order. It was the tire business that sparked an awareness of her in the Tucson community, which helped lead her to the Arizona legislature, which enabled her to reach the halls of Congress by age thirty-six.

"We're the buck-stretchers!" she'd say in El Campo's commercials. She wasn't the sixty-second philosopher her grandfather Gif Giffords had been. But she was telegenic and friendly; a natural with a pretty smile. By selling tires, she'd learn how to sell herself, and eventually, how to sell the issues, ideas, and values that would define her career as a public servant.

* * *

El Campo had about $11 million in annual sales when Gabby arrived, but the business was hemorrhaging, with significant losses every month. Her father, Spencer, was not in good health, and he was overwhelmed trying to manage twelve outlets and more than one hundred employees. He was admittedly burned out. Gabby's first order of business was to tell Spencer that he'd need to retire. "I can't really run the place if you'll be looking over my shoulder," she said.

Spencer didn't argue. It all felt familiar to him. When he took over the business more than three decades earlier, he had walked his father, Gif, to the door and sent him off into retirement. Spencer saw the sense in letting Gabby take the reins completely. He knew he could be ornery, difficult, and set in his ways. Gabby deserved to recast the operation as she saw fit. He was actually relieved when she asked him to step aside.

"Here are the keys," he told her. "It's all yours. Go for it. Thank you and I love you."

Gabby took no salary. She was there on a mission. Her goal was to get the business back into the black, and to preserve the family assets.

The business community took note of her age—just twenty-six—and her moxie. Early on, she gave an interview to the local paper, the *Arizona Daily Star,* about her return to Tucson and the family business. "I have a fresh eye for things, and I question why we're doing things a certain way," she said. "You only gain that perspective by being away from something, and then facing it head on. I have tremendous ambition, I'm enthusiastic, and I have great ideas, but I lack experience." She admitted that some key employees had left, and that she had jettisoned certain suppliers. "They worked for my father," she explained, "but I didn't get the sense they were going to work for me."

Sometimes, Gabby talked tougher than she acted. One woman in the front office had a drug problem and was routinely hostile to Gabby. People knew she needed to be fired, but Gabby couldn't let her go. It was partly because Gabby had a heart for working women, and partly because she would try, sometimes too hard, to see the good in people. The woman eventually quit.

One of Gabby's best business decisions was hiring Raoul to revamp the company's antiquated computer system. Back then, in the pre-Internet days, all the stores' computers were connected by phone line. It took Raoul hundreds of hours to modernize the place—he literally moved in and slept on the floor at night—and over time his friendship with Gabby grew.

Raoul noticed that many employees took a liking to Gabby quickly, drawn in by her friendliness and openness. Others found her to be too perky, too positive, too young. They seemed disdainful of her. They didn't know whether they should trust her, or whether her upbeat demeanor was just an act. Gabby didn't obsess about trying to win them over. She just continued being herself, and if her sunny disposition rubbed people the wrong way, she was OK with that. She was too busy to dwell on it.

Early in Gabby's tenure, she wrote a thick employee manual, the first in the company's history, so everyone would know the rules, expectations, benefits, and company philosophy. She also had children's play tables placed in the waiting areas of all twelve El Campo stores.

In any way she could, she tried to pay special attention to female customers. "The tire industry doesn't treat women customers the way they treat men," she observed. Salespeople would talk down to women or take advantage of them. At El Campo, most of Gabby's employees were men between the ages twenty and forty. Some looked like the roughest characters from a biker movie, with lots of tattoos and facial hair. Others were traditional family men who viewed the world as a patriarchal society. Gabby worked hard to change the culture within the company, reminding her workforce to treat women and men with equal respect.

She did a lot of reaching out to women, too. She bought a booth at the annual Tucson Business Women's Expo, set up a giant display of chrome tire rims, and stood there handing out El Campo refrigerator magnets and pamphlets with car-care tips. "We're locally owned and we're woman-owned," she'd tell passersby, conversing easily in both English and Spanish. "I just want you to know that we're a friendly tire company."

Gabby enjoyed being the face of El Campo, appearing not only in the company's television and radio commercials, but in print advertising, too. A part of her was still the kid who starred in *Annie*, and she liked that people did a double-take when they'd see a young woman on TV, looking so comfortable in front of a stack of tires. She felt like a groundbreaker. (Years later, after she met me, she said the commercials were too embarrassing, and she refused to track down the tapes for me to see them. I spent years begging to get a look.)

Not surprisingly, it was hard for Gabby to find a female mentor in the tire industry. There were almost no women in the business. So she looked elsewhere for a role model and found an older woman, Dorothy Finley, owner of a local beer distributorship in Tucson. Dorothy was an Arizona icon who turned from beer to philanthropy, serving on dozens of nonprofit boards. It was Dorothy who led efforts to stop the closure of Tucson's Davis-Monthan Air Force Base, saving thousands of jobs. Dorothy became Gabby's hero and confidante. They were an unlikely match, an octogenarian and a twenty-something, yet they connected with each other effortlessly.

Gabby knew she didn't want to stay in the tire business forever. Sometimes she felt antsy about that and sometimes she was more patient. She was pretty grateful, though. She recognized early on that she was learning skills in management, advocacy, and marketing that would serve her well up the road, no matter where her next stop would be. Running the tire business, she saw how vital it was to look at details, to harness the power of close observation.

At El Campo, she learned how to read a tire the way she'd eventually read legislation—with an eye toward identifying the weak spots. In a town where temperatures often topped 110 degrees in the summer, hot roads were tough on tires. It was in Arizona where the tires on Ford Explorers—the Ford Firestone ATX and the Wilderness AT— were first found to be deficient. Gabby and her employees saw how the tires repeatedly failed their customers. Eventually, the tires would be recalled nationwide.

In her first year at El Campo, Gabby increased annual sales by $1 million, and stopped the losses. She suspected, however, that such good news could be fleeting. She saw that the tire business was consolidating in the hands of a few national retailers. Family-owned businesses like El Campo would eventually be squeezed out. So once she'd gotten the business out of the hole, she decided that the best hope for preserving the family assets was to find a buyer for the whole operation.

She'd go to conventions of tire dealers, mingling with all the middle-aged men, trying to figure out who might be a good suitor for El Campo. She eventually set up meetings with both Goodyear and Firestone, and in July 1999, agreed to sell El Campo to Goodyear. Wisely, she sold only the business itself and not the properties where the stores were located. She figured that land values were going to keep rising in Tucson, and she was right. Her parents would be forever grateful to Gabby. They'd be able to enjoy retirement without having to worry about their finances.

Gabby also looked after El Campo's employees. She worked with Goodyear to make sure that her workers got to keep their jobs and retain their seniority. Some had been with the company almost four decades. Even those employees who weren't sure what to make of Gabby during her tenure were, by the end, very appreciative of her fierce advocacy for them. "You could have just walked away," more than a few told her, "but you didn't. Thank you."

As the sale of El Campo was being finalized, Gabby attended a meeting of the Arizona Women's Political Caucus. She went mostly out of curiosity. She had no firm plans to become a politician. But as she talked to the women there, she wondered if elected office might be the right next step for her. She'd been a Republican in her early twenties, but she now found herself in the camp with centrist Democrats. She felt more at ease with them, given her support of a woman's right to choose, and her belief that health care for the poor in Arizona had to be expanded. She'd been saddened, for instance, to learn that poor women with cervical or breast cancer weren't being insured. Democratic initiatives on these issues made more sense to her.

And so Gabby found herself at yet another turning point in her life.

Her move back to Tucson had reignited her heartfelt affection for her hometown. Her interactions with El Campo customers and employees had helped her understand the most pressing financial and social concerns swirling in the region. Her success running the company had emboldened her as a businesswoman and as a potential leader. She talked to her friends and family. "Look, I'm single. I have no children. Maybe now is the time I should be dedicating myself to my community."

After three years of focusing on tires, she widened her sights. She wrote down the issues that mattered most to her. She asked herself: If I ran for a seat in the Arizona House, what would be my platform?

She started scribbling. She'd make education her top priority, arguing for smaller class sizes and increased pay for teachers. She'd advocate for better health-care coverage for families living in poverty. She'd work to improve the state's mental-health system, which was in terrible shape. She'd get involved in making smart decisions about managing growth in southern Arizona. She'd help small businesses. Her list kept growing.

She was thirty years old, full of confidence, ambition, and enthusiasm, with a résumé that seemed like a dozen young women's résumés smashed together.

She felt different. She was no longer Spencer's younger kid, Gabby, back in town to sell tires.

She was no longer that cute "buck-stretcher" girl that people saw on TV.

She was now the candidate Gabrielle Giffords and she was ready to serve.

CHAPTER SEVEN

Big Dreams

In the early months of Gabby's recovery, I'd ask her, "Do you ever have dreams when you're sleeping?"

"No," she'd say, shaking her head.

One day, I pushed her a little. "Never? You never dream about anything? Your childhood, your life in Congress, the years we dated? Nothing?"

She thought for a moment. "No," she said. She seemed to understand my question. No was her answer.

I wondered: Was she having dreams but not remembering them? In her head at night, was she back to being her old self, conversing effortlessly? Or was she having nightmares, reliving or reimagining the shooting and the painful aftermath?

Her doctors said it was possible that she was having dreams she couldn't recall. It was also possible that the damage in her brain prevented dreaming. The brain is such a mystery. It was hard for them to say for sure.

"Well, I have dreams," I told Gabby. "I have recurring dreams."

Gabby didn't ask me, "So what do you dream about?" From the day she was shot, she had lost her ability to formulate any original questions. For those of us who love her, that was one of the most difficult aspects of her injury. She either had no urge to ask a question, or more likely, the broken pathways in her brain weren't allowing it. It was sad for us to see this. All her life, Gabby had been a woman fueled by her curiosity. Had she lost that piece of herself, or was she just unable to tap into it? We couldn't tell as we communicated with her, mostly in monologues. We talked. She listened.

On that day when I told Gabby that I have recurring dreams, she looked at me intently, waiting for me to say more. And so I answered the question she didn't ask. "I dream about you, Gabby," I said.

My recurring dreams were actually wonderful. In every one of them, Gabby would make an almost full and miraculous overnight recovery. The dreams were a little different each time, but the general theme was the same. I'd arrive somewhere, usually the hospital, and I'd be greeted by a nurse in the doorway of Gabby's room. The nurse would say something like, "You're not going to believe it. This is a really big deal! You've got to go in and see Gabby."

As I entered her room, I could immediately see that Gabby had morphed back into the person she used to be. She was almost completely lucid, talking in full sentences. "Hi, Mark. Sit down and talk to me. I'm feeling so much better today."

Interacting with Gabby in my dream, I could see that she still struggled with certain words, and that her right arm and leg were functional, but not yet totally back to normal. That didn't dampen my elation. I'd think to myself, "This is completely great! She's ninety percent there! And that's more than enough for me. Ninety percent? Gabby, we'll take that!"

Each morning, when I'd wake up, I had a sense of what I'd been feeling during these dreams: relief, exhilaration, appreciation. But within seconds, of course, I was back to reality. Gabby was certainly making meaningful progress every week, working as hard as she could in therapy. But mostly, she was taking baby steps. There would be no instant miracle.

That was not easy for me to accept, especially in the early stages of her recovery. I was demanding of doctors, always trying to determine the best treatments and the fastest paths to recovery. But eventually I adjusted to our new reality and, in the process, I learned things about myself.

One thing I discovered was that I have the capacity to be a patient guy. I learned to give Gabby the time she needed to say something, even if it was just one word. Often, that meant there were long, empty silences. I noticed that some visitors felt they had to fill those silences by chattering. This was frustrating for Gabby, who would still be trying to express herself. And so I had to become someone who taught patience to others.

It's funny that patience has become a virtue of mine, because in certain ways, a large part of me is very impatient. Starting in young adulthood, I was always so achievement-oriented, climbing each step of the ladder without slowing down or stopping. Always aware of "the urgency of now," I wanted to seize every opportunity. Maybe I was fearful that I'd lose everything I'd worked for if I allowed myself to relax.

Gabby, on the other hand, was always pretty patient, especially in her dealings with others. She'd let constituents say whatever they needed to say without interrupting them. She was wonderful interacting with people, whether young kids or old folks in nursing homes, always listening closely as they expressed themselves.

I also think back to the time, after my second space flight, in 2006, when Gabby and I got to have lunch with the legendary British astrophysicist Stephen Hawking, who is paralyzed due to a form of Lou Gehrig's disease. It takes him an excruciatingly long time to say anything, and I pretty much gave up on conversing with him beyond a few pleasantries. But Gabby was just incredible. She intuitively knew what to do.

After my failed attempt at interacting with Dr. Hawking, she kneeled down in front of his wheelchair and said, "Dr. Hawking, how are you today?" She then stared into his eyes and waited. As far as she was concerned there was no one else in the crowded room. She waited silently and patiently. Using a device that tracks the motion of a single facial muscle, he took at least ten minutes to compose and utter the phrase "I'm fine. How are you?" Gabby was in no rush. She could have kneeled there for an hour, waiting for his answer. I was so impressed.

After Gabby was injured, I found myself thinking about her encounter with Dr. Hawking. In fact, that memory helped me understand how I'd need to interact with her. It's almost like something out of *The Twilight Zone*: Dr. Hawking theorizes about time and space, and it was this moment in time that gave me a window into what our future would look like. It was as if Gabby was giving me a message back in 2006: "Watch me. I will be your teacher. Someday, you'll have to be patient with me and this is how you'll need to do it."

Emulating Gabby's gift of patience went beyond giving her time to talk. I also had to force myself to dial back my expectations, and to be patiently realistic. Doctors repeatedly said she was making remarkable progress. Just living through that kind of injury was rare. Still, I had to accept the obvious. Gabby would get better, but not at the pace I yearned for in my dreams.

I grew to accept that a lot of my efforts would seem fruitless, at least for a while. Breakthroughs would come when they came.

On the concept of asking questions, for instance, I had to commit myself to trying, day after day, to coax a question out of her. Doctors and psychologists advised us that until Gabby was able to ask questions on her own, we needed to refrain from giving her too much information about the shooting. It might be terrifying and even debilitating if we were to load her up with the particulars of the tragedy if she had no way of asking for more details or of expressing her grief. She also might feel very guilty, holding herself responsible for the six deaths and twelve other injuries, since it was her idea to host the Congress on Your Corner event.

If and when she was able to ask questions, we were told, she'd be better able to emotionally handle the full story of January 8. Until then, doctors instructed us to proceed gently.

And so each day I would work with Gabby, slowly and carefully explaining to her what constituted a question.

"Questions begin with the same words," I said to her one day. "Who, what, when, where, why, how. Let me give you some examples. *What* time is it? *Where* is my mom? *Who* is coming for dinner? *When* did it stop raining? Now you try, Gabby. Let's start a sentence. What . . ."

She looked at me and said nothing.

I gave it another shot. "What . . ."

"Tired," she said. "I'm tired."

"I know you're tired, Gabby, but let's try this. Try to start a sentence with the word 'what.'"

She struggled to think, and I could tell she wanted to please me by responding. A minute went by. Finally, she was ready to talk.

"What I'm tired," she said.

I shook my head. "Gabby, that's not a question."

She cast her eyes downward. She knew she hadn't come through the way I wanted her to, but the ability to ask a simple question was beyond her grasp.

Sometimes, I'd think about the fact that all my adult life, I'd been a guy whose dreams were big and ambitious. I used to dream of flying fighter planes, and that dream came true. I used to dream of being the first human to walk on Mars. Though I'm still about 40 million miles away from that one, I made a good effort.

But after Gabby's injury, I often felt as if my dreams had become completely basic. I spent my days hoping that Gabby would be able to end a sentence with a question mark. And then at night, after I'd drift off to sleep, she would appear to me, asking about everything.

*　*　*

When I look back at my life, I see certain experiences and lessons that helped prepare me to be a caregiver to Gabby. At the Merchant Marine Academy, I learned to appreciate that actions have consequences; how you respond in a situation determines the chain of events that follows. You can't just rely on your gut. You have to think about the ramifications of every decision. After Gabby was hurt, I saw that was especially true when determining her medical treatments and therapies.

Twenty-five years in the Navy and at NASA taught me to prioritize, to ask the question: "What's the most important thing I should be doing *right now*?" Sometimes that meant making a split-second decision, and it had to be the right decision because your life depended on it. But I also embraced the mantra of NASA's first flight director, Chris Kraft: When you don't know what to do, don't do anything. I kept that in mind, as I tried not to rush into decisions about Gabby. If there was time to collect facts and weigh data, I did it.

Training for and then flying the space shuttle, I learned how to think clearly under pressure, and how to avoid making mistakes when I was incredibly tired. That's a learned skill as well, and I'd need it in the early days after Gabby was shot, when I was functioning on just a couple hours of sleep.

During all my years of education, training, and flying, it wouldn't have occurred to me that I was also preparing to serve as a caregiver. But I was.

I entered the U.S. Merchant Marine Academy after graduating from high school in 1982. My brother, Scott, meanwhile, attended the State University of New York Maritime College. Throughout our younger years, we'd both become confident and able on the water, and we were influenced by our grandfathers. Our paternal grandfather served in the Navy in the Pacific during World War II, and our mom's dad served in the merchant marine before becoming a New York City fireboat captain. Their legacy led us to consider a career at sea.

The Merchant Marine Academy was a demanding institution with high academic standards. When my class of 350 midshipmen gathered together for the first time, we were given that old line "Look to your left. Look to your right. One of you won't make it to graduation." That turned out to be true.

I really buckled down when I was there and was near the top of my class academically. As a senior, I was named the regimental executive officer, which was the second-highest position in the military command structure among students. One of my duties was to oversee the indoctrination of the new midshipmen.

The first year was tough for them, along the lines of boot camp. My job as executive officer was to motivate them, to let them know what was expected, to hold them to high standards. My message was this: They were capable and smart, and if they followed instructions and worked hard, we'd all succeed together. (Decades later, I'd command the space shuttle using similar motivational tactics. And I'd spend countless hours reminding Gabby that, despite her injury, she was still capable and smart, and the harder she worked, the more she'd improve.)

What I loved best about the Merchant Marine Academy was that we were required to spend six months of our sophomore and junior years at sea aboard commercial ships. I made two trips through the North Atlantic on a container ship, carrying U.S. goods to Europe and then returning with European products for American consumers.

Long before I saw the world from space, I saw the world from these ships, and it was a great adventure—sort of like Gabby's forays through Mexico. I worked diligently, but I still hadn't shaken all of my juvenile-delinquent tendencies. One day, off the coast of Egypt, our ship was tied to a Saudi Arabian merchant ship so we could unload grain onto it. Late that night, the other midshipman at sea with me said, "I dare you to sneak onto that ship and steal the Saudi Arabian flag from the mast."

"You're on," I replied. I climbed on the Saudi ship, carefully avoiding the crew member on watch on the bridge. I quietly walked behind the pilothouse and up the stairs that went to the mast. I lowered the flag, stuffed it in my shirt, and got the hell out of there as fast as I could.

I'm lucky I wasn't caught, arrested, and sent off to Chop Chop Square in the Saudi capital, Riyadh, where public beheadings are conducted. They also cut off hands there, a bigger concern for a flag thief like me. (I kept that flag for years as a tangible keepsake of some of the idiotic things I did when I was young.)

On another ship, with twenty-five crew members, I made two trips through the Panama Canal to the west coast of South America. This was a six-hundred-foot-long "break-bulk" ship, which meant it carried cargo that needed to be loaded and unloaded individually, rather than in large freight containers. We'd head south with barrels of chemicals, a few cars, and someone's grandmother's junk in a trunk, and we'd return with a hold filled with bananas.

I learned how business was conducted in South America, at least back in the 1980s. The bananas could have been boxed up, put on large pallets, and loaded by crane onto our ship. That would have been quick and efficient. Instead, there'd be a string of guys loading two boxes at a time by hand, and it took forever. It was a way to keep more people employed, but it was maddening to watch. My experiences on those trips also taught me to always wash bananas. There weren't necessarily restrooms on the docks, so workers would disappear into a stack of thousands of boxes of bananas to relieve themselves.

I had considered myself street-smart as a teen, but in South America I saw that I was still a somewhat naïve nineteen-year-old kid from New Jersey. One day, along with the other midshipman at sea with me, I went to an Italian restaurant in Miraflores, a shopping district of Lima, Peru. A riot broke out, with hundreds of people piling into the streets and throwing rocks. We had no idea what the rioting was about, but it was quite a spectacle, and so we hung around to watch.

Eventually, a truck arrived and a bunch of military police got out the back of it. One officer stopped about twenty feet from us. He didn't say anything. He just pointed his gun at us, ready to shoot. In the mayhem as we ran away, it sounded to us as if he had fired that gun several times and that the bullets had whizzed over our heads. Maybe he was a bad shot, or else he was trying to deliver warning shots to break up the crowd. Either way, we quickly realized the risks of being tourists at a riot, and we took off back to our ship.

The day after graduating from the academy in 1986 with a degree in marine engineering and nautical science, I got in my car and drove from New York down to the U.S. Naval Air Station in Pensacola, Florida. While many of my classmates took the summer off to relax and clear their heads, I started training in Pensacola the following Monday. I had become too driven a guy to sit around and lose time. I had decided I wanted to fly, and I didn't want to wait.

During my training, however, I quickly found out that I wasn't a particularly good pilot. Boy, did I struggle. I failed a couple of check rides with instructors, and barely reached the point where I was considered safe enough to make an attempt on an aircraft carrier. When the Navy sends you out to the ship for the first time, there isn't anyone crazy enough to go with you. No instructor. It's just you, by yourself, with whatever skills you have accumulated from countless hours of practice.

So in July 1987, I flew out to the USS *Lexington* by myself. It was cruising in the Atlantic, and I was instructed to do two touch-and-go landings and four arrested landings. In arrested landings, you put down an extended hook attached to your plane's tail, and you're stopped by a long cable strung across the back of the ship. Then you taxi to the bow and are catapulted off to go around for another landing. After returning to shore you get debriefed by the instructor, who has been watching you from the deck. In my case, I'd been pretty awful. I barely passed.

I discovered during training that we all don't learn at the same rate. The student pilots who were great on their first aircraft carrier landings didn't necessarily go on to be astronauts. How well you perform when you start trying something difficult is not a good indicator of how good you can become. Looking back, I'm a prime example of someone who was able to overcome a lack of aptitude with persistence, practice, and a drive to never give up. By working hard, I went from a bad student pilot to an OK test pilot to a pretty decent astronaut.

* * *

In December 1987, after eighteen months training on the T-34C Mentor, the T-2B Buckeye, and the TA-4J Skyhawk, I was designated a naval aviator. I spent all of 1988 training to fly the A-6E Intruder attack aircraft, after which I was assigned to the "Eagles" of Attack Squadron 115 in Atsugi, Japan. It was from there that I'd be deployed twice to the Persian Gulf aboard the aircraft carrier USS *Midway*.

Iraq invaded Kuwait on August 2, 1990, and for a few months, the international community tried diplomacy and sanctions to convince Saddam Hussein to withdraw his troops. In November, our ship was sent to the Gulf, where we waited to see if the United States and a coalition of thirty-four other nations would opt for military action. On January 17, 1991, at about 3 a.m., the Persian Gulf War began with a massive aerial bombing campaign. My first flight into battle would begin much later that day, at 9 p.m. I was twenty-six years old, the same age Gabby was when she returned to her dad's tire store.

The A-6E was a two-man aircraft, and my bombardier/navigator was a smart, laser-focused guy named Paul Fujimura. While many of us were from the service academies or ROTC programs, Fuj was a rarity—a graduate of the very liberal University of California, Berkeley. Back at his alma mater professors and students were mounting antiwar protests. And here he was with me, planning to fly into Iraq carrying twelve thousand-pound bombs.

Fuj was steady. I felt I was a bit more nervous. I kept thinking, Well, this is the real deal.

We flew north toward our target, an airplane maintenance hangar at the Shaibah military airfield, southwest of Basra. I wasn't thinking about how many Iraqi soldiers or civilians might have been in that hangar late that evening. I wasn't thinking of the politics of the war. I'd just spent five years training for one purpose: to drop bombs on a target when my country asked. Now I was going to try my best to do just that.

As we got to within fifteen miles of the target, I looked over my left shoulder and saw a white dot snaking through the sky and coming directly at us. It was a Russian surface-to-air missile fired by Iraqi forces.

Earlier, I had turned down the volume on our plane's antimissile countermeasure system because another U.S. plane had been tracking us with its radar, and the resulting noise had been a distraction. I had forgotten to turn the volume back up, so I never heard the warning about the missile.

But now the thing had my attention. "Fuj," I said, "there's a missile coming at us."

"Roger," he replied. "Tracking the target."

The missile got closer. "Fuj, this isn't good," I said. Again he told me, "Tracking the target."

"Fuj, I'm going to have to do a last-ditch maneuver to beat this thing!"

His job was to run the weapons systems and track the target. So that's what he did. "Roger, tracking the . . ."

OK, I heard him!

I'm sure my heart rate shot up. In addition to high explosives, this kind of missile had an expanding rod, which is a circular wire-cutting device designed to slice through an airplane and its crew.

We hadn't practiced for this. You can practice dropping bombs, flying low in formation, dealing with bad weather in mountains. But there's no good way to prepare for a real surface-to-air missile.

We were at about 15,000 feet, and I rolled inverted, added full power, and planted the stick in my lap, trying to confuse the missile into avoiding us. It worked. The missile missed us and exploded above our aircraft. I saw the flash as it detonated, but fortunately, as I scanned the engine instruments, I could see that it hadn't done any damage.

I was relieved, of course, but now we had a job to do. We had to drop those bombs. Fuj remained focused, never taking his head out of the radar boot.

Just then, damn it, I spotted another missile. Having survived a near miss with a Russian SA-6 surface-to-air missile, there could be no worse feeling than to see a second one coming your way.

I did the same last-ditch maneuver that worked earlier, and the missile missed us. I was pleased. Having learned from my encounter with the first missile, I avoided the second one more easily. It was on-the-job training. As Fuj and I encountered this fusillade, another A-6 in our strike group jettisoned his bombs and high-tailed it home. He'd seen the missiles guiding on and detonating near us, and he wanted no part of it.

We were able to get the nose of the plane climbing again, so we could get back to the right altitude to roll into our 30-degree dive and drop our bombs. If Fuj hadn't been so focused through those two missile attacks, we'd never have been able to hit the target.

When we came through the clouds, with our target ahead of us, it was a sobering sight. It looked as if all of Iraq was on fire, and we were about to add to the chaos. At 6,000 feet, I pulled the trigger, directing the computer to release the bombs. The airplane hangar was destroyed.

Now we had to get back safely to the USS *Midway* out in the Gulf. Our planned egress route was the same as the route we took to the target, but there was no way I was going to fly back through the area where the Iraqis were launching those missiles. So I flew as far east as possible, forty or fifty miles into Iran, before making a right turn to head south, where the aircraft carrier was waiting.

That's when I heard on the radio that an enemy airplane had been spotted by U.S. forces, and they were preparing to shoot it down. When they gave the aircraft's altitude and airspeed, I noticed, Hey, that's my altitude and airspeed. That's when I realized: Because Fuj and I were speeding toward the Persian Gulf from Iranian airspace, they thought we were an enemy fighter. They were getting ready to shoot us down.

Nearly getting shot by the enemy is one thing, but being blown out of the sky by your buddies is a recipe for a bad night. Iraqi missiles I could deal with. Air-to-air missiles from a U.S. Navy F-18 Hornet or F-14 Tomcat would present a much more difficult challenge. Once they got their missiles in the air, Fuj and I would certainly be dead.

"FUCK!" I said to Fuj as I realized how badly we had screwed up by not letting our guys know that we had sneaked into Iran. Two decades later, I can't recall exactly what I said on the radio at that moment, but it was immediate, loud, and conveyed this message to everyone listening: "Please don't shoot down the morons in Iranian airspace!"

After my radio transmission was acknowledged, we slowed down and took a deep breath. "It's not a good idea to fly out of Iran looking like an enemy aircraft to coalition forces," I told Fuj, stating the obvious. He agreed. We quietly flew back to the ship and landed without incident.

I didn't find it easy to fall asleep knowing I was almost killed three times that night.

It was the first combat mission of my life. I'd fly thirty-eight more before the war ended six weeks later.

*   *   *

Some missions are a blur. Others, like the one on January 30, 1991, remain clear in my head. On that day, Fuj and I spotted two ships motoring together toward Iran. They appeared to be Russian-made Polnocny amphibious personnel carriers. Were they carrying Iraqi troops? We had to make certain.

From 5,000 feet I could see that one of the ships was flying a flag. I dropped to just a hundred feet above the water, and got out a picture guidebook I had of the flags of every nation. Middle Eastern countries have flags that look strikingly similar. It can be maddening to figure out which is which. Iran, Iraq, Jordan, Kuwait, Syria, United Arab Emirates—they've all got blocks or stripes of red, white, and green.

I flew right alongside the ship, from stern to bow, as fast as the A-6 would go, and held up my picture of the Iraqi flag to compare it to the flag on the mast. "Yep," I said to Fuj, "it's an Iraqi ship." In hindsight it was very risky to fly so close to that ship, giving its troops such a clear shot. But we were young and felt somewhat invincible after a couple weeks of combat.

We flew higher and radioed what we'd seen back to the *Midway*. Minutes later, we got clearance to sink both ships. We rolled into a 10-degree dive and let loose a thousand-pound, laser-guided bomb. Unfortunately, it missed the ship. These things don't always go as planned. The bomb pierced through the water a couple hundred feet away. It was the first time we had missed in fifteen combat missions and neither of us was happy about it.

The Iraqis weren't happy either. They began shooting at us with the antiaircraft artillery gun mounted at the center of the ship. We pulled up and jinked a few times to maneuver and avoid the enemy fire. Fuj quickly reconfigured our weapons system so I could deliver the two cluster bombs that remained by visually aiming for the target. I pulled hard on the stick to keep the A-6 turning, trying to make the shot more difficult for the Iraqi gunner. Then, as one of our more colorful squadron mates liked to say, "Now we're on government time." (By that he meant: We are serving our country, and whatever happens, happens.) That was the crappy part of these bombing runs, where we had to stay pointed at the target, get to the correct release conditions, and hope that those bullets coming at us just plain missed.

This time, our weapons hit the target and we sank one of the ships. The other was sunk a short time later by another aircraft from our squadron.

I ended up getting an award from the Navy for "heroic achievement" on that mission. You can't celebrate awards like that. I was doing what my country asked me to do, and I recognize that there was great violence inherent in my act.

I have no idea how many people were on those two ships. I did see men jumping into rafts as we flew away, so I know some of them lived.

When the war began, a couple of men in our air wing decided they couldn't serve in battle. They were left back on the *Midway,* standing watch as duty officers, ostracized by some of their comrades. Whether they were scared or just disagreed with the legitimacy of the war, they made a decision I wouldn't make. As I saw it, I was trained as a combat pilot for a singular purpose—to deliver weapons to an enemy target when my country called. It wasn't my job to question the decisions that put us in that position, at least not at twenty-six years old.

I believed that 1991 war with Iraq needed to be fought. I still believe that. I was proud to serve. But I never lost sight of the sobering fact that I had a job, sanctioned by my government, that required me to kill a lot of human beings.

I know the magnitude of what it means to use destructive force against people. I saw it as a twenty-six-year-old pilot flying combat missions off an aircraft carrier. I saw it again at age forty-six, on that terrible Saturday in Tucson.

After Gabby was shot, and eighteen others were killed or wounded alongside her, I did a lot of thinking about the violence humans are capable of committing. Much of it is beyond senseless, like the gunman's rampage in Tucson. But even violence with a purpose—including my missions in the skies over Iraq—requires solemn reflection. It can never be taken lightly.

* * *

In my Navy career, I logged nearly six thousand hours in the air, flying fifty different aircraft. I landed planes on aircraft carriers 375 times. I'd risen to the rank of captain and was able to earn a master's degree in aeronautical engineering from the U.S. Naval Postgraduate School. I also attended the U.S. Naval Test Pilot School. By 1994, I was a project test pilot on a variety of aircraft. My training and experience had left me with a pretty formidable résumé.

The following year, at age thirty-one, I decided to apply to be an astronaut. Ever since I was a boy, I'd dreamed about the possibility that I'd be chosen. The job of an astronaut involved everything I was interested in: adventure, risk, speed, the unknown, and massive amounts of adrenaline. My high school girlfriend remembers me promising her that I'd be the first human on Mars. Back then, I had more confidence than experience, knowledge, or sense.

As an adult, though, I knew the odds were long that I'd actually make it into the program. First, the Navy had to agree that I was qualified enough to have my application packet forwarded to NASA. About 2,500 military personnel and another 2,500 civilians apply for each NASA class. For the upcoming class, NASA would end up taking just thirty-five Americans and nine international candidates—two Canadians, two Japanese, an Italian, a Frenchman, a German, a Swede, and a Spaniard.

I was lucky, though. The first step went my way. The Navy agreed to send my application on to NASA. A few weeks later, I was having dinner with my brother, and I told him he ought to apply, too. He and I had similar résumés; he was a naval aviator and a test pilot. The Navy agreed to send in his application, too.

I continued my military duties as an instructor at the U.S. Naval Test Pilot School in Patuxent River, Maryland. Almost a year later, out of the blue, I got a call to head down to Houston for a weeklong NASA interview. I didn't have a business suit, so I borrowed the one suit my brother owned.

I was nervous. I knew this was a real opportunity—a childhood dream within reach—and I didn't want to screw it up. But I also knew that of the 120 candidates they were bringing down for interviews, half would be disqualified for medical reasons. It didn't matter if you were in great health. They'd find some minor condition or something you didn't even know you had—a heart murmur, imperfect vision, a missing kidney—and they'd cross off your name.

The testing was intense and comprehensive. They took a lot of blood. They did a colonoscopy. They hooked me up to an EKG and put me in a sphere, curled up in the dark like a ball, while they watched my heart rate. If it went above a certain level, they'd figure I was claustrophobic and they'd dismiss me. I was pretty good in there. I just relaxed and went to sleep.

Once I made it through the medical tests, the interview process followed. It was a twelve-on-one interview: twelve of NASA's top officials and one of me.

One of my inquisitors was John Young, the legendary astronaut who flew the first manned Gemini mission in 1965, went to the moon twice, and was the first commander of the space shuttle. He asked me a very technical question about the frequency of the flight-control computer on a plane I was flying then, the F-18 Hornet. I wasn't sure, but I made the most educated guess I could. I must have been close because he seemed happy with the answer.

The next day they told me they planned to invite my brother down for an interview, too. I thought that was a good sign that I'd done well in my interview. If I had done poorly, why would they want another one of me?

When it was time for Scott's interview, however, he realized he had a problem. He had just one suit, and I'd already worn it to my NASA interview. He thought it would be ridiculous to show up wearing the same suit his twin brother had worn.

"Buy another suit," I told him.

"You should have bought another suit!" he said.

He ended up wearing the same suit, and I let him borrow the shoes I'd worn down to Houston. It was a bit nuts. He decided to bring the matter to people's attention before they noticed. "I bet something looks familiar," he said, "and it's not just my face."

Scott thinks that we both benefited from each other's interview. Most candidates who get called down to Houston are technically qualified. Acceptance hinges on whether NASA officials and veteran astronauts connect with you and like you. Because they got a double dose of me and Scott, they had more time to get to know us, and we had more time to try to impress them.

In the spring of 1996, I got the call first. It was Dave Leestma, head of Flight Crew Operations. I had learned that Dave would be placing calls to all those who were accepted, while the chief astronaut would call the candidates who were rejected. I was obviously thrilled to hear from Dave.

"You did very well in the interview process," he told me, "and we hope you'll want to come down to Houston and work here as an astronaut."

I accepted immediately, trying to find the right words to express my gratitude. We talked for a few more minutes, and then I had to address my curiosity. I knew I normally wouldn't get anywhere asking about another candidate for the job, but I couldn't help myself. So I asked Dave: "Will you be calling my brother?"

Dave answered, "Well, I usually wouldn't say this, but yes, I need to talk to him as well. Do you know where I could find him today?"

He didn't say the chief astronaut—that bearer of bad news—would be looking for my brother. He said *he'd* be making the call. So I knew Scott had been accepted, too. I was incredibly proud and thrilled for both of us.

Other twins may know what I was feeling. It was like a double triumph.

*   *   *

Years later, after I met Gabby, I described for her the emotions I felt when I learned I'd been accepted into NASA's astronaut program. "It felt better than winning the lottery would," I told her. "I wouldn't have traded that job offer for anything in the world."

My career path was slightly more conventional than Gabby's—I never lived with Mennonites—but she saw us as kindred spirits. It wasn't just that we were both ambitious and driven. It was also because, even though she was liberal arts and I was the sciences, we were fascinated by each other's life and career choice. We were each other's cheerleader.

It was especially thrilling for me to watch Gabby fall in love with the space program. My enthusiasm became hers and hers became mine. Her district had many connections to space research, from the local astronomy culture to the University of Arizona's lead role in the Phoenix Mars Mission, which studied the history of water in the Martian arctic's icy soil.

In her congressional career, Gabby turned out to be both a geeky policy wonk and great advocate, serving as chair of the House Subcommittee on Space and Aeronautics. Again and again, she spoke about the benefits of space exploration, and about the need to continue an ambitious and coherent national space policy. She could be tough, angry, and exasperated when NASA and its funders in government lost sight of the lofty goals of the nation's earliest space pioneers. In congressional hearings, she never minced words.

At one hearing regarding NASA's uncertain future, in February 2010, she pointed to a proverb on the wall behind her: "Where there is no vision, the people perish."

"These words," she said, "are as true today as when our forefathers undertook a voyage of discovery, when they landed on this continent and founded America as a city upon a hill, a beacon of light for the future world. . . . Our job as servants of the people, as members of this subcommittee, is to allow our scientists, our engineers, our researchers, our visionaries to be as bold in this undertaking as our faculties will allow."

Some of Gabby's advocacy efforts were rooted in her understanding of me. She knew the grittiest details of my trajectory from directionless kid in New Jersey to military pilot to shuttle commander. Understanding how my dreams came true, she often thought about the young people today who deserve a chance to be the next generation of explorers. At that 2010 hearing, she said: "My concern today is not numbers on a ledger, but rather the fate of the American dream to reach for the stars. Should we falter, should we slip, should we let our dreams fade, what will we tell our children?"

In the months after Gabby was shot, I'd think back to how she was always such an eloquent idealist. She had a contagious enthusiasm and a true gift for encouraging others, including me. And now, sadly, she had no choice but to focus on herself, to hope she'd again be able to master the simplest tasks.

When I'd feel disheartened about all of this, it was helpful for me to think about Gabby kneeling beside Dr. Hawking, patiently waiting for his words to come. I may have rocketed into lower Earth orbit, but he had explored the entire universe from his wheelchair.

Maybe big dreams were still possible—for me, for Gabby, and for our life together.

CHAPTER EIGHT

Baby Steps

By late March, almost three months after Gabby was injured, she had graduated to more complex tasks in speech therapy. For instance, rather than just trying to identify and say words she saw in a series of photos, she was asked to think more deeply about what was going on in the pictures.

In one session, her speech therapist, Angie, showed Gabby a photo of an envelope about to be mailed. It had an address on it. "What is missing from this letter?" Angie asked.

Gabby brought the photo close to her face. She read the recipient's address on the envelope. "Kansas," she said.

"Yes, the letter is going to Kansas," Angie answered. "But what is missing?"

Gabby studied the photo. She didn't know what was missing, so Angie told her. "It's missing a stamp. What will happen if an envelope is mailed and has no stamp on it?"

There was no response from Gabby. Maybe she knew and couldn't find the words. Maybe she didn't know. Angie moved on.

The next photo showed a motorcyclist. "What's missing?" Angie asked.

It seemed like Gabby knew the answer, but her word choice wasn't exactly right. "Medical. Medical," she said, waving her left hand over the photo.

"It could be a medical issue, yes. Tell me what is missing."

"Scary. Scary. Medical," Gabby said, and then touched her head. "Glasses," she said, but as soon as the word came out, she knew it was wrong. She tried again. "Helmuh . . ."

"Yes!" Angie said. "The motorcyclist is missing a helmet. And without a helmet, he could hit his . . ."

"Head," Gabby said.

"And what would happen?"

"Bump, bump," Gabby answered.

"What else?"

"Brain injury. Brain injury." Gabby had come to know those two words very well. They came easily to her. Her answer was a good one.

Angie held up a third photo. It was a picture of someone drinking a glass of water. "What's the matter with this?" Angie asked. "There's a safety concern with this glass. Try to use words to tell me."

Gabby couldn't answer.

Angie prompted her. "The glass is . . ."

"Green," said Gabby. She could often come up with a common phrase or a snippet of a song lyric, though not always precisely.

"Well, the grass is green, yes," Angie said to her, "but this glass is . . ."

Now Gabby found the word in her head. "Broken."

Angie wanted Gabby to think through the steps. "If you're out for dinner and they give you a broken glass and you drink out of it, what might happen?"

"Brain injury," Gabby said. That was her fallback affliction.

"No, not a brain injury, but you could get . . ."

"Cut," Gabby said.

"What would you cut?"

"Cut lip. Lip," Gabby said.

She'd gotten it. Angie smiled at her.

When I sat in on such sessions, I was pretty good at being upbeat and encouraging, complimenting Gabby on her progress and urging her on when she was frustrated or tired. But it could be dispiriting sometimes, watching how tough this whole process was for her.

Most of us have contemplated what it would be like if we were blind or deaf. I certainly have thought about that. But until Gabby was injured, I had never once considered how disabling it is to be unable to speak. What Gabby was dealing with was more debilitating. Those who are blind or deaf can engage with the world, they can communicate their needs and feelings. They can express themselves creatively.

But especially in those early months, Gabby was locked inside herself. And that could be terribly disheartening, even for someone as optimistic and innately cheerful as Gabby.

At one low point, I fantasized about making a deal with God. If Gabby could just regain the full use of language, it would be OK if she'd never walk again. I thought Gabby would make that agreement without hesitation. To be able to talk, she'd give up the ability to walk.

There were no deals to be made, of course. All we could do was hope and pray and offer Gabby our optimism.

It was important for us to keep reminding her that she was definitely making progress. That's why I'm glad I had a lot of her therapy sessions taped. She was far more on target in this late-March session than she was just one month before. I had the old footage to prove it. Eventually, I showed Gabby some tapes, so she could see for herself.

My forty-seventh birthday was February 21, and the day before, Gabby was in therapy with Angie, and they were singing together. My digital recorder captured it all.

"You are my sunshine, my only sunshine . . ."

Gabby was singing softly, but she seemed to be hitting every word. She wore a green sweater and a khaki cap over her short hair. She looked tired, but she was trying.

Then Angie asked her to practice "Happy Birthday" so she'd be ready to sing for me.

Angie and Gabby sang together, but when they got to the third line, Gabby sang, "Happy birthday, dear chicken . . ."

"You'd better not say that on Mark's birthday," Angie said. "It's 'Happy birthday, dear Mark.'"

Gabby tried again. Again she said "chicken" instead of "Mark." Angie wrote my name on a piece of paper and held it up for Gabby. Again, she sang "chicken."

You could see how frustrated Gabby was. Angie decided to move on to looking at photos. She held up a photo of a hairbrush.

"Comb," Gabby said.

"It's not a comb, it's a brush," Angie told her.

Gabby said the words "boo hoo" and seemed ready to cry. She looked miserable.

"Gabby, you've been amazing," Angie told her. "It's been just five weeks since you were hurt. It's a long road but we can do it. Are you a fighter?"

"Yes," Gabby said, and used her left arm to deliver a positive fist pump.

Angie showed some more photos. Gabby looked at a photo of a set of car keys and said "Tooth berry." She looked at a photo of a desk lamp and said "Tooth berry" again. She'd been saying those two words together a lot. We didn't know why and she didn't either.

Angie tried to get her more focused. "What are you wearing on your head?" she asked.

"Chicken," Gabby said, but then she tried to force the right word out of her mouth. She furrowed her brow and squinted her eyes as she thought. "Hack," she said, finally.

"Not hack," Angie told her.

"Hat," Gabby said. She'd gotten it right, but she was overcome by a wave of emotion. She started crying.

"You're doing amazing," Angie said. "Can I tell you something? It will get better. You've come a long way." Angie rubbed Gabby's back, then brought her a tissue. "Do you need a hug?"

She and Gabby hugged, and as they did, the water bottle in front of Gabby fell over. Gabby's tears were interrupted by a little giggle.

"You look much prettier when you smile," Angie said. "Now wipe your eyes and let's sing."

Angie began slowly singing "This Little Light of Mine"—they'd practiced it before—and Gabby joined in. "This little light of mine, I'm gonna let it shine, this little light of mine, I'm gonna let it shine . . . let it shine, let it shine, let it shine . . ."

When they finished, Gabby was very subdued. "I know it's frustrating," Angie said. "But you're going to get through this."

"Yes," Gabby said, but softly.

"Say it like a congresswoman!" Angie instructed.

"YES!" Gabby replied, with a little more enthusiasm.

Watching old footage of herself in therapy was not easy for Gabby. She could certainly see the strides she had made from February to March, and that was encouraging. But at times, she couldn't help but cry while the video played. Watching herself saying the wrong word then the right word then a word that made no sense at all, she saw clearly that she had a long road ahead. It would take a great many baby steps—and much bigger steps, too—to get back to the woman she had been.

* * *

Gabby's first run for public office was in 2000, when she sought a seat in the Arizona House of Representatives. Before the election, she knocked on as many doors as she could. She spoke to any group that would have her, touting her business experience at El Campo and her volunteer work. (Only thirty years old, she served on the boards of the YMCA, the Tucson Regional Water Council, and a support group for the Arizona Air National Guard.) She explained to people that she was a moderate Democrat who until 1998 had been a registered Republican. Growing up, she was the daughter of a Republican mother and Democrat father. "I learned about bipartisanship at the kitchen table," she'd say.

Gabby was determined. Her strategy to win the election was to talk to every single person in the district of about 172,000 people. Each day for weeks, she'd put on her white tennis shoes and a pair of shorts, she'd pull her hair back in a ponytail, and she'd walk. And walk. She walked door to door, all day, almost every day, for weeks. She walked from one end of the district to the other, and by election night, she truly felt like she had spoken to every registered voter—or at least she had tried. Maybe they didn't like her or agree with her positions on every issue. But thousands of them did meet her, and got a firsthand impression, which they'd hold on to when she'd later run for the U.S. House.

The *Arizona Daily Star* in Tucson endorsed her, writing: "Giffords is the youngest of the four candidates, but she has packed a lot into her years." Gabby won the election and threw herself into learning the intricacies of state government.

In the spring of 2002, she decided to run for the Arizona state senate, and she was required to collect four hundred valid signatures on her nominating petition. She went walking again. Whenever she had free time, she'd cover herself in sunscreen and take to the streets. On more than one day, she encountered Jehovah's Witnesses also going door to door. They were a hard act to follow. She had to convince residents that she'd come to talk about issues and ask for support, not to proselytize.

The process was tedious and slow. Some people weren't home and some closed their doors after ten seconds of conversation. There were a lot of barking dogs. Some remembered her from the last time she came by (or from her old El Campo commercials), and told her they admired her efforts. But if they weren't registered voters, they couldn't sign her petition.

Gabby figured out that she was collecting just seven usable signatures per hour of canvassing; she'd have to log about sixty hours in the streets to get the four hundred names she'd need. She wondered if the Jehovah's Witnesses had a better sign-up ratio.

A highlight for her was coming to the home of four retired nuns. They were Democrats, they knew who she was, and they were happy to sign. She left their front porch feeling giddy. As she later described it, four signatures in one swoop was "the mother lode!"

After three weeks, she got her four hundred signatures and ran on a platform opposing trims to state social service agencies, advocating for better funding for public education, and supporting continued Native American gaming agreements. On the stump, she'd tell constituents about her experiences at El Campo. "More than half of the people applying for jobs at my family tire business were so poorly educated that they couldn't fill out our application," she'd say. "We have to find ways to help our public schools do a better job. It's outrageous that they're graduating so many young people from high schools who can't read or write."

Gabby spoke with passion, and from her own experiences. She won that election easily, too.

Once she joined the thirty-member senate, Gabby immersed herself in the issues, including some that many people didn't pay attention to. For instance, she introduced a bill to minimize light pollution, asking that government buildings and parking lots in major Arizona cities be required to put shields over outdoor lights. The reason: Arizona is home to a large number of astronomers, and a growing optics industry.

Though they're drawn by the clear desert sky, astronomers are handicapped by the light in inhabited areas. "Darkness," Gabby liked to say, "is one of our greatest natural resources."

Opponents of Gabby's bill called it "frivolous," but it passed and she continued to advocate for the "dark sky" movement throughout her career. It's meaningful to me that Gabby believed in the importance of studying the stars even before we met.

Gabby had an easy smile with people, but she was tough, too, and took more than a few unpopular positions. She wanted police to be able to stop motorists for not wearing seat belts. Arizona state law prohibits police from citing drivers for seat-belt infractions unless they have committed another infraction first. Gabby thought seat-belt use would increase if people feared getting ticketed. "We as consumers end up paying for people who do not wear seat belts," she said. "It costs either in increased insurance premiums or costs taxpayers for emergency services."

Observing the government at work could be disheartening for Gabby. While legislators should have been diligently crafting a state budget, she couldn't believe the inane issues they chose to focus on. She complained publicly: "We're bogged down in debates about whether businesses should allow armed patrons to bring their guns into bars—but only if they don't order a drink!—or whether people can bring bottled water into baseball games. These are the kinds of debates that give the legislature a bad reputation."

When the senate was in session in Phoenix, Gabby shared an apartment with another legislator, Linda Lopez. Gabby was a night owl, staying up late reading legislation. She'd Rollerblade around downtown Phoenix. Once, she banged herself up pretty badly—she scraped her knees and arm, and had road burn on the side of her face—but she got back on her skates even before she fully healed. On a lot of fronts, Gabby was undeterred.

Though she was devoted to her job as a senator, she also kept her options open. At one point she decided that she wanted to moonlight by skating for a roller derby team.

I was incredulous when she gave me the news. "The roller derby?" I said.

"It'll be fun," she answered. "I want to try it."

She figured she'd do it part-time for the kicks. She drove Linda and some other friends to a roller derby practice, where they watched young, tough female skaters slamming into each other and body-checking the air right out of each other's lungs. These roller derby women were tough; they had more tattoos than teeth. Any chance of Gabby actually signing up for this punishment ended as one skater left the rink and, in her drunkenness, vomited into a trash can right in front of Arizona's youngest female state senator.

Gabby smiled sheepishly at her friends. "I guess maybe I need to reconsider this," she said.

She still wasn't sure politics would be her career for life, but others saw she had a gift for it. She began getting noticed in Democratic circles nationally. In the fall of 2003, the Democratic Leadership Council selected "100 New Democrats to Watch." One of those named was Barack Obama, then a state senator in Illinois. He got a few paragraphs in the DLC's brochure. Gabby got a whole page.

In May 2005, an *Arizona Daily Star* editorial gave mock awards to politicians and dubbed Gabby Arizona's "Cheeriest Lawmaker." It sounded slightly condescending, but the editorial also pointed out: "Giffords wins praise from people on both sides of the aisle for her intelligence, her diligence at research and the way she treats state senator like a real job instead of a title."

On weekends, Gabby wouldn't stay in Phoenix. As soon as the legislature recessed, she'd bolt out the door and head south on I-10, home to Tucson. She and I were in the early stages of our relationship then, and we'd do a lot of speaking by phone on those drives. It was romantic. We'd talk about what our future together might look like. We talked about how hard Gabby worked, and how low the pay was in state government. (She was earning about $24,000 as a state senator.) She told me repeatedly that she looked forward to someday earning more money.

I saw that Gabby had a lot of things figured out, but at the same time, she had a lot of figuring out to do. Though I had just entered her life, part of what made her exciting to me was watching her mull all those options of hers. There was so much about her that impressed me—her work ethic, her genuine concern about so many issues, her enthusiasm for a variety of things, and, frankly, her ambition, too.

I was the new boyfriend, yes. But I also had become an admirer of Gabby, both the public servant and the private citizen. I wondered where all of this would take her.

* * *

On November 23, 2005, Gabby and I were hiking together in Sedona, Arizona's Red Rock country. She had left her phone in the car, and when we returned to it after our hike, she had thirty missed calls. At first it was disconcerting. Why were thirty different people trying to get in touch with her?

Turned out, they had all called for the same reason. Word had just gotten out that Jim Kolbe, the eleven-term congressman from Arizona's 8th District, was not planning to seek reelection in 2006. A very popular moderate, and the only openly gay Republican serving in Congress at the time, Jim was just sixty-three years old. It had been assumed that he'd serve for another decade, maybe longer. His announcement was a great surprise, and all of Gabby's friends and colleagues who'd left her a voice mail had the same message: Here's your chance.

Registration in the district was 39 percent Republican, 35 percent Democrat, and 25 percent independent. As a centrist Democrat, people told her, she had the ability to woo just enough independents and Republicans to win the seat.

"What do you think?" Gabby asked me as we sat together in the car. "Should I run?"

"Well, you never expected you'd have this opportunity to run in your home district," I told her. "You thought you'd have to wait ten or twenty years for Kolbe to retire. You have this opportunity, you should take it."

"Will you support me?" she asked.

"Of course," I told her.

"Will you support me to the maximum?" she asked, and I saw a devilish smile forming on her face.

"I'll support you completely," I said.

"Good," she said, "then get out your checkbook. You can donate a maximum of twenty-one hundred dollars for the primary and twenty-one hundred dollars for the general election. That's forty-two hundred."

I was still just her boyfriend at the time. We weren't yet engaged. And as an astronaut, I was living on the salary of a civil servant, so $4,200 was not inconsequential to me. But I saw that if I wanted to show Gabby that I truly loved her, I'd be smart to become the first contributor to her newborn congressional campaign. I obediently took out my checkbook and wrote the check.

Gabby sat in the car, on the phone, for the next three hours, picking the brains and the purses of everyone she knew in political circles. Within a week, just calling the names in her cell-phone address book, she had raised $200,000 from more than four hundred contributors.

She wrestled with the question of whether to leave her job as a state senator to make the run for Congress. If she stayed on just one more month, Gabby would have served five years in office and been entitled to a state pension. But in the end, she decided she couldn't serve her constituents well if she was busy traveling the campaign trail in a district that stretched nine thousand square miles. She resigned on December 1, which allowed a replacement to be selected before the legislative session began in January. She will never see a penny in pension money, but she knew she'd done the right thing.

Gabby formally announced her candidacy at the landmark Arizona Inn, which was built by Isabella Greenway, Arizona's first female congresswoman. Greenway won the seat in 1932, and only one other woman in Arizona was elected in all the years since; Karan English served one term, from 1993 to 1995. Launching her "cactus roots campaign," Gabby hoped to be the third female congresswoman in state history.

Among those there to support her that day was Dorothy Finley, the octogenarian beer magnate who mentored Gabby during her El Campo years. Dorothy was active and powerful in Republican circles, and her endorsement reminded voters that Gabby was working to be a candidate who transcended party labels. (Dorothy frequently invited us to join her at the Mountain Oyster Club. It's a private facility devoted to supporting Southwestern heritage, including the consumption of bull testicles, which are known as Rocky Mountain oysters. Dorothy loved that place and Gabby loved Dorothy. I went, too, but took no pleasure in eating "cow balls.")

In the primary, Gabby ran against five candidates, including Patty Weiss, a former TV news anchorwoman with almost 100-percent name recognition. Yes, some voters recognized Gabby from her 10- and 15-second El Campo commericals, but she was considered a long-shot underdog compared to Patty, a well-regarded TV journalist who had anchored newscasts in Tucson for more than three decades. Gabby hustled day and night—meeting voters, raising money, and convening twenty-three policy roundtables with a diverse group of local experts.

Gabby ended up winning the election easily, with 54 percent of the vote, 23 percent higher than Patty, the second-place finisher. The Democrats united behind Gabby very quickly. Patty very generously came over to her headquarters on election night and publicly pinned a "Giffords for Congress" campaign button on her suit.

The general election was far more combative. Gabby's opponent was Randy Graf, a former state representative. He was a far-right con-servative; it was Randy who had introduced that bill seeking to allow Arizonans to carry guns into bars. His platform was centered on his get-tough stance on immigration, and on painting Gabby as soft on the subject.

From the start, Gabby spoke of the need for realistic immigration policies, but it was hard to be heard and easy to be misinterpreted. Her positions were nuanced. She said employers who hire illegal workers should be sanctioned with fines, or should even lose their licenses to do business. But she felt there also needed to be guest-worker programs so Arizona businesses would have access to needed legal, qualified work-ers. (It is especially hard to find enough Americans willing to work on farms bringing produce out of the fields; Mexican labor is crucial to parts of the Arizona economy.) Gabby also thought that hospitals and law-enforcement agencies in the district that were affected by illegal border-crossers needed to be compensated by the federal government.

She was not in favor of the sort of unconditional amnesty that Pres-ident Reagan granted in 1986, but felt there should be a reasonable path to citizenship for the millions of illegal immigrants living in the United States. She favored a plan that would require people to register with the federal government, agree to criminal background checks, pay fines and back taxes, learn to speak English, and get in the back of the line. "It's a path to citizenship," she'd say, "but it's not an easy path."

Gabby's views on immigration led to her being targeted by ads paid for by the Minuteman PAC, a group seeking stricter immigration policies. They called her "out of touch." She responded: "Building a wall across the entire expanse of the border is not going to fix the problem."

In a red state like Arizona, no politician is easily elected without supporting gun rights, and Gabby did, too. But she wanted to be rational. "I take my cues from law enforcement," she'd say. "The mentally ill and convicted criminals shouldn't have access to firearms."

Gabby stayed on message. When she was criticized, she'd say she understood people's frustrations. When she was taunted, she'd try to stick to the issues. She was tactful. She resisted getting irritated. As a military man, I was impressed by her discipline.

In campaign literature and at appearances, Gabby made sure she was referred to as Gabrielle Giffords. Her given name made her seem more serious, more mature. And that's why many in the opposing party relished calling her "Gabby." They hoped the nickname would make her seem girlish, younger, more frivolous. Voters were reminded that Gabby was the name of a character on TV's *Desperate Housewives*. It didn't sound like the name of a congresswoman.

Some of Gabby's supporters thought the opposition was using "Gabby" in the same patronizing and sexist way they'd say "sweetie" or "honey." Gabby didn't let it get to her. She soldiered on.

Before friendly groups, she'd sometimes joke that her friends called her Gabby because she talked a lot. She'd get a few laughs by saying that. But mostly, she stuck with Gabrielle. A man named Lincoln can go by Abe instead of Abraham, a man named Carter can be Jimmy instead of James, but a woman named Gabrielle thought it best to wait a few more election cycles before she publicly allowed herself her nickname. I believe she was right in that decision.

Over the course of the campaign, I went with Gabby to several dozen appearances. Standing in the back of the room, I was always struck by the ease with which she held on to the audience, and how carefully she listened to people. I marveled at how fresh she could sound, repeating the same lines and answering the same questions. After a while, I could have delivered her entire twenty-minute stump speech. "When your family calls, you go," she'd say. "That's what you do. So I put on my boots, I got back in my pickup truck, I drove across the country, and I started changing tires the next day."

I'd kid her. "So what did you do? Did you put on your boots? Did you get back in your pickup truck? When did you start changing tires? The next day?"

But Gabby knew what she was doing. She knew how her words and her story resonated. She had almost pitch-perfect instincts for politics, and for people's needs and dreams. She won that election by 12 percentage points.

Her victory speech on the night of November 7, 2006, still viewable on YouTube, shows Gabby at her best. She was charismatic and poised, ready to start the job. She looked like a young woman who was going not just to Congress, but maybe to places beyond.

"I'm humbled by the support you've given me and the confidence you've granted me," she told the cheering crowd at Tucson's Doubletree Hotel. She thanked those who voted for her, "not just the Democrats, but the independents, the Republicans, the Greens, the libertarians, the vegetarians." That was pure Gabby, giving a shout-out to the vegetarians.

She saluted Arizona political legends who'd come before her, including the late, longtime congressman Mo Udall. They'd shown her, she said, that she'd need to have "a gut to tackle the tough problems and the chutzpah to be able to stand up and say it like it is."

Jim Kolbe, the outgoing Republican congressman, was kind enough to stop by the celebration, and after thanking him for his decades of service, she brought him onstage and hugged him.

She vowed she would not go to Washington as an ideologue. "In my TV ads, you saw that there are some lines I just won't cross," she said. "But there is one line I will never be afraid to cross. I will always extend my hands across the aisle to do what's right for the American people, to build consensus, and to get the job done."

I watched how Gabby ended her eight-minute speech. It was almost like she was shouting out her own countdown, and she was about to be launched right to Washington.

"I'm ready to roll up my sleeves," she said, "to work hard for our troops now serving in Iraq.

"I'm ready to roll up my sleeves to get to work for the children in our country, who deserve the best schools, the best education." The cheering almost drowned her out.

"I'm ready to roll up my sleeves for those of us who live in border regions and who deserve a practical solution to a complicated problem.

"I'm ready to roll up my sleeves and get to work for future generations who deserve to inherit a planet as beautiful and extraordinary as the planet that all of us were born into!"

When the cheering subsided, she was more pensive. "We have a lot of work to do," she said. "I just want to thank each and every one of you for making tonight possible. And I'm ready to get to work for all of us."

She left the podium and I hugged her only briefly, knowing there were so many others in the room who wanted to shake her hand or hug her themselves.

Five years later, she'd be a woman taking baby steps through a torturous recovery. But on that night, so ready to roll up her sleeves, she had the stride of a giant.

Six-year-old Gabby is pensive in a straw hat. (Giffords Family)

As a fifth grader at Tanque Verde Elementary School in Tucson, Gabby was the "obvious choice" to play the title character in the musical *Annie*. Her half-shepherd, half-Airedale terrier starred alongside her as Sandy. (Giffords Family)

Gabby, age eight, proudly sports a cap from El Campo Tire and Service Centers. For many years, El Campo's slogan was "The Buck-Stretchers." (Giffords Family)

Mark *(right)* and Scott look ready to race in August 1964. They are six months old. (Kelly Family)

On the back of this snapshot from August 1970, Mark's mother wrote: "Twins are ready to take these fish over to a neighbor." Their dad and their paternal grandfather caught forty fish on an all-night charter boat. (Kelly Family)

The eight-year-old Kelly twins (Mark, *left*) got snow cones on the boardwalk in Wildwood, New Jersey. (Kelly Family)

Mark likes this photograph of Gabby with her "wild, frizzed-out '80s hair." (Giffords Family)

Gabby wore this traditional Mennonite dress while living with Mennonites in the Mexican state of Chihuahua during her year as a Fulbright Scholar in 1994. (Giffords Family)

Gabby knew how to ride scooters and motorcycles, and how to fix them. (Giffords Family)

The message her parents wrote next to this photograph of Gabby and her mom in her 1993 Scripps College yearbook reads: "Gabby . . . You've given us so much more than we could ever reciprocate. But beyond all that, thanks for just being you." (Courtesy of Scripps College)

Gabby graduated from Scripps, the all-female college in Claremont, California, in 1993. Her family was there to celebrate (*from left to right,* Spencer, Gloria, and Melissa). (Giffords Family)

Gabby and her dad were together on the day before she earned a master's degree in regional planning from Cornell. Her degree helped her land a job at Price Waterhouse in New York City. (Giffords Family)

Mark *(left)* says that "even though both my mother and father were cops, some people considered Scott and me to be borderline juvenile delinquents." (Kelly Family)

Mark *(right)* flew thirty-nine combat missions during the Gulf War, most with Paul Fujimura. They were stationed on the aircraft carrier the USS *Midway*. (Kelly Family)

Richard Kelly was there to see his sons Mark *(center)* and Scott graduate from test-pilot school at the Naval Air Station in Patuxent River, Maryland, in 1994. (Kelly Family)

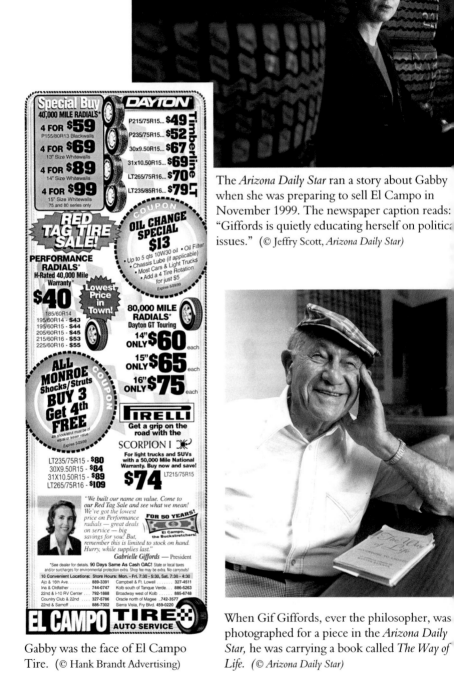

The *Arizona Daily Star* ran a story about Gabby when she was preparing to sell El Campo in November 1999. The newspaper caption reads: "Giffords is quietly educating herself on political issues." (© Jeffry Scott, *Arizona Daily Star*)

Gabby was the face of El Campo Tire. (© Hank Brandt Advertising)

When Gif Giffords, ever the philosopher, was photographed for a piece in the *Arizona Daily Star,* he was carrying a book called *The Way of Life.* (© *Arizona Daily Star*)

Gabby and Mark returned to China and visited the Great Wall in 2005. The couple met on a 2003 trip to China sponsored by the National Committee on United States–China Relations. (Giffords/Kelly Family)

In May 2005, an *Arizona Daily Star* editorial gave mock awards to politicians and dubbed Gabby Arizona's "Cheeriest Lawmaker," writing: "Giffords wins praise from people on both sides of the aisle for her intelligence, her diligence at research, and the way she treats state senator like a real job instead of a title." Gabby also earned a real award from the Arizona State Senate. (Raoul Erickson)

At their wedding on November 10, 2007, the emcee at the reception, Robert Reich, toasted "to a bride who moves at a velocity that exceeds that of anyone else in Washington, and to a groom who moves at a velocity that exceeds seventeen thousand miles per hour." (Marc Winkelman)

Scott *(left)* was "my twin brother and best man," says Mark. (Marc Winkelman)

Mark's daughters Claire *(left)* and Claudia were nine and twelve years old when Mark and Gabby married. (© Daniel Snyder Photographer)

CHAPTER NINE

With This Ring

Gabby always loved playing with my wedding ring. After we got married, we'd go out to dinner by ourselves and hold hands across the table. At almost every meal, she'd slip the ring off my finger and move it from her thumb to her forefinger to her middle finger. It was her little ritual, her way of fidgeting.

I understood it.

Gabby loved being married. She had waited until she was thirty-seven before settling down, and having gone all those years without a wedding band, she enjoyed the way her hand felt now that she had two rings at her disposal—hers and mine.

Her ring is a lapis-studded gold band with an inscription inside it, and Gabby was very touched when she first read the words I'd chosen to press against her finger: "You're the closest to heaven that I've ever been." I meant it as the ultimate compliment, considering that I'd already flown more than 10 million miles in space.

Gabby wouldn't take off her own ring to play with it. But my tungsten ring, larger and looser, was like a favorite toy in her hands, something she'd borrowed from her closest playmate.

From the day we got married, she was drawn to my ring. She still is.

On January 13, 2011, five days after Gabby was shot, I was sitting with her in her hospital room, holding her left hand with my left hand. She had opened her eyes very briefly the day before, but she still remained in a mostly comatose state. She made no sounds. She hardly moved. We didn't know if she'd make it back at all.

But then, suddenly, as she held my hand, she recognized something familiar. I could feel her fingertips exploring my ring, and then, despite seeming as if she was unconscious, she actually pulled the ring off and began to move it around in her fingers, just like always. She easily moved it from one of her fingers to the next for the next five minutes. She didn't drop it once.

Her eyes remained closed, tubes were everywhere, but she was somehow able to direct the fingers of her one good hand to rediscover her old pastime. I was more than surprised. I was overwhelmed. For the first time since she was shot, I felt as if I had a clear reason for hope. "She's still Gabby," I thought. "She's going to pull out of this."

After she returned the ring to me, I had to tell her doctors. I called them into her room and tried to move the ring from one of my fingers to the next, one-handed, just as Gabby had done. I didn't have the dexterity to do it. I ended up dropping the ring.

By then, Gabby had returned to the stillness of her comatose state. But the doctors told me that her performance with the ring was a hugely encouraging sign.

Every day after that, I'd hold Gabby's hand, and she continued to take off my ring and play with it. At that point, she was unable to speak, and she didn't seem as if she understood much of what anyone said to her. And yet she'd move that ring up and down my finger, and then onto her fingers, and then she'd place it back where it belonged, on my hand. It was a lifeline for her. And for me, too.

* * *

Gabby and I were married on November 10, 2007, and my ring actually went missing just before we said our vows. The evening ceremony was outdoors at an organic-produce farm thirty-five miles south of Tucson, and our ringbearer was the four-year-old son of one of my fellow astronauts.

The kid was named Laurier in memory of our friend Laurel Clark, an astronaut who was killed in 2003, when space shuttle *Columbia* disintegrated on reentry into Earth's atmosphere. I understood the sentiment behind this, but I also thought Laurier was too close to "A Boy Named Sue" for a kid growing up in Texas. We all know how that story ended; I pictured this poor kid showing up at school and getting his ass kicked. I did him a favor and gave him the nickname "Buster" before he was born.

Anyway, as our wedding approached, I had some concerns about our choice of ringbearer. Buster was a good kid, but I thought he may have been too young and not capable of making it down the aisle without incident. "What if he drops the ring?" I asked his mother.

"He won't drop the ring," she assured me.

Sure enough, he dropped the ring in the grass right before he needed to hand it over to us. Three hundred guests were left rustling and giggling while my brother and Buster's mom looked for it. It seemed like five minutes before they found it.

It didn't matter. Our wedding was such an eclectic mix of people, customs, cultures, and unconventional touches that a renegade ringbearer just added to the festivities.

Gabby, of course, was the mastermind of the whole event. Though long retired from the role of "Annie," she still liked to put on a show. She didn't need or want a lavish wedding. But she loved the idea of making the wedding a statement about our roots, our personalities, and the causes that mattered to us.

She arranged for a "low-carbon-footprint" wedding and tried to make everything recyclable or reusable. The utensils and plates were made of biodegradable sugarcane and cornstarch. Flower arrangements were homemade, and wedding favors were simple jars of honey from the Santa Cruz River valley. "I'm trying to tread lightly on this Earth," Gabby explained to people when they asked how the planning was going. "I'm looking for ways to minimize the impact of the wedding."

Gabby decided to borrow a Vera Wang gown from the daughter of Suzy Gershman, her wedding planner. She liked that I would be wearing my formal dress Navy uniform, also white and reusable.

Gabby's mom, Gloria, came up with the idea for our wedding invitation. In Mexico, Spain, Germany, and Italy, when something wonderful or miraculous happens, there's a tradition that a small painting, a "retablo," is created describing it. People hang it in their church, giving thanks. In Mexico, one popular and humorous version of such a painting features a dashing young man, a sombrero in one hand and flowers in the other, courting a lovely woman in a courtyard. She sits on a bench with a shawl on her shoulders, her head turned toward the man. The image of a saint is in a nearby tree, looking over them. But the painting also contains some tension. Around the corner is a man with a gun in his hand, undoubtedly the young woman's father, ready to chase the male suitor away.

Gabby and Gloria thought it would be amusing if they used this painting on the top flap of the invitation. With Photoshop, they removed the father's hair so he'd look more like Gabby's balding dad, Spencer. And the woman in the courtyard, originally a brunette, was turned into a blonde so she'd look more like Gabby. (I nixed Gloria's idea of putting a NASA patch on the man's jacket. NASA is careful about the use of its logos and designs. I'd become sensitive about the minutiae that could earn an astronaut a trip to the front office.)

At the time, not all of our guests knew what to make of this image. They just figured, correctly, that it was Gabby and her artistic mother doing something creative that reflected "borderland" culture. Looking at that invitation in retrospect, of course, yields a different impression, as if it foreshadowed what was to come. The painting now feels stark and troubling. A man and a woman have fallen in love, that's obvious, but their relationship is being threatened by a hairless, sinister-looking man holding a gun.

* * *

The farm we rented for the wedding was called Agua Linda, and Gabby thought the setting she chose for the ceremony was perfect: a mesquite-covered lawn with the Santa Rita Mountains behind us. The food she ordered from Las Vigas, a local restaurant, was a regional Mexican-American mix of steak, potatoes, and made-on-the-spot tortillas.

Our wedding party was a little different in that each of us had a member of the opposite sex among our attendants. Gabby's friend Raoul stood up for her—a bridesmaid in a suit—along with three of her friends, her sister, and my daughters, Claudia and Claire. Three of my four groomsmen were astronauts, including my brother and Buster's mom, a groomsman in a dress. I also asked Mark Baden to stand up for me. He was the guy who dared me to steal that Saudi flag, and he later became a Navy A-6 Intruder pilot, like me, and then a pilot for United Airlines. We all walked down the aisle accompanied by the music of a mariachi band.

It was also important to Gabby that we be married in a Jewish ceremony.

She was raised as the product of a mixed marriage; Spencer, a Jew, and Gloria, a Christian Scientist, had encouraged their daughters to make their own decisions about faith. By the time Gabby reached young adulthood, she had fully embraced her Jewish background. She even had a formal naming ceremony in which she took the Hebrew name Gabriella, which means "God is my strength."

She'd gone to Israel for the first time in 2001 and described the visit as "life-changing." The journalists and politicians on the trip with her said she asked more questions than anyone, and she came away feeling a kinship with Israelis. She was especially taken with the Jewish concept of *tzedakah,* which speaks to our obligations to be charitable.

Though she cast her lot with the Jewish people, Gabby being Gabby, she remained curious and open-minded about other religions. She took a liking to the Catholic priest who was the chaplain of the U.S. House of Representatives. She wanted us to go to him for premarital counseling.

"Let me get this straight," I said to her. "You want me to go to marriage counseling with a guy who has never had a relationship with a woman in his life?"

"Well, it's only ten classes," she said.

"Ten classes? In Washington? How am I going to get from Houston to Washington for ten classes?"

"Maybe we can do it by video conference," Gabby said.

We met with the chaplain, a very nice man. I thought I could talk him into giving us the abbreviated version of marital counseling, but he wouldn't go for it. He also wanted to see us in person. We had to back out.

Gabby still liked the idea of counseling, though, so she turned to her rabbi at Congregation Chaverim, the Reform temple in Tucson where she is a member. Rabbi Stephanie Aaron has an interesting backstory. She was born Catholic, converted to Judaism after marrying a Jewish man, later divorced him, became a rabbi, then married a different Jewish man. Gabby really liked her, and I thought maybe a rabbi with this background would understand where I was coming from as a Catholic marrying a Jew. From her own life, Rabbi Aaron knew about divorce and finding love on a second try. I also appreciated that she didn't ask us to commit to ten sessions. We ended up meeting with her a couple of times, and it went fine. She agreed to conduct our wedding ceremony.

Just before our ceremony, we signed our *katubah,* which in essence is a Jewish marriage contract. Gabby had asked me to write the vows for the document, and this is what I'd come up with: "We pledge to love, respect, and support each other. We shall endeavor to be understanding, and will work hard to build a strong and loving family, a family that fills a home (or three) with laughter. We will help each other with our wishes, dreams and goals.

"We will support each other as we navigate this world, and will try our best to leave it a better place than we found it, a place that is more good than bad, more light than dark. As friends, we promise to be honest, forgiving, and devoted to each other. We will share whatever wisdom we may possess, and will grow together on this incredible journey of marriage and life."

After the *katubah* signing, it was time for the wedding ceremony.

We were married on a cool desert evening under the traditional chuppah, a canopy that in Judaism symbolizes the home we'd create and the children we might bring into our lives together. When the ceremony ended, we kissed and then walked back down the aisle as the mariachi band played the Hebrew folk song "Hava Nagila."

My military comrades had arranged a traditional "saber arch," in which officers in formal dress honor a bride and groom by holding up swords or sabers. They did a good job with it, positioning their swords with tips nearly touching and blades up, as Gabby and I walked hand-in-hand underneath. They were joined by Laurier/Buster, the ring boy, who held a toy sword. It was something of a surreal scene—a Jewish wedding with military touches and a mariachi band providing the soundtrack.

Marc Winkelman, a Texas businessman and our good friend, was one of the four people we honored as a chuppah pole-holder during the ceremony. As he mingled afterward, Marc couldn't stop smiling, and he was struck by the fact that the other guests—astronauts, politicians, Navy guys, my old buddies from New Jersey, Gabby's friends from Tucson—all had similar expressions on their faces. "Everyone was smiling from ear to ear," Marc later told us. "There was just so much love and affection in the air."

The reception was held in the courtyard of the hacienda, and the evening's emcee was Robert Reich, a very funny friend of ours best known as President Clinton's secretary of labor. Bob and Gabby had met years earlier when she spent time at Harvard's John F. Kennedy School of Government.

When Bob raised his glass for a toast, he alluded to the pace of our crazy lives. Gabby, a member of the House Armed Services and Foreign Affairs committees, returned from a visit to Iraq just days before the wedding. In a week's time, she'd gone from power suits on Capitol Hill to camouflage and body armor in Baghdad to a borrowed white dress in Arizona. As for me, I was deep into training for my third shuttle mission. We were so overwhelmed with responsibilities that our honeymoon had to be postponed indefinitely.

Bob concluded his toast by saying, "To a bride who moves at a velocity that exceeds that of anyone else in Washington, and to a groom who moves at a velocity that exceeds seventeen thousand miles per hour."

Gabby and I sat together, her hand on mine, as Bob spoke. We were both moving at zero miles an hour, not our usual pace, but we felt completely content.

* * *

On the day Gabby was shot, before I arrived at the hospital to see her, my mind raced with all kinds of terrible thoughts. But even in that early chaos, there was a moment when our wedding vows came into my head. We had promised to be faithful partners "in sickness and in health, in good times and bad . . ."

I wasn't sure how I'd find Gabby that day, but I expected the worst, and I knew our future had changed forever. "So this is what those vows mean," I thought.

In the months that followed, I often told Gabby, "I'm here for you. We're a team." That's what we had promised each other when we exchanged wedding rings—to be there for each other in the worst of times.

Though she couldn't fully articulate it, I knew Gabby often felt like a burden. I'd remind her that she had been there for me in my times of need. After my brother was diagnosed with prostate cancer in 2007, I figured that as his twin, I'd better get myself checked. Sure enough, I had it, too.

Gabby came with me to my doctors' appointments, she searched the Internet for medical information, and she kept on me to get second opinions. In 2008, after a mission in space, I elected to have surgery to remove my prostate. In the months that followed, I coped with all the troubling side effects familiar to prostate cancer patients, from incontinence to sexual dysfunction. The urologist had me taking Viagra every day for more than a year, and I even had to regularly give myself very unpleasant injections in very private places.

This experience taught me a lot about myself and the process of recovery. One thing that stuck with me was that if you are religious about rehab and if you follow a prescribed course of treatment, you can recover completely, despite the odds or the conventional wisdom that might leave you thinking otherwise.

Throughout my medical odyssey, Gabby was incredibly supportive. She had faith that I'd fought off the cancer and would get completely back to normal. "But no matter what happens," she told me, "I'm in this with you for the long haul." It wasn't immediate, but I did make it back to 100 percent.

Now it was my turn to be there for Gabby. In the wake of her injury, without hesitation, I said those same words to her. "I'm in this with you for the long haul."

I'd even kid with Gabby about my cancer scare. As a result of her injury, she had to get regular shots of Botox in her arms and legs to help with spasticity and to deaden her nerves. It was no fun getting the shots, and from time to time she'd complain about them.

"Listen, Gabby," I said to her one day. "Your shots are easy. Do you remember where I had to give myself shots?"

She remembered and laughed. She grimaced through the next needle with little protest.

There was another time, three months after Gabby was shot, when I found myself thinking again about our wedding vows. As always, I was trying to determine what Gabby understood and what she recalled about her life. So I asked her a few questions.

"Hey, sweetie, do you remember our wedding?"

"Yes," she said.

"Do you remember your wedding dress?" I was probing.

"Yes."

"What kind of dress was it?" I asked, and she paused for a long time. No answer.

"Did you buy it?"

"Nooooo," she said. "Borrowed."

"Yes! That's right. And what kind of dress was it?"

She couldn't answer, so I gave her a hint. "Ver . . . Ver . . ."

"Vera Wang," she said. She got that right, too.

"So, Gabby, do you remember what happened that day?"

"Married," she said.

"Yes, we got married. But there was something magical that happened as we were getting married. Do you remember what it was?"

She thought for just a few seconds and then she smiled. "Rain," she said.

I was so thrilled to see that she remembered and could say it.

That night we got married, we were under the chuppah, which was all lit up, and we were about to begin saying our vows. Just then, as we looked into each other's eyes, the lightest sprinkle started to fall from the sky. It lasted only the length of our vows, about forty-five seconds, before it stopped.

It really was magical. As I gazed at Gabby, thinking how gorgeous and happy she looked, the air was sparkling from the lights and the misty raindrops. And then the rain passed and we were husband and wife.

Some cultures consider rain at a wedding to be good luck or an indication of fertility. The Italians even have a saying: *"Sposa bagnata, sposa fortunata."* A wet bride is a lucky bride.

"Rain," Gabby said again, and I could see she was thinking back to that happy moment.

I reached for her hand, and as always, she found her way to my wedding ring, which she slipped off easily, onto her waiting fingers.

CHAPTER TEN

The Ace of Spades

In the spring of 2011, I was simultaneously the commander of space shuttle *Endeavour* and the assistant chief of encouragement at Gabby's bedside. During the workday, her mom, Gloria, was on duty as chief encourager and cheerleader while I was at Houston's Johnson Space Center, training for my upcoming mission.

Doctors at TIRR, the rehab hospital, told us that our optimism and encouragement could make a great difference in Gabby's recovery, and they suggested specific, meaningful things we could do.

For instance, we were told to encourage her not to forget about the right side of her body. Because she was shot on the left side of her head, it was the mobility on her right side that was severely compromised. That's just how the wiring in the brain works. There was another issue, too: A bullet passing through a brain is just the beginning of the injury process. That wiring in the brain suffers even more damage in the days that follow.

After Gabby was shot, brain tissue bruised by the bullet continued to swell for days, killing additional cells in the left side of her brain. That likely caused more impairment to the right side of her body. (Gabby was lucky that the bullet did not cross the geometric center line which splits the brain's left and right hemispheres. That likely would have been fatal, because both sides of her brain would have swelled.)

A lot of traumatic-brain-injury patients ignore the side of their body opposite their brain injury. Gabby understood this impulse and fought it, making efforts every day to move her right leg and to try to move her right arm. Our job was to urge her on.

"Hey, Gabby," I'd say when we were both just sitting around. "Try to move your right hand."

She'd give me a look of weariness, and issue a sigh that suggested, "OK, but don't expect too much. We've tried this before, and we know how it turns out."

Still, she'd make a gallant attempt. She'd stare at her hand for a little while, as if she was using telepathy to will it to move. She could sometimes get it to twitch slightly, but it usually just remained still.

"Come on, Gabby, try to move it," I'd say again.

And that's when she'd do exactly what I asked. She'd use her good left hand to grasp her floppy right hand. She'd pick it up from her wheelchair armrest and place it on her lap. Then she'd smile at me playfully, as if to say, "You asked me to move my right hand. Well, I did. Now stop bothering me!"

She still had her sense of humor.

In those months, Gabby and I followed pretty much the same daily routine. Because my house in League City is far from the downtown hospital, I was staying at the home of our friends Tilman and Paige Fertitta, in Houston's River Oaks neighborhood. I'd wake up each day at 6:00 a.m., and by 6:30 I'd be at the Starbucks in the Highland Village Shopping Center, picking up a cup of coffee for Gabby. I knew just what she wanted: a nonfat grande latte with two raw sugars and cinnamon powder on top.

Early on, the baristas recognized me, and they'd nod politely. After they realized I was buying coffee each day for Gabby, they began decorating her cups with different messages. They'd write "Have a great day, Gabby" or they'd use colored markers to draw simple illustrations—a rising sun or a smiley face.

Gabby was touched by their efforts, and she enjoyed each day's new message or design. After I told this to Jim Bradley, the manager at Starbucks, he decided to expand the creative process. Another regular customer was a second-grade teacher, and Jim wondered if her students might pitch in by designing cups. The kids loved the idea and got to work.

After that, Gabby was always glad to see me each morning, but she seemed more interested in the colorful Starbucks cup in my hand, designed with butterflies, rainbows, stars, flowers, a cactus here or there, and my favorites, rockets, space shuttles, and astronauts. Gabby not only loved the illustrations, but as a visitor from Arizona, she appreciated the welcoming embrace of the children of Houston.

I'd hang out with Gabby for forty-five minutes or so as she ate breakfast, then I'd give her a kiss goodbye, wish her well in therapy, and drive thirty-five minutes south to NASA. Once at work, my days were spent training in the space shuttle mission simulator with my crew, as we tried to master every detail and potential hazard that awaited us in space.

After a long day at NASA, I was usually pretty weary when I arrived back at TIRR each evening. Gabby's parents, who were logging fourteen-hour days with her, would fill me in on the day's successes and setbacks, the meals and the visitors. Then they'd take off for a while to give Gabby and me some private time together. The nurse would leave the room, too.

Some nights I'd climb into bed with Gabby before she fell asleep, and we'd talk.

Well, mostly, I'd talk. Back then, it took her an enormous amount of effort to try to articulate anything close to a complex thought, so she was usually pretty quiet. But she listened.

To fit together in the bed, we'd both lie on our sides, and I always made sure I was on her right side. That way, I could get her to focus more on the right side of her body.

One night in mid-April, we were in her bed together, face-to-face, just inches apart. We were both pretty tired, and we were just relaxing, not saying anything. Then I realized that Gabby was looking closely at something on my face.

"What is it?" I asked.

"Hair," she said.

She reached over and started to mess with an extra-long hair in my right eyebrow. Gabby had developed a keen eye for detail since her injury—she'd notice the spot on a doctor's tie or the scuff on his shoes. Now she had zoned in on my eyebrow.

The next word out of her mouth was "scissors." She leaned toward her nightstand in search of a pair.

YIKES!

"Gabby, hold on!" I said. "Let's think about this. You're newly left-handed, your vision is damaged, you're not wearing your glasses, I'm about to launch into space, and you want me to let you come at my eye with a pair of scissors? Are you crazy?"

She and I laughed and laughed and laughed. The bed was shaking from our laughter. It was a nice moment.

* * *

Astronauts do a lot of joking around, and we have a shared appreciation of gallows humor. That's because we know the odds of our chosen occupation. A visually impaired spouse coming at us with a pair of scissors is among the least of our worries.

In my fifteen years at NASA, I found that behind the jokes there was a sobering reality that we didn't often address. We loved our jobs, we knew we were helping mankind increase its knowledge of the universe, and we were proud when our efforts inspired children to dream. But we also knew that the achievements of the space program came with human costs—and always will.

There were 135 space shuttle missions. Two of them resulted in the deaths of all crew members. Fourteen astronauts in total. Of the five orbiters built in the history of the shuttle program, two were destroyed during missions—*Challenger* in 1986 and *Columbia* in 2003.

In the astronaut office at NASA, we knew the statistics. Each mission had a "demonstrated risk" of 1 in 67.5, meaning that was the probability we wouldn't make it back alive. Our "calculated risk"—the likelihood of a catastrophic failure on any given mission—was thought to be 1 in 57 for each mission, according to NASA data crunchers. I flew a total of four shuttle missions, which suggests that I had somewhere between a 1-in-14 and a 1-in-17 likelihood of not surviving my NASA career.

To understand the risks of space travel, I'd sometimes ask friends who aren't astronauts to consider a deck of cards. "Imagine that I offered you a million dollars if you pick any of the fifty-two cards except the ace of spades," I'd say. "A million dollars just like that. But the deal would be: If you pick the ace of spades, you'd lose your life. Would you take that risk—one out of fifty-two?"

Some would. Most wouldn't. Even for a million dollars.

Then I'd ask: "Would you take those same odds for a ride in the space shuttle?"

Not many people said yes. But that's the unspoken deal astronauts choose to take.

Our families knew the statistics, too, of course. By tradition, the day before liftoff, we'd be permitted to step out of quarantine and say good-bye to our spouses and children. The hugs were long. The mood would be joyous but stressful. Tears were common. There was a poignancy even in mundane directives: "Don't forget to put out the garbage cans." All of us were aware that fourteen of our comrades went through this same goodbye ritual, the hugs and the kisses, but didn't make it home.

Gabby used to tell me that she never slept well when I was in space. She felt nervous and, for a take-charge person, uncomfortably helpless. She'd be glued to NASA TV in the middle of the night. During my 2008 mission, she talked about her worries in an interview on CNN. "I wake up every couple hours," she said. "I check e-mail. Check the news. Make sure everything is going OK. You never really relax until you see the vehicle touch down, the parachute deploy, and it fully rolls to a stop."

I'd sometimes talk to Gabby about my experiences on February 1, 2003, the day *Columbia* disintegrated during reentry into Earth's atmosphere. The disaster happened because a piece of foam insulation not much bigger than the size of a pizza box had broken off from the shuttle's external tank when it launched sixteen days earlier. This piece of debris had struck the left wing, damaging the vehicle's thermal protection system, which we call TPS. The TPS was designed to protect the shuttle from the intense heat that results during reentry.

Columbia's crew members had been aware that they were having serious problems. As the orbiter sped across New Mexico and then Texas, the crew was confronted with failures that we often see in the simulator. In this case, however, the failures were real and *Columbia* was quickly coming apart.

The last audio transmission came just before 8 a.m. central time, about sixteen minutes before the planned touchdown at the Kennedy Space Center in Florida. *Columbia*'s commander, Rick Husband, said "Roger" and then was abruptly cut off. About five seconds later, *Columbia* was out of control. Hot plasma had entered the wing and was melting the vehicle's structure from the inside out. Over the next forty-two seconds, the crew fought desperately to salvage a rapidly deteriorating situation. At about 180,000 feet and Mach 15, the crew cabin began to break up. More than 84,000 pieces of debris would fall over east Texas.

Within seconds of hearing that we had lost communication with *Columbia,* and more ominously, that we had also lost tracking, I was in my car rushing to the NASA office. I joined another astronaut, Mike Good, in our contingency action center, where we started going through the mishap checklist. Over the next thirty minutes, nearly everyone in the astronaut office arrived to help.

We had never planned for the possibility that this sort of accident would happen within a two-hour drive of where we were sitting in Houston. It's a big planet. The likelihood of the space shuttle crashing this close to home was minuscule. I said to Andy Thomas, then the deputy chief astronaut, "We never planned for this, but I think we need to get someone there right now."

"OK," he said. "You go."

I immediately called Harris County's Constable Bill Bailey. He was a great option if you needed something done fast. There isn't a law-enforcement official in the state of Texas who looks more the part than Bill Bailey. Big hat, big boots, big belt buckle, BIG man. I said, "Bill, this is Mark Kelly. I need a helicopter right now."

No explanation was required. He just said, "I'll call you right back." Within minutes Bill had a car on the way to the Johnson Space Center to bring me to a waiting U.S. Coast Guard helicopter. A short time later I was on my way to the debris field.

We headed for Hemphill, Texas, population 1,100, because we'd gotten word that the crew compartment may have landed near there. (In the early going, the media speculated about whether any of the crew members could have survived. We knew better.)

Three of the seven crew members started with me and my brother in our astronaut class back in 1996; they were our friends. I tried, not always successfully, to set aside my emotions as I helped look for their remains. The area was very remote, and the debris was spread widely. An FBI agent and I had to take dirt roads and then go off into the woods. We recovered the remains of Laurel Clark, my very good friend and a U.S. Navy flight surgeon, on one of those dirt roads in Hemphill. She was the coworker whom our wedding-ring bearer would later be named after. Another search party found the remains of *Columbia*'s pilot, Willie McCool, in a wooded area not far away. I immediately went to the scene to help with the identification and to make sure things were handled appropriately.

On the second day, the FBI agent and I recovered the body of Dave Brown, a Navy captain who had been conducting science experiments on the mission. I spent two hours in the woods, sitting next to Dave's body, while the owner of the property cut back trees to get a larger vehicle to our location. I'd wished Dave well before the mission. Now, sixteen days later, all I could do for him was to make sure that his remains could be returned to his family. Most astronauts write a letter to their families to be opened only if they don't return from their missions. I sat with Dave's body, thinking about whether he'd written a letter, and what it might have said.

Like the *Challenger* accident seventeen years earlier, the loss of *Columbia* came in the wake of signs that were ignored. This wasn't just a random accident. NASA certainly could have done a better job of addressing the long-term problem of foam liberating from the external tank. While the space shuttle is an incredibly complex machine that can fail in thousands of catastrophic ways, it sometimes tries to tell you ahead of time what's coming. I think this was one of those times. We had seen foam problems again and again on successive launches and done little about it. Poor decision-making contributed to both tragedies, *Challenger* and *Columbia*.

From all my conversations with her, Gabby knew how I felt about the failings within NASA. I learned there that a well-meaning team of people can sometimes make horrible decisions that no single individual would make. Groupthink, and an unwillingness to disagree with the bosses, was too often a problem at NASA. It may be oversimplifying to say it this way, but in my years as an astronaut, I learned that none of us is as dumb as all of us. That phrase is now clearly posted in the room at NASA used by the Mission Management Team. (When Gabby was injured, and a large medical team needed to be assembled to treat her, it was very helpful to me to keep this mantra in mind.)

In the wake of *Columbia,* I had a hard time fully reassuring my daughters that everything would be OK. Though thousands of good and talented people played a role in each shuttle flight, each astronaut was at the mercy of a million decisions. My girls intuitively knew this.

Claudia, my older daughter, then nine years old, was especially adamant. She begged me to quit the astronaut program. She knew Laurel Clark well through astronaut family gatherings, and was friends with Laurel's son, Ian. "That could easily have been you on that mission," she said. "I could be like Ian, the one without a parent!"

"NASA is fixing this problem," I'd say, and that was true. But we all knew there was no way to make the shuttle fail-safe.

I did my best to speak honestly and directly to my kids. The shuttle is a complex machine with hundreds of thousands of parts. It operates near the limit of what humans have been able to engineer. "Design changes are going to help stop the shedding of foam from the tank, so what happened to Columbia is far less likely to happen again," I told them. "I know I'm in a risky business, but sometimes we have to take risks in life, because the rewards are so big. Those of us who are astronauts, that's how we feel about the importance of space exploration."

For a while, I thought about the Columbia disaster every single day. Now, maybe it comes into my head a couple times a week.

Gabby knew when she met me that there were dangers in my line of work, from my thirty-nine combat missions in the Navy to my missions into space. And though she accepted the anxiety that comes with being an astronaut's spouse, she also felt a need to be proactive. As ranking member of the House Subcommittee on Space and Aeronautics, she held hearings on flight safety, focusing not just on NASA but also on the commercial rocket companies now gearing up to deliver astronauts into space.

Gabby began one of her hearings by saying, "I am under no illusion that human spaceflight can ever be made risk-free. Nothing in life is . . . But this subcommittee is holding today's hearing because we need to be sure that any decisions being contemplated by the White House and Congress are informed by our best understanding of the fundamental crew-safety issues facing our human spaceflight program. And in making those decisions, we should not let either advocacy or unexamined optimism replace probing questions and thoughtful analysis."

It's ironic. When Gabby was elected to Congress, we didn't consider that she was the one with the risky job, or that she'd be the one nearly losing her life while serving her country. We never imagined that it could be Gabby who'd draw the ace of spades.

* * *

My maiden mission into space was as the pilot of *Endeavour* in December 2001. It was the first shuttle flight after the September 11 attacks, and we were told that security was higher than at any time in NASA history.

The U.S. government was so concerned about a terrorist's aircraft flying into the space shuttle on the launchpad that it allegedly positioned antiaircraft artillery around the Kennedy Space Center. At least, that was the word that leaked out from government sources. It wasn't until years later that I found out there were no antiaircraft guns. It was just misinformation. Tricky but effective. We were all fooled.

That's not to say there wasn't tight security. Guards with automatic rifles escorted us when we departed for the pad. On the road, we passed a Humvee with a .50-caliber machine gun. During the countdown, fighter jets and helicopter gunships were on patrol.

It was a time of high emotion for the country, of course. We'd carry with us six thousand postcard-size flags, which would be distributed after our flight to the relatives of 9/11 victims, and to some survivors of the attacks. (There aren't many things that have left the planet and safely returned. From the Mercury program to today it has been a tradition to take items into space that can be given away as mementos. People collect and treasure these keepsakes.)

We also brought along a flag that had flown at the World Trade Center on September 11. It was torn and still smelled of smoke. We worried that unpacking it in space might actually trigger smoke alarms.

Our commander, Dom Gorie, spoke beautifully for all of us just before we launched. He saw a vital message in that ripped flag. "Just like our country, it's a little bit bruised and battered and torn," he said. "With a little repair, it's going to fly as high and as beautiful as it ever did, and that's just what our country is doing."

I was able to mostly put the possibilities of terrorism out of my head. But because it would be my first flight, I couldn't fully shake my feelings of anxious uncertainty about what was ahead. Most every sensation on my journey, from liftoff to long-term weightlessness to reentry, would be new to me. What would it really feel like once I was sitting atop 500,000 gallons of rocket fuel, waiting to go?

My brother had beaten me into space—his first mission was in 1999—and before my liftoff he warned me about the first two minutes of flight. He said there's no real way to describe what it would be like. "You'll feel like maybe something is going very wrong," he warned. "You'll feel every pound of thrust. It's full power, instantaneously."

On the day of the flight, when I was strapped into my seat on the space shuttle, at first I was just hyperfocused on my job. It takes three hours to turn everything on. Then, as the countdown clock approaches zero, things start to get really busy. At six seconds, the three shuttle main engines start producing about a half-million pounds of thrust each. At zero seconds, the solid rockets ignite, and with 7.5 million pounds of thrust you jump into the air. It is an amazing, wild ride that takes you from 0 to 17,500 miles per hour in just eight minutes and thirty seconds. The best way that I've been able to describe this experience to nonastronauts is to have them imagine being on a runaway train going down the tracks at 1,000 miles an hour. And it keeps getting faster.

That mission lasted twelve days and orbited the earth 186 times. After we landed safely back at Kennedy Space Center, Scott was waiting to greet me on the runway, and my first words to him were, "Boy, you were right about liftoff!"

My next flight was on July 4, 2006, the first time a crew had launched from this planet on Independence Day. It was the second "Return to Flight" mission after the loss of *Columbia,* so it was understandably nerve-wracking. Had NASA fully corrected the problems that led to *Columbia*'s destruction?

Our mission brought thousands of pounds of supplies and a German astronaut to the International Space Station, but its primary purpose was to test new safety and repair procedures instituted in response to the failures that brought down *Columbia.* We did lose small pieces of foam during our launch—we knew that during the mission—but there was no significant damage to the orbiter. We traveled 5.5 million miles and landed without incident. The mission was deemed a great success because it gave NASA confidence in a new set of inspection and repair procedures.

One fellow crew member on that mission was Lisa Nowak, who made news a year later because of her obsession with a fellow astronaut. Police said Lisa drove from Houston to Orlando, Florida, with a black wig, a BB pistol, pepper spray, rubber tubing, and a hooded trench coat to confront a woman the astronaut was dating. News reports said she had worn diapers so she wouldn't have to stop on her long trip; she later denied that was true. Lisa was charged with attempted kidnapping, spent two days in jail, and later pled guilty to lesser charges. She received one year of probation, and NASA terminated its association with her.

It was an embarrassing occurrence that led to an independent panel reviewing the mental health of astronauts. Sometimes I wonder if I could have done something to help Lisa before she got herself into trouble. Those of us who knew her saw that she wasn't doing well emotionally in the months leading up to the incident, and I wish I had talked to her about what was going on in her personal life. This episode reminded us that just as the machinery of the shuttle program was imperfect, so were we as astronauts.

Gabby was my girlfriend when she attended the 2006 launch. By my next launch, on May 31, 2008, she was my wife. With the exception of a fictional character in James Michener's novel *Space,* Gabby was the first member of Congress in history to be married to a spacebound astronaut.

When *Discovery* blasted off, Gabby was in the family viewing area, simultaneously gripping my mother's arm and her mother's hand. It took her a while before she exhaled.

I had arranged for a friend from the astronaut office to present her with roses and a card, which reminded her that I loved her and that I'd see her again in two weeks. I instructed him not to deliver the flowers until Mission Control announced we were safely in orbit, just over eight minutes after liftoff. If the launch had gone awry, I didn't want her holding my flowers and my card during a hard moment.

Being married to me, Gabby saw both the soaring possibilities of space travel and the life-threatening challenges. She also saw that there was a dispiriting lack of vision inside NASA. The space shuttle era was ending, but in the increasingly rudderless space program, there was no clear consensus about what should follow. Gabby took a lot of her inside knowledge back to Congress.

"What is most striking about the [NASA] budget is the lack of over-all vision," she said in a hearing, ten months before she was shot. "We went to the Moon with a vision of exploring our first heavenly body. We flew the shuttle and the International Space Station with the vision of living continuously in space. What is our vision now? Where will we go? How will we get there? And when will we go? It is simply unfair to ask the American people to hand over billions of dollars for something that isn't even detailed enough to qualify for a loan from a loan shark."

Gabby knew well that the achievements of every generation of NASA astronauts and engineers were rooted in great risks. She knew that risk is often a necessary component of vision. I loved to talk to her about all of these issues. She understood.

I do a lot of thinking now, comparing Gabby today to how she was before. Since her injury, the rest of us have been called upon to encourage her to walk those extra steps or to move her right hand or to find the right words in her head and to say them out loud. We're constantly encouraging her. But before the shooting on January 8, it was Gabby who was the great encourager. She saw it as her job to encourage her staffers, her constituents, and her colleagues in Congress to be bold, to take risks, to think big. And that was especially true when she thought about the space program.

One day in July 2009, Gabby was in the cloakroom, the gathering area for members of the House of Representatives. *The Tyra Banks Show* was playing on the television, and that annoyed her. She had nothing against the talk show, but it just seemed frivolous.

"I switched the channel," she told me later. "I put on NASA TV."

"Good choice!" I said.

It was the fortieth anniversary of *Apollo 11*'s landing on the Moon, and NASA's channel was offering a retrospective. "While we were between votes, I thought it would be nice if my fellow members were exposed to coverage of the anniversary, rather than just watching Tyra Banks," she said. "Maybe they'd learn some things. Maybe they'd be inspired."

All around her in the cloakroom, representatives were socializing, eating snacks, or even napping. But Gabby was there on a mission, switching the TV channel and turning up the volume. Neil Armstrong was standing bravely on the Moon, and she wanted him to be heard.

CHAPTER ELEVEN

Second Chances

My daughters, Claudia and Claire, were very attentive to Gabby after she was injured. They sat by her bed and held her hand. They gave her hugs. They told her they loved her.

I was touched to see their compassion and concern. You don't always know how your kids will react in tough situations, and they made me proud.

For Gabby, though, their affection was a different experience. In fact, it was so unexpected that it was almost disorienting for her. Before January 8, Gabby had tried her best to connect with my kids. Sometimes she was able to engage them. Often, she was not. They wouldn't be rude. They just weren't receptive.

Gabby understood their reluctance about building a relationship with her. She was the stepmother, arriving in the girls' lives after their mom and I had divorced. The divorce was amicable, but the girls didn't need or want another mother figure. It's a familiar story, of course, after a parent remarries.

I understood how everyone was feeling. It was hard for Gabby. It was hard for Claudia and Claire. It was hard for me.

I'd let the girls know that Gabby truly wanted to reach out to them. She was determined. "There's nobody on the planet who asks about you more than Gabby does," I'd tell them. "She asks about your schoolwork, your friends, your activities. She's always asking."

The girls would just shrug when I said that.

As they saw it, Gabby was busy with her career. She didn't live in Houston or visit very often. How truly interested in their lives could she be? And because I'd travel to Tucson or Washington to be with

Gabby, she was responsible for taking me away from the girls, who split their time between me and my ex.

The events on January 8 changed everything.

The girls were shaken up by the sheer violence of that day: six people dead, thirteen injured. It pained them to see me so distraught and emotional, especially early on. And they also felt great regret about their dealings with Gabby. They desperately wished they'd been more willing to give her a chance, but she was in a coma, unable to understand or acknowledge their apologies.

Once Gabby started to heal and was more aware of her surroundings, the positive changes in the girls' interactions with her were so pronounced that Gabby didn't know what to make of them. She couldn't articulate her thoughts, but sometimes she and I would make eye contact. Her look said it all, as if she had stepped into an alternate stepdaughter universe.

As Gabby improved, she recognized that Claudia, sixteen, and Claire, fourteen, were trying hard to make up for lost time. But Gabby was in a different place, unable to talk to them about much of anything, feeling vulnerable and helpless, struggling with so many emotions. She still yearned for a child of her own, and knew that dream was now unlikely, given her injuries. She wondered if my kids had changed only because they felt sorry for her. In truth, their newfound affection and empathy made her uncomfortable. I sometimes had to ask the kids to back off, and that request, though carefully delivered, was hurtful to them.

Meanwhile, through it all, Claudia kept in her purse a folded-up piece of paper that she read to herself several times a day. She wondered if she'd ever find the right moment, or the courage, to read it aloud to Gabby.

*   *   *

Just as some employees at El Campo Tire didn't know what to make of Gabby's cheerful personality, neither did my kids. Claudia was especially suspicious.

She used to keep her thoughts to herself. But after January 8, she talked through her feelings. "I always thought Gabby was fake," she admitted. "She was so animated. No matter what you'd tell her, she'd have this warm smile on her face the entire time. I never knew if it was real."

As Claudia reached her teens, she almost never initiated a conversation with Gabby. If Gabby asked her something, she'd give a short, basic reply. Otherwise, she kept her stepmother at arm's length.

The girls were busy with school, friends, sports, and cheerleading. Gabby would ask them questions about their activities. Often it seemed they were answering only out of obligation.

But Gabby was always looking for common ground. When Claudia said she was considering a run for student council president in eighth grade, Gabby lit up and immediately offered advice for the campaign.

"You should run," Gabby said. "You'd be great!"

"I don't know," Claudia answered.

"You'll need to get your name out there. Tell everyone the positive things you'll do for the school."

"Yeah, I'll probably make some posters," Claudia said.

"Posters are good," Gabby told her. "But you should also figure out what bugs the kids." She suggested that Claudia set herself up at a table during the lunch hour to interact with her fellow students. "They can tell you what's on their minds, and you can talk about how you might help improve things."

"I don't know," Claudia said.

"Think about it," Gabby said. "It could really help you understand the kids at school. And once you're president, you'll be a better leader."

Gabby was enthusiastic, brainstorming about speeches Claudia could give, and ways she could turn lunchtime at the League City Intermediate School cafeteria into a miniature Congress on Your Corner.

"I'm not sure I want to do that," Claudia finally said. "I'll probably just stick to the posters."

Claudia saw Gabby's political spirit, but it all seemed too much for middle school. In the end, Claudia decided not to even run.

Claudia and Claire understood that issues mattered to Gabby, but that could be annoying to them, too. As a conservationist, "Green Gabby" wasn't happy when the girls stood for a while in front of the refrigerator with the door open, trying to decide what to eat. She'd playfully tell them, "You don't need to keep the refrigerator door open that long." They'd close the door and try to resist rolling their eyes.

But Gabby was very conscientious about her impact, and ours, on the planet. We'd even discuss with the kids the man-made devastation I'd observed from space. From my first shuttle mission in 2001 to my last mission in 2011, I clearly saw the deforestation in the Amazon. By my last trip, there were many more big blotches of nothing. Gabby understood how troubling this was, and couldn't resist reminding the kids of how we all need to do our part to save the environment. She'd say, "Don't throw that plastic bottle in the trash. It'll sit in a landfill for a hundred thousand years!" Or: "If you're leaving the room, turn off the light!"

Gabby was a stickler for other things, too. She didn't like the girls putting their shoes on the couch, or up against the back of the front seat in the car. They didn't like when she called them on it.

Gabby tried to be a positive influence for the girls, and sometimes she'd say things that got through to them. When Claudia was having trouble with a teacher and wanted to switch out of the class, Gabby told her, "All through your life, you're going to find people you don't like or who don't like you. You just have to figure out a way to suck it up and deal with it." Claudia found Gabby's advice useful, and remained in the class.

Each year in mid-February, Gabby was always the first one looking ahead, asking, "What should the kids do this summer?" You could almost set your watch to the moment she'd start planning. She'd ask, "Should the girls go to camp? How about some sort of service organization? We need to figure out how they can have a productive summer." Gabby suggested that Claudia consider a "wilderness" hiking expedition sponsored by the National Outdoor Leadership School. "You'll learn a lot and it'll be fun," Gabby told her. "Just ask your dad."

As an astronaut, I had gone on three trips with that organization. We spent several days backpacking while getting an education on expedition behavior, conflict resolution, and team building—stuff that's important in space. Claudia did end up going twice on the teen version of that trip and she loved it.

Then, in the summer of 2010, Claudia went on a community service trip to Nicaragua, where she and other teens helped build retaining walls in poor villages. Claudia stayed with a villager and ten members of his extended family in a home with just three rooms and dirt floors. At night they'd sit around the kitchen table, under a lone light-bulb, peeling black beans to make meals for the next day. Claudia sat with them, peeling and listening. One night she'd have beans for dinner. The next night she'd have rice. Some nights, for variety, her hosts would serve beans and rice together.

This was just the sort of eye-opening adventure that appealed to Gabby, of course, and that made for common ground. "I once lived with the Mennonites in Mexico," she told Claudia, and they talked for a while, comparing their experiences.

The girls, Gabby, and I did have some good times together. Claudia, Gabby, and I enjoyed hiking together to the bottom of the Grand Canyon. Claire liked visiting Gabby's parents, who live well outside of Tucson, in the middle of nowhere. We'd all go hiking out there, and when Claire complained that she was tired, Gabby was her cheerleader. "Come on, you can do it!" We'd struggle through the heat, the swarms of wasps and yellow jackets, the pokey cacti, and eventually reach a waterfall, where we'd eat lunch, and Gabby would tell Claire she was proud of her for not giving up.

Those moments were positive memories. But mostly, the girls weren't interested in bonding with Gabby. And they didn't.

"I understand," Gabby said. "They're kids and I love them. I'm patient. I'll wait for them to come around."

She continued to reach out. She'd buy them little gifts. She'd ask about their lives. She tried to have no expectations.

Then came January 8.

The girls had flown with me that day from Houston to Tucson. It was the first time they'd ever seen me cry. That afternoon, they visited Gabby—bandaged, battered, comatose—in her hospital room. They had never before seen anyone who was that close to death. It was shocking and scary, and they were both shaken.

Back at the hotel, just before midnight, Claudia was unable to sleep. She thought about how she had never allowed herself to get close to Gabby. She thought about the things she admired about her stepmother but had kept to herself. She wished she could go back in time and have a second chance. All she could do, through her tears, was to take out a piece of paper and start writing.

Dear Gabby,

You are the strongest, most incredible woman I have ever met. I love you so much. I am thankful to have someone like you in my life. I know we have not been extremely close in the past couple years and I am really sorry. That is going to change immediately.

I took such a wonderful person for granted and I feel horrible. I have been praying for you all day. I am going to visit as much as possible. Thank you for supporting me in everything I do and for believing in me. I can't wait to see you again and give you the biggest hug and kiss ever. I can't wait to hear your voice again. Stay strong. I love you. —Claudia

She rewrote the letter in neater handwriting and stuck the rough draft in her purse. She gave me the original, and weeks later, I read it to Gabby, who listened and nodded. Gabby was still in the early stages of her recovery, so she didn't respond with words. But I sensed that she understood and appreciated Claudia's efforts.

Claudia, meanwhile, kept that rough draft in her purse for months. She'd take it out several times each school day, just to reread it. It almost always made her teary.

She told her pole-vaulting coach that she was struggling with guilt. "I'm ashamed of how I acted before this all happened," she said. The coach, Chad Hunt, offered perspective and advice. "Don't punish yourself anymore," he said. "You can't think about what your relationship has been. You have to think about what your relationship with your stepmother is now, and what it's going to be. That's the only thing you can control." (Claudia and Claire's mom—my ex, Amy—also encouraged the girls to build new bonds with Gabby, for which I am grateful.)

Claudia chose never to discuss her letter with Gabby. She explained that she had made a decision: "I want to show her I've changed and that I care through my actions, not my words." Among her friends, Claudia became an advocate for repairing relationships with parents and step-parents. "I took Gabby for granted for so long," she'd say, "and I'm lucky I got a second chance to build a relationship with her."

* * *

For her part, Claire continued to struggle with feelings of sadness and guilt. At age fourteen, she had difficulty understanding how this could happen. How could a madman attack someone she knew so well? How could something so bad happen to someone who tried so hard to improve the lives of others?

The Monday after the shooting, Claire returned to school. She was grateful for all the supportive text messages and Facebook postings her friends had left for her over the weekend, but she knew it would be a terribly hard day. She went to school promising herself she wouldn't cry, but the tears came as soon as she arrived and embraced a good friend. Her first-period teacher, Mrs. May, whom Claire loved, gave her a hug when she got to class. One student asked why the teacher was hugging Claire, and another student blurted out, "Her mom got shot in the head!"

"That broke me," Claire later said. "I had to leave the room, tears streaming down my face. I was an emotional mess."

Another teacher gave Claire a box of tissues to carry with her from class to class. "I know Gabby would have wanted me to have a normal and productive day," Claire decided, and through her tears, she tried to do just that.

In the months after the shooting, Claire was sad on another front. She didn't like that I was unavailable for her, given how busy I was caring for Gabby and training for my space shuttle mission. "You have so much on your plate," she told me. "I feel like there's no room for me."

Claire tried not to be resentful, but the changes in our lives after January 8 were very tough for her. All I could do was hug her, tell her I loved her, and promise that I'd try harder.

* * *

As Gabby's recovery continued, she became more comfortable with the girls. She enjoyed when they came to see her. She told them "I love you." But Claudia still wrestled with her emotions and her regrets. Like me, she was having dreams about Gabby's full recovery. In my dreams, I was overjoyed that Gabby was almost back to normal. "Mine are more like nightmares," Claudia said. "Gabby is fully recovered, but she doesn't want a relationship with me. She can't forgive me."

She didn't need to worry. I had no doubts that the relationship between Gabby and the girls would continue to blossom. I saw it happening day by day.

Meanwhile, our lives remained split between before and after.

There were little things the girls reflected on. Before the shooting, they knew that people sometimes described me and Gabby as a so-called power couple. If they typed "astronaut Mark Kelly" and then "Rep. Gabrielle Giffords" into the Google search engine, we both had a similar number of entries. We were each mentioned on websites here and there, but like a lot of ambitious B-listers, our online presence was fairly modest. After Gabby was injured, the number of entries about her on Google exceeded eight million. None of us could have predicted that Gabby would charge ahead on the Googling front because of such an anguishing event for our family and eighteen other families. But the Internet is a heartless inventory. It tallies entries, not grief. It hurt to think about Gabby's mushrooming online presence.

My girls lost their innocence in the wake of the shooting. They grieved for the children of the other victims in Tucson, and for the parents and brother of Christina-Taylor Green, the nine-year-old girl who died that day. They saw how, in retrospect, our lives had been easy and idyllic. We didn't fully know it, but we'd all been very lucky, and lucky to have each other. We see that clearly now.

* * *

As Claudia began looking at colleges, there were a few that rose to the top of her list. One was the United States Naval Academy in Annapolis. Another was the University of Arizona in Tucson, where she considered joining the ROTC program.

She liked the idea of U of A because she already had a network of family and friends there. While it was far from home, it was a place she'd find her dad, her stepmom, Gabby's parents, and other familiar faces. She could hike with Gabby's friend Raoul, or he could lend a hand if her car needed to be fixed. Another friend of Gabby's, Nelson Miller, a retired Navy SEAL, would be there for Claudia if she needed help or guidance. And she knew Gabby would want to offer her advice on places to see, things to do, and people in Tucson to meet.

Just sixteen years old, Claudia had time before she'd have to make a decision. But she enjoyed contemplating that possible life in Tucson. She pictured herself biking the same Tucson trails that Gabby loved. It might be a long while before her stepmother could get back on a bike, if ever, but Claudia could take those rides and enjoy all the scenery. Then she and Gabby could talk about what she saw or who she met along the way. Claudia would enjoy that, and it lifted her heart to think that Gabby would, too.

CHAPTER TWELVE

Higher Callings

As Gabby fought for her life in the early days after the shooting, she had no idea that she was at the center of a boiling nationwide debate. Political discourse in America had become increasingly angry and belligerent, the rhetoric mean-spirited and threatening. The question of the moment: Had hateful, confrontational politics played a role in the shooting in Tucson?

Some argued that a troubled twenty-two-year-old man went to that shopping center to assassinate my wife and to murder and maim other innocent people solely because he was mentally ill. It wasn't the influence of political rhetoric. It was schizophrenia.

Gabby couldn't speak for herself after she was shot, but I knew exactly how she felt about the toxic political climate and the use of violent imagery in campaigns. She hated it. And she worried that some people, influenced by what they heard and read, could be motivated to respond with violence. She'd already seen it in her own congressional district, in her own office.

She was well aware that unstable people, like everyone else, watch the news, see campaign commercials, and seek information on the Internet. They are sometimes obsessive followers of politics. And because they may have a skewed way of processing information, it's possible that angry, violent words could motivate them to do disturbing or terrible things. Gabby didn't just talk to me about this risk. She also spoke publicly about it.

Especially during the debate over the controversial 2010 health-care bill, Gabby paid close attention to the threats and violence in other congressional districts. Pictures of nooses were sent to congressmen in

Michigan and South Carolina. A New York congresswoman received a telephone message mentioning snipers, and a brick was thrown into her office. A shot was fired into a Virginia congressman's campaign office.

For weeks leading up to the health-care vote, protesters had gathered outside Gabby's office in Tucson, jeering loudly and angrily. They held nasty signs, including some that showed Gabby dressed as Death and carrying a scythe. Checking messages on the office answering machine, Gabby's staffers would have to log calls such as: "Is that c— going to vote for the health-care bill?"

Some angry callers would demand to talk directly to Gabby. "Is that Communist bitch there?" more than one asked. Gabby's staffers tried to remain cool. Her communications director, C. J. Karamargin, had an urge to answer, "Which Communist bitch are you looking for?"

Staffers joked about their efforts to sweet-talk "crazy callers," but they were nervous, too. At times things felt sinister. During health-care forums, C.J. thought the hostility "was rumbling like a volcano." He wondered when the lava would flow. But he was struck by the ways in which Gabby worked to ease the tension. When people were rude at the forums, Gabby responded forcefully and firmly, but in a way that was quintessentially her. She wouldn't scold or wag her finger. Instead she would cajole her audiences. "Hey, guys, let's try not to be rude here, OK?"

Bill Clinton used to talk about himself as being like an inflatable clown; if you punched him, he came right back up. Gabby's staffers said she reminded them of Clinton in that regard. She endured verbal blow after verbal blow, and she bounced right back up, trying to smile. "I'm here to listen," she'd say. "I'm here to understand."

When Gabby was alone with me, though, she spoke more candidly. Like her staffers, she felt the rumbles of the volcano and feared that it might blow.

She was troubled that her district was one of twenty targeted on Sarah Palin's Facebook page and website, Sarahpac.com. Gabby understood that politics is a rough game. But she was taken aback by the image on Palin's website. It featured a United States map with gun sights over the districts where Sarah Palin hoped her supporters would defeat Democrats who had supported President Obama's health-care plan. The headline was "We've diagnosed the problem . . . Help us prescribe the solution." Palin also sent out a Twitter message—"Don't Retreat, Instead—RELOAD!"—encouraging her followers to visit her Facebook page.

Gabby told me that Palin's rhetoric had no place in political discourse. "It sends all the wrong messages," she'd say. "It's a dangerous thing to do."

In March 2010, a few hours after Gabby voted to approve the health-care overhaul, someone shot out the glass door and side window of her office. Police suspected a pellet gun was used, though the perpetrator was never caught. That, more than anything up to that point, was distressing for Gabby's staffers. They feared for their safety.

After the attack on her office, Gabby was invited to go on MSNBC to talk about it. One of the interviewers, Chuck Todd, asked her, "Are you fearful today?"

"You know, I'm not," Gabby answered. "We have had hundreds and hundreds of protesters over the course of the last several months . . . The rhetoric is incredibly heated, not just the calls, but the e-mails, the slurs."

Rather than talk about fear, Gabby wanted to appeal to people's better instincts and ideals. "You've got to think about it," she said. "Our democracy is a light, a beacon really, around the world, because we effect change at the ballot box and not because of these, you know, outbursts of violence."

Gabby didn't want to make this a partisan issue. She mentioned that she had seen "extreme activism" and efforts to inflame emotions among both Democrats and Republicans. "I think it's important for all leaders, not just leaders of the Republican party or the Democratic party, to say, 'Look, we can't stand for this.'"

During that interview, Gabby decided to mention her feelings about the Sarah Palin website. "For example, we're on Sarah Palin's targeted list. But the thing is, the way she has it depicted has crosshairs of a gun sight over our district. When people do that, they've got to realize the consequences to that action."

Todd pointed out that "in fairness, campaign rhetoric and war rhetoric have been interchangeable for years." He asked Gabby if she thought Palin really intended to suggest violence.

Gabby held her ground. "You know, I can't say. I'm not Sarah Palin. But what I can say is that in the years that some of my colleagues have served—twenty, thirty years—they've never seen it like this. We have to work out our problems by negotiating, working together, hopefully Democrats and Republicans. I understand that this health-care bill is incredibly personal, probably the most significant vote cast here for decades, frankly. But the reality is that we've got to focus on the policy, focus on the process. Leaders—community leaders, not just political leaders—need to stand back when things get too fired up and say, 'Whoa, let's take a step back here.'"

On the day Gabby was shot, Sarah Palin's rhetoric came quickly into my head. In fact, when President Obama called that afternoon to offer his help and his condolences over the tragedy, I told him that Gabby and I had found Palin's website very disturbing.

"Sarah Palin actually has a map with gun crosshairs over people's districts!" I said.

I had woken up that morning never imagining that by sunset I'd be talking on the phone with the president about my critically wounded wife. But now, as Gabby struggled to stay alive and I had my cell phone pressed hard against my ear, I needed to vent and President Obama let me. I was stressed out and pissed off.

It was just a few hours after the shooting, but I felt as if I already had gone through the early stages of grief—disbelief, shock—and had settled firmly into the anger stage. I didn't know who this guy was who had shot my wife. (I wouldn't even learn his name until days later.) I didn't know why he had done it. But I did know that there had been an environment that encouraged hatred, a lot of it focused on my wife. I needed to talk about it.

"You know, Mr. President," I said, "politics in Arizona has really gotten out of control." I recounted for him my disgust over a fundraiser held by Gabby's opponent, Jesse Kelly, in the 2010 race for her seat. A candidate with heavy support from the Tea Party, Kelly had invited supporters to "Get on Target for Victory in November" by paying fifty dollars to shoot a fully automatic M16. His ads invited shooters to "help remove Gabrielle Giffords from office." A six-foot-eight former U.S. Marine, Kelly was featured in his ad campaign holding a gun, with the tag line "Send a Warrior to Congress."

President Obama listened when I told him about Kelly and Palin. I don't remember him commenting on them directly. He did ask questions about the others who were killed and injured, and about Gabby's care. Before we hung up, he said, "You have the full resources of the United States government. Call me if you need anything. You and Gabby have a friend in the White House." I thanked him for listening—we'd been on the phone less than ten minutes—and then an operator came on the line and gave me a direct number I could call if I needed to reach the president.

In the days that followed, Sarah Palin received a great deal of media attention about the crosshairs controversy. In response, one of her aides said that the bull's-eyes on her website map were actually surveyor's marks, not gun crosshairs. (The map had been taken off the site the day of the shooting.) Palin herself posted an eight-minute video online in which she said her "heart broke for the innocent victims" in Tucson. "It's inexcusable and incomprehensible why a single evil man took the lives of peaceful citizens that day," she said. But she also had a message for those who questioned her rhetoric, adding: "Within hours of a tragedy unfolding, journalists and pundits should not manufacture a blood libel that serves only to incite the very hatred and violence they purport to condemn. That is reprehensible."

Gabby and I both were aware that there are mentally ill people who do horrible things. I don't know if the shooter in Tucson ever looked at Sarah Palin's website, or any others that targeted Gabby. Whether he did or he didn't, he pulled the trigger again and again and again. He is to blame. He did it. That goes without saying.

And yet, at the same time, I agreed with what Gabby said before she was injured. All of us, especially those who want to be leaders, have a responsibility to the higher callings of democracy and civility. We need to tone it down, speak more respectfully, and fully recognize that words have consequences.

I've been told by John Coale, a Palin advisor, that Sarah and her husband, Todd, were "devastated" by the tragedy in Tucson. Coale, a

Washington attorney and the husband of Greta Van Susteren of Fox News, was sincere when he reached out to tell me that. I don't doubt his description.

In the early days after Gabby was shot, I thought Sarah Palin might call me to say she wished Gabby well and that she was praying for her and the other victims. We heard from many Republicans offering heartfelt messages. Given that a lot of the discussion in the wake of the shooting had singled out Palin, I expected she might also want to clear the air.

As Gabby remained in her coma, and I sat by her side, I found myself thinking about what I would say if the phone rang and it was Palin. I even ended up constructing a few precise words.

"Thank you for reaching out," I planned to tell her. "Gabby is hanging in there. Thank you for asking."

I would have listened to what Palin had to say, graciously accepted her words of consolation. Then it would be my turn. I vowed to myself that I would address the violence in Tucson head-on.

"You are not responsible," I planned to tell Sarah Palin. "But you *are* irresponsible."

I don't know how she would have responded to me. She may have been insulted. She may have been open to discussion. She may have said things that would resonate with me. As it turned out, she never called.

* * *

In the years before the shooting, Gabby knew politics often required forceful language and scrappy interactions. She was a policy wonk, but she was also a woman who spoke frankly and fearlessly. Many found her refreshing. Others were put off by her.

When she got to Washington, Gabby didn't mind taking on the federal government. She'd go on radio and TV and make pointed statements. She explained to NPR that she represents one of the longest U.S./Mexico border districts in the United States. "The federal government has essentially failed the people of Arizona," she said. "We have over twice the number of illegal entrants as California, Texas, and New Mexico combined. Yet the federal government has not reimbursed Arizona for the costs of health care, for the costs of our schools, for the costs of first responders and law enforcement."

She fought over issues that people outside border states didn't even know existed. For instance, a lack of cell-phone service plagues sparsely populated areas of Gabby's district near the border with Mexico. When a rancher went missing in 2010, poor coverage made it impossible for anyone to call law-enforcement agencies for help. The rancher was found dead, allegedly murdered by a border-crossing smuggler.

"This murder is the latest in a disturbing trend of home invasions, burglaries, assaults and other lawless activities along the international border," Gabby wrote in a letter to Lowell McAdam, president of Verizon Wireless. Ranchers carry cell phones but have no service, she wrote, leaving them "isolated and endangered when they encounter drug- and people-smugglers on their lands . . .

"I am aware that Verizon has portable cell phone towers that can be located in areas where coverage is inadequate or unavailable. These towers were installed in Arizona to provide critical security during the most recent presidential campaign. There is a need to do so again to provide security to the families who are under fire from smugglers in Southern Arizona . . . I look forward to your earliest response and the support I am sure you will want to provide." (McAdam promised to study Gabby's request, as did the president of AT&T. Since the shooting, Gabby's staffers have remained on the case.)

Gabby always had a pile of issues such as this on her plate, and she was a workaholic. I used to say if she was awake, she was working.

Each week, she was asked to make appearances at about fifty meetings or events, and she'd try to accommodate as many as she could. She had trouble saying no, especially if it involved constituents, and her schedule was overwhelming. Her staff kept track of all the numbers. In 2009, for instance, she appeared at 530 events and meetings in Washington and 216 in Arizona. On top of that, she also attended 231 "private events," usually get-togethers with community leaders and constituents. Her staff even kept track of her days with me on their color-coded calendar. I had my own color: purple. The records show Gabby spent fewer than a hundred days with me in 2009, mostly in Arizona or Washington. She came to Houston for just a dozen of those days.

Gabby's weekly trips back and forth between Washington and her district were not easy. She'd wake up at 5:00 a.m. in Arizona, catch a

7:00 flight to Dallas, where she'd connect to a Washington, D.C., flight. Door-to-door it took her eight to nine hours. She preferred a window seat on early morning flights so she could lean against the window and catch a few minutes of sleep. On afternoon flights, she wanted the aisle so she'd have more room to work. She could spend a whole flight composing e-mails, which would be delivered the moment she landed. Her staffers knew when she'd arrived because a flood of e-mails would fill their in-boxes, often with detailed directions on how to focus their efforts on improving constituents' lives.

Ron Barber, Gabby's district director, once got into a philosophical discussion with her about the meaning of life. Why are all of us brought into the world? Why do we exist? They went back and forth on the question, and then Gabby finally said, "I think it comes down to this: We are here to care for each other."

To that end, Gabby was also a diligent thank-you-note writer. She'd typically write or sign five hundred a week. On the plane, at the kitchen table, in the car, she'd have a giant stack of paper in front of her. Each one would have a personal note scribbled at the bottom. To me, it seemed as if she remembered something about everyone. She sent many thank-you e-mails and notes to her thirty-five staffers and interns, too. She was loyal to them and they were loyal to her.

Some staffers felt that Gabby was a perfectionist. It wasn't easy for them when they had to wait longer than they liked for her authorization to send a press release or schedule a meeting. She also had a policy that if a constituent from Arizona was visiting Washington and stopped by the office, unless it was impossible, she wanted to see them. That included kids on school trips. She met with a couple hundred to a couple thousand constituents each month in her office, and she wasn't good at moving on. She'd be chatting away and her staff had to point at their watches or wave their arms to let her know she was throwing off the whole day's schedule.

Gabby's staffers came to understand that she was motivated by an urge to do it all. And she stayed so busy in part because she had a mantra: "Nothing can replace firsthand knowledge of an issue. To understand something, you have to see it." So, unlike a lot of Arizona politicians, she toured long stretches of the U.S.-Mexican border. She even went to places that are accessible only by mules because the terrain there is too rocky for horses. (Mules are more stable, and better at making their way through creek beds.)

A couple times, Gabby took me with her on border visits. We stayed at the home of Warner and Wendy Glenn, whom Gabby visited so often that they'd become close friends. Warner is a seventy-something rancher and mountain-lion hunter. This guy is the definition of tough; he makes Clint Eastwood look like Lady Gaga.

Warner and his daughter Kelly took Gabby and me out to the border for hours, and we'd see illegal immigrants waiting on the Mexican side to make their crossings. I waved at them and said *"Hola,"* but Gabby, as a representative of the U.S. government, didn't think it appropriate to engage in conversation with people preparing to enter the country illegally.

At one point I got off my mule, tied it up, and told Gabby I was going to become an illegal immigrant to Mexico. "Don't do that!" she said. But I went under the pathetic barbed-wire fence and strolled about a hundred yards into Mexican territory, then came back into the United States, just to test how easy it is.

"You shouldn't have done that," Gabby told me when I returned. But I think she was glad I now had a sense of how porous our border is. In her district alone, hundreds of people a day are caught trying to cross. It's hard to say how many get through. In some spots, the border is nothing more than a couple pieces of barbed wire.

When President Obama spoke about fixing the immigration system in 2010, Gabby issued a tough statement. "Arizonans have heard it all before," she said. "We listen closely to speeches and then wait for Washington to act. We're tired of waiting. The crisis on America's borders won't be addressed with words. . . . Today we have two border problems: security and reform of our broken immigration laws. I reject the call by some that we must focus exclusively on one without addressing the other. We are a smart country. We can multitask. We can and we must address both of these problems."

Gabby spoke sharply on other issues, too.

She called U.S. energy policies "potentially disastrous" unless more money is invested in renewable energy. She'd point out that her dis-

trict has 350 days of sunshine a year. "Every single new house con-
structed should have solar panels on the roof," Gabby said.

As a member of the Space and Aeronautics subcommittee, she paid
attention to the issue of safety in space, and held a hearing in April
2009, after two satellites collided. She talked about the 19,000 objects
in Earth's orbit that are tracked by the U.S. Space Surveillance Network, and the 300,000 other pieces of debris—some as small as a half
inch in size—that no one is tracking. Gabby wanted witnesses from the
space program to address whether that satellite collision was a harbin-
ger of life-threatening disasters to come. "What is needed and how do
we go about getting it put in place?" she asked.

One thing I always loved about Gabby was the way she focused her
attention on the biggest issues and the smaller ones with equal passion. In 2009, two British tourists were hit by a truck and killed while
crossing State Highway 80 in Tombstone, the historic Western town
in Gabby's district. There had been three other fatalities there in recent
years. Gabby wrote to Governor Jan Brewer asking her to act quickly
to install a crosswalk and lighting. The Arizona Department of Transportation had conducted two studies at that location and determined a
crosswalk was not justified.

"Tombstone, known internationally as 'The Town Too Tough to
Die,' must not become known as a place where tourists and residents
risk their lives when they cross the street," Gabby argued. ADOT studied the issue again, but didn't agree crosswalks were necessary.

Gabby knew she wouldn't win every issue, but she woke up each
morning ready to keep trying. She really did. Whether she was focusing on a vast stretch of outer space, her district's 114-mile border with
Mexico, or the few dozen yards from one side of a busy street to the
other, my wife was relentless.

* * *

When it came to the biggest and toughest policy issues, I watched how
carefully and thoughtfully Gabby made up her mind. TARP and the stimulus package were particularly difficult votes for her. In 2008, TARP—
the Troubled Asset Relief Program—was designed to strengthen the
financial sector by allowing the government to buy assets and equities
from financial institutions. Given her concern that the government often

does a poor job spending taxpayers' money, and that the bill didn't have sufficient accountability measures, Gabby initially voted no. The bill failed. Then the stock market plummeted and President Bush couldn't get enough Republican support for a new version of the bill.

Gabby knew it was a politically unpopular thing to do, but given how critical that moment was, she felt the right decision was to support the president and the house leadership in both parties. She also felt the changes in the bill had made it a better piece of legislation. If the new bill had failed, our banking system and the entire economy may have failed, too.

As a fiscal conservative, Gabby wasn't one to vote for new spending unless the situation was dire. That's why President Obama's economic stimulus package in 2009 was such a difficult vote for her. It gave her sleepless nights. She collected input, pro and con, from her constituents. Then, worried about a recession or even a depression, she voted for the plan.

Like all of us, she wanted to be liked, but she wasn't afraid to be unpopular as long as she was given a chance to make her case. And she liked the challenge of changing people's minds.

She was repeatedly invited to speak before the Tucson Chamber of Commerce, and even though the chamber always endorsed her Republican opponents, she appreciated the opportunity to be heard by these conservative business leaders.

At one speech, near the end of her first term, she began by covering all her bases: "I am honored to be here today as a third-generation Tucsonan, a product of our public schools, a former local small-business owner, and now as your member of the United States Congress.

"Since I was elected, people keep asking me if I'm having fun yet and I never know quite what to say. The 110th Congress's schedule is grueling, traveling home on the weekends exhausting, and my D.C. apartment is worse than my freshman dorm room in college."

But then she talked of racing from meeting to meeting, passing reminders—a statue, a painting—of legendary Arizona lawmakers from the past. "I aspire to live up to the legacy of those who came before me," she said, "and to set a new standard for those who will come along in the future."

As the Chamber of Commerce audience listened, she took them on a "tour" of her district by describing people who were doing important work at places such as the VA Medical Center and Hendricks Elementary School. Gabby always had a performer's sense of theater, and she arranged to have special people in the audience—heroes from her district she wanted to introduce. There was a third-grade teacher from Hendricks, Jay Stanforth. "Jay, will you please stand to be recognized."

There was a veteran of the war in Afghanistan, Tommy Mendoza, who served on the Veterans Advisory Council, which Gabby had created. "Tommy, please stand. Thank you for your service and for your commitment to making lives better for all returning soldiers."

Gabby talked about how Arizona is the fastest-growing state in the nation, and that some towns in her district are "exploding overnight." She mentioned Benson, with a population of about 5,000. "Now over fifty thousand homes are slated for construction there," Gabby said. She explained the issues of infrastructure, water conservation. "Folks, we have some choices to make," she said. "The tension between growth and nature can be lessened through smart policies and collaboration." Then she introduced Katharine Jacobs, a woman heading a consortium of universities and state agencies that is studying water issues. "Katharine, will you please stand and be recognized."

Many members of the Tucson Chamber of Commerce weren't ever going to vote for Gabby, but they had to admit she put on a good show.

In her own way, Gabby was actually a one-woman Chamber of Commerce. Her day wasn't complete unless she had spent some time proselytizing about southern Arizona. Gabby loved the people, the land, the history, the industry, the weather, the food, the culture.

"It's the best place in the world," she'd always say to Pia Carusone, her chief of staff, who was raised in upstate New York. "Don't let people tell you that Arizona is too hot! The weather here is great and people like it hot anyway. You can have a year-round tan, and use solar panels to cut your electric bills way down."

Gabby loved that her constituents were such a diverse crowd. Her district is home to an Air Force base and an Army post. Her constituents are ranchers, retirees, artists, college students, professors, astronomers, union members, public-sector workers, and a lot of hardworking, low-wage blue-collar types. Pia marveled at how adept Gabby seemed to be at relating to the "crunchy people in clogs" who thought she wasn't liberal enough, and the grumpy old Republicans with guns on their belts who distrusted Washington. She called them her "bubbas."

She could talk about military benefits with veterans, details of missile-production with Raytheon engineers, and Department of Defense policy specifics of the new Joint Strike Fighter with Air Force generals. She could nurse a beer with her bubbas at Trident Grill, a favorite Tucson watering hole owned by her friend Nelson Miller, or at the Shanty, owned by her friend Bill Nugent. She was just as comfortable sipping wine out in the foothills with retired investment bankers who'd moved to town from back East and wanted to discuss tax policy. And because Gabby spoke Spanish fluently and knew Hispanic culture well, she related easily to Latinos in her district.

She had a lot of warm feelings for the people she represented. It saddened her, though, to see the darker side of her district.

There was one highly charged Congress on Your Corner event in 2009 where people were arguing about the health-care bill. A man's gun dropped out of its holster and slid across the floor of the Safeway supermarket. That was a scary moment for Gabby and her staffers; they realized people could be coming to COYC events armed.

On that particular day, there had been a group of people of Mexican descent waiting two hours to talk to Gabby. When they got to the front of the line, they hugged her and she spoke to them in Spanish. They related to her very warmly.

An angry Tea Party supporter watched Gabby interact with this group of people and shouted at her, "That's why you're going to lose in November—because the Mexicans love you!"

Gabby knew well that fringe elements were damaging Arizona's reputation. She accepted that she'd have to live with sizable pockets of zealots. Some were vociferously anti-immigration, seeing no areas for compromise. Others were so pro-gun that they thought any laws requiring background checks or waiting periods were a threat to society. There were those who so hated Obama's health-care bill that the veins in their necks bulged when they yelled at Gabby about it.

Gabby knew she represented these people, too. She often spoke about that to me. "I represent everyone who voted against me in the last election as equally as I represent my closest supporters," she'd say. She hoped people's anger could be tempered, that there was room for understanding. Publicly, she spoke of hope. Privately, she was sometimes less optimistic.

On Friday, January 7, 2011, the night before Gabby was shot at her Congress on Your Corner event, she received an e-mail from Kevin Bleyer, a writer we know who works for Jon Stewart's *Daily Show*. The Comedy Central program had made fun of Arizona thirteen times in 2010 for its reactionary politics, its die-hard extremists, and the silly antics of some lawmakers. Kevin sent us a news link about an Arizona state representative we know who had said his goal for the upcoming session of the state legislature was "to try to keep Arizona off *The Daily Show*."

From my observations of the state, I thought this was an impossible goal. I also thought it was all kind of funny.

But Gabby saw the note from Kevin in very personal terms. At 7:15 p.m., she replied to Kevin's e-mail and cc'd me.

"My poor state!" she wrote. "The nut jobs have stolen it away from the good people of Arizona."

That turned out to be the last e-mail I received from her.

CHAPTER THIRTEEN

"I Wonder What Happened"

In the days after Gabby first came out of her coma, she became aware, in the haziest of ways, that she was seriously injured. She recognized that she was hospitalized. She knew her loved ones had gathered around her. But she was not in a position to understand what had happened, and we offered no details. She wasn't ready.

"I was a zombie," Gabby would say, seven months later, when she tried to describe how she felt after waking up.

For our part, we didn't know what she was thinking in those first weeks following the shooting. She may have assumed she was in a car accident or that she'd had a stroke. Perhaps she didn't even consider how she was injured. Her brain wasn't functioning yet at that level of awareness. And even if it was, a tracheotomy tube prevented her from speaking.

Jerome Caroselli, her neuropsychologist at TIRR, told us that when she was ready to absorb the news, it was important for her recovery that she know what happened to her. She didn't need to be given the full story anytime soon, or any details about the fates of all the people around her. Almost certainly, that would be too difficult for her to process, especially because she wasn't able to ask questions. But she deserved to be told how she had been hurt.

"She should know it wasn't a stroke and it wasn't a car accident," Dr. Caroselli said. "You'll need to tell her she was shot."

I first attempted to have this discussion with Gabby in early February, less than a month after she was injured. Pretty quickly, I realized that she could not comprehend what I was saying. She looked at me blankly. I gave up.

Ten days later, I tried again. "Gabby, there's something important

165

that you need to know," I said. "I'm going to tell you what happened to you."

She looked at me and waited.

"You were at your first Congress on Your Corner event of the new term," I said. "It was January eighth at the Safeway on Oracle. This man came up to you with a gun and he shot you. He shot you in the head. We don't know why he did that. I'm sorry it happened. We all are. But he's in jail. You're safe."

Gabby looked shocked and surprised, but only for a minute. Then it was as if the news wore off and escaped from her mind. She gave no further indication she had heard me.

I tried a third time a week or so later, and it didn't go well. After I spoke, Gabby began crying uncontrollably, and she kept crying for about a half hour.

I told her neuropsychologist what happened, and he was pleased. "Great," he said. "That's an appropriate response. She understood what you said and she cried about it. I'm happy to hear that." But again, her sadness passed and within hours Gabby seemed to have forgotten what I told her.

Then on March 12, a Saturday, I was sitting with Gabby, and as usual, I was encouraging her to try to ask a question. She looked at me for a while in silence before she spoke. "I wonder," she said. "I wonder what happened to me."

It wasn't really a question, but I gave her credit for it.

I decided to take a different approach to help her understand what she was wondering about. This time, instead of telling her what happened to her, I'd tell her what happened to me. I'd share the story of the shooting from my perspective.

So I didn't start by mentioning the Congress on Your Corner event. Instead I said, "A couple months ago, I was home on a Saturday morning and the phone rang." I explained that Pia, her chief of staff, was on the line. "She told me you'd been shot, and that I needed to get to Tucson." Gabby seemed to be following the story more closely this time.

"Do you remember being shot?" I asked her.

"Yes," she said. It was hard to know if she really remembered, but she was insistent. "I remember."

"What do you remember?" I asked.

"Shot. Shocked. Scary," she said, very clearly, pausing between each word.

I still didn't tell her that others had been injured and killed. Her doctors had warned us that she might hold herself responsible for their deaths, having hosted the event. How would she handle feelings of guilt and sadness, given her inability to say much or ask questions? We were told we had to proceed very carefully.

A little later that morning, however, Gabby took charge of the flow of information into her life.

For a few weeks, I had been reading articles to her from *The New York Times, The Wall Street Journal,* the *Arizona Republic,* and Tucson's *Arizona Daily Star.* Every day, she seemed to be getting a clearer sense of the stories. She even looked at the front-page headlines and photos on her own, and read the words to herself. It was hard to know just how much she comprehended, but she was definitely engaged in the newspapers.

On this Saturday, there happened to be a teaser at the bottom of the front page of *The New York Times*: "Doctors Detail Giffords's Progress." It pointed to a story on page A-13.

Gabby saw that and started frantically leafing through the paper to find the page. Just then, Angie, her speech therapist, came into the room to bring her to a session. Sitting in her wheelchair, Gabby latched her good left hand onto the railing of her bed, giving all of us the firm message "I'm not going anywhere!" To me, it seemed as if she was thinking, "Everyone has been lying to me about my condition. But now I'm going to get the real story!"

"OK, Gabby," I said. "Let's find the story and I'll read it to you."

I turned to page A-13 and Gabby watched as I read the story aloud, paragraph by paragraph. Her eyes remained focused on the newspaper. The story was mostly about a news conference held by her doctors at TIRR the previous day. Saying Gabby was "making leaps and bounds," they explained that her cognitive level and long-term memory seemed good, that she was walking with assistance, and that her personality had reemerged. They called her progress "quite remarkable."

Gabby listened as I read. When I got to the second column, I knew what was ahead. I was going to come to a paragraph about the people who were killed and wounded in Tucson. I thought I'd smoothly and seamlessly skip over those sentences, but Gabby had been following along. She watched me bypass that paragraph. That's when she grabbed the paper, ruffled it, and glared at me. Using her middle finger and forefinger, she forcefully and abruptly tapped the paragraph in question.

I had made a decision after she was injured that I wouldn't mislead her. If she asked me a question, I'd give her an answer. Now here she was, nonverbally, asking me for the truth. And so I read to her, slowly: "Ms. Giffords was one of nineteen people shot in January while she was meeting with constituents in a supermarket parking lot in Tucson; six died."

I looked up from the page and took Gabby's hand. She didn't ask, "Who died? Did I know them? Were they strangers?" She couldn't formulate a question or express herself at that level. But now she knew that she wasn't the only one shot that day.

She sat for a moment, digesting the news, and then Angie asked, "Gabby, are you ready to go to speech therapy now?"

"Yes," Gabby answered, but I could tell her thoughts were elsewhere.

As Angie wheeled her to therapy, Gabby began crying. I sat in on her session, and she was very emotional. She had trouble getting through her verbal exercises.

That night, I was lying in bed with Gabby and I asked her how she felt about what we'd read in the newspaper. "Awful, awful," she said. "So many people hurt."

"Yes," I told her. "It was a very terrible day."

"Die," she said. "So many people." She cried and I held her.

* * *

On the morning of the shooting I was home in Houston. It was my weekend to have the kids. Claire was sleeping and Claudia was sitting with me, talking about a boyfriend I didn't approve of. (It wasn't totally the boy's fault. I don't approve of any of them.)

That's when my cell phone rang. It was Pia. "I don't know how to tell you this, so I'll just say it," she said. "Apparently, Gabby has been shot at the Congress on Your Corner."

She was in Washington and had no other information. She said she had just received a call from Mark Kimble, Gabby's senior press advisor, who was at the Safeway but uninjured. Mark said he was standing behind a pole with bodies all around him. It was about four minutes after the shooting. The police hadn't even arrived there yet.

Pia recalls that I was calm while hearing the news. She told me she had no other information. The call was over in fewer than thirty seconds.

"Claudia!" I said. "Wake up, Claire." And then, strangely, I thought to myself that maybe I had just imagined my short conversation with Pia. For a few seconds, I wondered whether I'd been hallucinating. I got out my cell phone and looked at it to make sure Pia's phone number was my most recent call.

I hit redial. "Tell me this again," I said to Pia, and she repeated what she had said.

This time, she added that she'd heard Gabby may have been shot in the head. I'm an optimist. Maybe that information was wrong. Maybe the injury wasn't life-threatening, and the bullet had just grazed her. Pia could only tell me what she'd heard from Mark Kimble.

I hung up and immediately called Gabby's parents in Tucson. When something terrible happens to your child, I believe you have a right to know immediately. Spencer answered the phone and took the news hard. He began sobbing. He said Gloria was at a dry cleaner in Tucson, so I called her on her cell. She was shocked, but she's like me. She was thinking, "What do I do next?"

For me, the first question was "How do I get to Tucson?"

The next commercial flight wouldn't get me there for six hours. If it had been a weekday, I could have flown myself in one of NASA's T-38s. I always needed more training hours on the jet; I had to log forty-five hours per quarter. In my emotional state, however, I'm not sure how that flight would have gone that day. In any case, because it was a Saturday, the T-38s were in the hangar and unavailable.

That's when my friend Tilman Fertitta came into my head.

Given his restaurant and casino businesses all over the country, he had his own plane. When I told him about the shooting, he jumped into action. "The plane is about to be taken apart for maintenance," he told me. "Let me call them right this minute."

He stopped the mechanics in time and had the plane fueled while I packed two suitcases. I didn't know how long I'd be in Tucson, so I figured I'd better be prepared. The girls begged to come with me, and I finally relented. After my mom offered to join us and look after them, the four of us jumped into my car and headed for Houston's Hobby Airport.

At first, there was nothing on the news about the shooting. We were listening to CNN on the car's satellite radio. But then, shortly before we arrived at the airport, the first "breaking news" from Tucson was reported. It was about forty-five minutes after the shooting began.

Once the news was out, my cell phone started vibrating as friends and colleagues learned what had happened and tried to reach me. I didn't answer any of their calls. We were too frantic rushing to get onto the plane. Once it was in the air, I tried to figure out if the TV system on board would work. It turned right on, and we were able to get CNN and Fox News.

In hindsight, however, watching the television was a great mistake.

We had the TV set to Fox, which at first had limited information, but then reported news that had just aired on National Public Radio: "Congresswoman Gabrielle Giffords of Arizona has been shot and killed during a public event in Tucson, Arizona."

It was the most shocking moment of my life.

My mother screamed and the girls began crying. I was so distraught I didn't know what to do except to stand up and go into the plane's tiny restroom.

I sat in there on the lid of the toilet with my head in my hands. I cried. Gabby was the most amazing person I had ever met, full of life and optimism. Now she was gone. What would the coming days look like? I didn't know what to do or what I could say to my kids and my mom. Through the bathroom door they could hear the muffled sounds of my grief, and I could hear theirs.

After a few minutes, I wiped away the tears, splashed some water on my face, and pulled myself together the best I could. I came out of the bathroom and hugged the girls. Claudia later said it seemed as if my whole body was crying.

We switched on CNN, which also was reporting that Gabby was

dead. "I should tell you," said the CNN anchor, Martin Savidge, "that NPR is now reporting that Congresswoman Gabrielle Giffords has, in fact, died, as have six other people." A few minutes later, he said: "For those of you tuning in, CNN has confirmed that Congresswoman Gabrielle Giffords was killed at a shooting that took place at a grocery store."

"Confirmed." That was the word CNN was using.

Minutes later, one of the pilots, Dave Dinapoli, yelled back to us in the cabin, "Tilman is on the phone."

I picked up the phone and Tilman said, "I'm watching the news and they're saying Gabby died. I don't believe it. Something is screwed up here." Other news outlets had been reporting that Gabby was taken to the hospital. Dead people aren't usually taken to hospitals. Tilman told me how to use the phone on the plane so I could try to call Pia.

Pia answered right away. "I've spoken to Gloria," she told me. "She's at the hospital now. Gabby is there and she's alive. They've taken her into surgery."

I repeated what Pia had told me to Claudia, Claire, my mom, and the pilots. We were numb but relieved. Hearing that Gabby was dead had been rock bottom for us. After we learned that she was still breathing, at least for my family, there was reason for hope.

From the plane, I was able to send an e-mail to Scott Simon, my friend at NPR. His show, *Weekend Edition,* airs on Saturdays, so he was at work when the news broke. "Where is NPR getting that info?" I wrote. By that point, several major news outlets, including *The New York Times* website, were also pronouncing Gabby dead, crediting NPR for breaking the news. It was one of the worst possible examples of pack journalism. We had to get NPR to disclaim its false report.

Scott called the NPR newsroom and asked how they had received information Gabby was dead. "It's solid, Scott," he was told. "We have two sources." Scott later told me that he got the impression they were humoring him on that call. They were almost dismissive. As a top NPR personality, they thought he was trying to "bigfoot" them—poking around on the news side, where he didn't belong.

Scott then had his producer call the newsroom to push harder. Turned out, NPR's two sources had no real knowledge of what was going on. The first was somebody employed by the Pima County Sheriff's office. The second worked for another Arizona congressperson and wasn't even in Tucson. From those two flimsy "sources," NPR chose to broadcast confirmation of Gabby's death to the world.

Within the next twenty minutes, the network realized it had rushed its erroneous news onto the air irresponsibly. Scott e-mailed me back: "NPR now withdrawing its report." (The incident was so distressing to Scott that he considered whether the network, his home for almost thirty years, was a place where he still wanted to work. In the end, though he told his bosses that NPR's recklessness was "indefensible and reprehensible," he did not resign. He was the conduit for a letter of apology that Gabby and I received from the president of NPR.)

From the plane, we watched the cable networks pull back on their reports about Gabby's demise. But even though we knew Gabby was alive, we still had no idea how serious her injuries were, or whether she'd still be alive when we reached Arizona. We sat there, mostly in silence. It felt surreal to be stuck in that cabin, 30,000 feet in the air, watching TV footage from the scene of the attack interspersed with old photos of Gabby, smiling happily. I wished the plane could move faster.

It takes two hours and fifteen minutes to fly from Houston to Tucson. We still had an hour until we'd arrive.

CHAPTER FOURTEEN

Tucson

On January 8, there was no countdown clock. I'm used to lots and lots of preparation for big events. They typically culminate with the winding down of a tiny digital clock on one of the displays on the flight deck of the space shuttle orbiter. As the clock strikes zero, 7 million pounds of fire and thrust are unleashed in an instant, sending me on a planned trajectory at a very high rate of speed. Then, once I arrive in space, I have multiple critical decisions affecting the lives of me and my crew.

On January 8, however, instead of a clock, there was just the ringing of my phone. "Mark, it's Pia . . ."

That phone call sent me hurtling on a path with no clear trajectory, but with multiple critical decisions that would need to be made on behalf of the woman I loved.

I often think of how Gabby described that day: "Shot. Shocked. Scary."

In some ways, January 8 is now a blur. In other ways, so many moments feel heightened and will never leave my memory.

* * *

The shooter had bought his gun, a 9mm Glock 19 semiautomatic pistol, at a sporting-goods store. He purchased his bullets the morning of January 8 at a Walmart. He traveled to the Safeway in a taxi, wearing a dark, hooded sweatshirt. He came to kill, bringing four magazines containing ninety bullets. The rest of his story—his past, his problems, his frightening behavior before the shooting—is all available elsewhere. Hundreds of thousands of those entries online that now mention my wife also mention this man. So there is no need to give more space to him here except to say that at about 10:10 a.m. in Tucson, as Gabby began cordially meeting her constituents, he shot her at point-blank range and she fell to the ground.

Gabby had been standing in front of the glass window of the Safeway, between the American flag and the Arizona state flag. She was the shooter's first victim.

The man fired thirty shots randomly into the line of people gathered to talk to Gabby. Police said every one of his bullets pierced a human being. Five people died at the scene, and those of us who love Gabby grieve deeply for all of them. There was a richness to each of their lives.

Gabe Zimmerman, Gabby's community outreach director, was shot in the head and died not far from where Gabby fell. It was Gabe who had cheerfully organized the Congress on Your Corner event. At age thirty, he was handsome, charismatic, and engaged to be married. Trained as a social worker, he had a contagious devotion to public service, and Gabby really admired him and appreciated the work he did assisting her constituents. He was almost like a younger brother to her, and she saw him as an empathetic extrovert who was going places. No one knew it, but Gabby had planned that one day Gabe would become her district director, after Ron Barber retired. Had Gabe lived, there's no doubt he would have continued to contribute to the world in meaningful ways.

John Roll, a sixty-three-year-old Republican, was the chief federal judge in Arizona. He had just attended mass and came by the event to thank Gabby for a letter she had written requesting a judicial emergency in Arizona. He and Gabby had been discussing the large volume of immigration and drug cases in Arizona's overstretched federal courts, and she had advocated for increased funding, which Judge Roll appreciated. He had served with distinction on the federal bench since he was appointed there in 1991 by President George H. W. Bush. As a jurist, he was considered fair-minded and compassionate, a man who always tried to find time to talk to law students and answer their questions. He was the father of three sons and had five grandchildren.

Phyllis Schneck, seventy-nine, was a homemaker from New Jersey who came to Tucson each winter. She had lost her husband to cancer after a fifty-six-year marriage, and her life was now focused on her church and her three children and seven grandchildren. Her family later described her to the media as a voracious reader and "a frustrated librarian." She had even catalogued her collection of *National Geographic* magazines according to the Dewey Decimal System so her kids could easily find information for their school reports. Phyllis was a Republican who wasn't politically active. Still, she came to meet Gabby to discuss her concerns about border security.

Dorothy Morris, a seventy-six-year-old retired secretary, had attended the event with her husband, George, a retired United Airlines pilot. They'd been married fifty-five years and friends said they were inseparable. George, a former Marine, instinctively tried to save Dorothy's life by pushing her to the ground and covering her with his own body. He was shot in the shoulder, had a broken rib and a punctured lung, but survived. Dorothy, known affectionately as "Dot," died underneath him.

Dorwan Stoddard, also seventy-six, came to meet Gabby with his wife, Mavanell. The couple had known each other in high school, but spent most of their lives married to other people. They reconnected after they were both widowed, and married in 1996. Dorwan, a retired road-grader, traveled the country with "Mavy" in a motor home. When the shooting started, he and Mavy dropped to the ground and Dorwan got on top of her to protect her. Mavy was shot three times in her legs. Dorwan died while saving her life.

The youngest shooting victim, nine-year-old Christina-Taylor Green, was shot in the chest. She had come to the event with a fifty-eight-year-old family friend, Suzi Hileman, because she had a growing interest in government and politics. On the drive over to the Safeway, she was still unsure of what question she'd ask Gabby. While she was standing in line, Suzi leaned down next to her and said, "Someday, when you grow up, you could be like Gabrielle Giffords." Suzi later told me those were the last words the little girl heard before she was shot.

Christina-Taylor was, by all accounts, very special. She served on her school's student council and played on an all-boys baseball team. She was born on September 11, 2001, but never let the date of her birth define her. In the aftermath of her death, much would be made of the fact that she came into the world on a day marked by violence, and left the world on another tragic day. But those who loved her spoke of her urges "to be a 9/11 baby who represented hope and peace." She carried herself with maturity and had a winning sense of humor. She was patriotic and loved wearing red, white, and blue. She liked to tell her parents, "We are so blessed. We have the best life." What might she have offered the world if she had been given a chance to grow up?

The thirteen people who were injured at the Congress on Your Corner event included Suzi Hileman, shot three times while she tried to shield Christina-Taylor with her body. Ron Barber, Gabby's district-office director, was shot in the face and leg. Gabby's community-outreach coordinator, Pam Simon, sixty-three, was shot in the wrist and chest. One of the bullets lodged in her hip. Others were wounded in their arms, legs, feet, backs, and knees. A bullet grazed the head of a retired Army colonel. All of these victims, along with those who were murdered, were in a mostly enclosed space between concrete pillars and the wall of the Safeway. There was no easy escape.

After the shooter ran out of ammunition, he had tried to reload, but a woman named Patricia Maisch risked her life and grabbed the clip. Other constituents, Bill Badger and Roger Salzgeber, bravely fought the man to the ground. They held him down until police arrived. "You're hurting my arm," he said to them.

When emergency crews arrived, they found bodies and blood everywhere. It was chaos, with a lot of bystanders trying to do whatever they could. As three medical helicopters landed in the parking lot, paramedics had to figure out who was still alive, and of them, which victims were "immediates"—those who most urgently needed help. Seven of those alive, including Gabby, were deemed "immediate."

After a paramedic named Colt Jackson got to Gabby, he asked her, "Can you hear me?" In response, she squeezed his hand. One of Gabby's interns, twenty-year-old Daniel Hernandez, had remained at her side, his hand pressed against her head to contain her bleeding. As Daniel lifted Gabby up and cradled her, Ron Barber, on the ground and wounded in the face and leg, looked over at them. Ron noticed that Gabby's skirt was hiked up in the wake of her fall, and he watched her pull down the skirt with her left hand. Gabby was always modest in how she dressed. While Ron tried to will himself not to pass out from blood loss, he thought to himself: "Maybe there's a sliver of hope for Gabby. She's still who she is, striving to remain modest even in the wake of a horrific injury."

At about 10:40 a.m., Daniel accompanied Gabby to the ambulance, and she was rushed to the University Medical Center.

Meanwhile, nine-year-old Christina-Taylor was given CPR at the scene, and then loaded into a separate ambulance. Paramedics continued CPR on her during the ride to the hospital.

Medical guidelines suggest that shooting victims can be declared dead if they don't respond after fifteen minutes of CPR. Christina-Taylor had been receiving CPR for more than twenty minutes when she arrived at the hospital, but given her age, doctors didn't want to let her go without the most aggressive attempts to save her. After opening the little girl's chest, Dr. Randall Friese, a trauma surgeon, used his hand to massage her heart. He had blood pumped into her heart through an IV line, but it wouldn't beat. The chief resident took over and kept trying, as Dr. Friese learned that another severely injured victim had arrived.

That victim was Gabby.

When Dr. Friese reached Gabby, he took her left hand and twice asked her to squeeze it. Still conscious, she complied but could not follow his commands to squeeze her right hand. The brain injury had already severely damaged her ability to control the right side of her body.

A breathing tube was inserted in Gabby's throat as doctors worked frantically to determine the extent of her injuries. Her skull was fractured and her brain was swelling. She had fractures in both eye sockets.

Gabby was taken into surgery right away, where doctors removed much of the left side of her skull, in pieces, to relieve the pressure caused by the swelling of her brain. The pieces of skull were placed in a freezer in case they later could be used in reconstructive surgery. Even though bone and metal shards from the bullet had gone deep into Gabby's brain when she was shot, the surgeons didn't attempt to remove what they couldn't easily reach. Yes, there was a risk of infection. But doctors knew they could do further damage to Gabby's brain if they tried digging for stray pieces of bone or bullet.

As all of this was going on, and I was on that plane bound for Tucson, Gabby's parents were making their way to the hospital. After Gloria had gotten the news that Gabby had been shot, she had begun to pray. As she described it, she had gone into a metaphorical "closet" and closed the door. She's a Christian Scientist and she prayed silently to herself. "I knew Gabby was OK," she later told me. "She was God's child."

At the hospital, as Gloria and Spencer waited for Gabby to emerge from surgery, a psychologist approached Gabby's sister, Melissa. "I think your mother is in shock," he said.

Gloria heard him. "I am not in shock!" she said. "I am praying."

After a while, Gabby's family was moved to another room. "Are you putting us in this room because our daughter is dying?" Gloria asked the nurse on duty there.

"No, but expect the worst," the nurse said. Gloria returned to her private prayers and meditations.

Meanwhile, Pia, Gabby's chief of staff, was still in Washington, arranging to fly to Tucson. On her way to the airport, she stopped at Gabby's office on the Hill, where about ten staffers and former staffers had gathered. Gabby had hired a young, energetic, idealistic group. They tended to be people who felt things deeply. When Pia arrived, the emotions in the room were overwhelming. It fell to her to tell them that Gabby was alive, though critically injured, that two fellow staffers were also shot, and that Gabe Zimmerman had been reported dead.

It was a crushing announcement for the group. Gabe was their friend. For some, he was a mentor. Jennifer Cox, Gabby's loyal operations director, had even dated Gabe for a while. Everyone was crying about Gabe, crying about Gabby, crying about Pam and Ron, cursing the senselessness of it all.

Before Pia left, she told them, "Take care of each other."

Just about then, at 2:30 p.m. Tucson time, the plane carrying me, my mother, Claudia, and Claire landed at Tucson International Airport in the area reserved for private planes. Two police cars were waiting for us.

We were driven straight to the hospital, where I arrived feeling very apprehensive and scared about what the doctors would say. Having been an emergency medical technician when I was a teen, dealing with gunshot wounds in the inner city, I knew what a bullet to the head usually means: long-term disability, paralysis, an inability to speak, a loss of cognitive function. It was likely very bleak. But then I thought about Gabby: She's tough. She's a fighter. She's a tireless worker. I had a clear, uplifting epiphany that Gabby would do what she needed to do to claw her way out of this.

I was ushered into a room at the hospital where I met her doctors, all of them weary from the day they'd just been through. Besides Dr. Friese, there was Marty Weinand, Mike Lemole, and Peter Rhee. They showed me her CAT scan. I'd recently had an MRI of my own brain for some space research on the optic nerve, so I was familiar with the landmarks and some of the anatomy. "Your wife is going to survive," Dr. Rhee told me. "But she could be in a coma for four to six months."

By that point, Gabby had been taken out of surgery and was on her way to the intensive-care unit, but we still weren't allowed to see her. All we could do was wait.

In my mind, I was thinking of how I'd need to prepare myself mentally for the long haul, of how I'd have to pay close attention to every medical decision to help Gabby recover. That would be my job. As Gabby's mom prayed silently, I told myself: "Focus, focus, focus."

*　*　*

Seeing Gabby for the first time that day was a great shock. Even when you know what to expect, nothing fully prepares you for seeing someone you love in such a critical state.

The doctors had done an emergency shave of all the hair on the left side of Gabby's head, which was bandaged. She still had her hair on the right side. She was comatose, hooked up to a tracheotomy tube and other lines.

Her face was black-and-blue and her head was terribly swollen. It looked as if it was twice its normal size. I took it all in and then I told her how much I loved her. I knew she couldn't hear me, but I had to say it.

"You're going to make it through this," I told her, my voice breaking, "and we're all going to help you."

I took Gabby's hand and noticed that there was caked blood under each of her fingernails. I thought about everything that she and the other victims had endured that day. I tried not to cry.

As I stood there at her bedside, a slight bloody tear fell from her left eye. I reached over and, very tenderly, wiped it away.

CHAPTER FIFTEEN

Sunrise

I made no attempt to sleep the night of the shooting. I just sat in the chair by Gabby's bedside, holding her hand. I slept a couple of hours the second night, still in the chair.

In those first few days, Gabby's skin was alarmingly yellow. Her eyes were closed, bruised and bulging. She had tubes in both arms, and as a precaution, doctors had her connected to a breathing tube. She was able to breathe on her own, but they hoped the ventilator would prevent windpipe infections and pneumonia. Eventually, they'd do a tracheotomy.

On the second day, doctors adjusted Gabby's level of sedation so they could draw her out of her medically induced coma to do some testing. "Show us your fingers," Dr. Rhee said to her, and Gabby, eyes still closed shut, was able to weakly lift two fingers on her left hand. She did it one time. "That's a great sign," the doctor told us. The part of her brain that processes instructions was not fully damaged, even though the bullet had traveled the full length of her left hemisphere at a thousand feet per second. Also, all things considered, she was phenomenally lucky: The bullet hadn't sliced a major vein or artery in the brain.

Had the bullet passed through the area connecting the two hemispheres of the brain, it is unlikely Gabby would have survived. There would be too much damage. But the doctors told us that her ability to follow a command meant the centers in her brain were at least partially intact and communicating with each other, a positive sign. By keeping Gabby mostly in a medically induced coma, doctors were able to limit the electrical activity of her brain, which would help her brain tissue heal. The biggest risk: In the days ahead, tissue that surrounded the bullet's path would be dying, exuding fluid, which would lead to more swelling. If the swelling got too bad, additional surgery would be necessary.

On some fronts, Dr. Rhee was positive almost from the start. "Your wife has a 101 percent chance of survival," he said. "She will not die. I do not give her permission." We knew that nine out of ten people shot in the head don't survive. So Gabby was a success story just by virtue of still being in this world. But we all wanted more, and Dr. Rhee couldn't say for sure that she wouldn't end up in a semivegetative state. "It's too soon to tell," he said.

Those of us who love Gabby had a lot to learn about the brain, and part of what we learned was that so much is unknown. The brain has "redundant circuits" for some functions, such as walking. So it was possible that Gabby would be able to walk again. Language, which is far more complicated, could be harder to recover.

Even when doctors remove a piece of skull and look inside someone's head, they don't discover much that can predict a patient's likely progress. During brain surgery after people suffer a bullet wound, it's hard to tell which parts of a brain will recover since, as Dr. Lemole said, "It all looks bad." The doctors reminded us that the scars we saw on the outside of Gabby's body reflected what was going on inside her body. The trauma was severe.

How far might Gabby go? How close could she come to returning to her former self? Could she meet the expectations of her constituents? "Those answers won't come until rehab in the weeks and months ahead," the doctors said. "Some answers may not come for years."

My resolve defined me in those first days. My instinct was to take charge. I was going to supervise Gabby's recovery and get her back as quickly as possible. Maybe I wasn't always realistic, but that attitude helped me stay focused in the early going. I was tired, I was angry, but I just kept running on adrenaline. I was on a mission.

* * *

I had a place to stay at the Arizona Inn, but I never went there until about a week after the shooting. I just couldn't leave Gabby. On the third night, hospital staffers kindly found an empty room for me in the pediatric intensive-care unit. I was able to sleep there for several hours each night, and I developed a routine. On my way to or from bed, I'd stop by the nurses' station to see how all the little patients were doing. "How are the babies today?" I'd ask the nurses.

"They're going to be OK," they'd say. "And how is the congress-woman?"

I'd see young mothers holding their babies, most born prema-turely or with serious health issues. Those mothers were like Gabby's mom, wishing they could take away their children's pain, hoping that their love would serve as a form of medicine. When I was away from Gabby, Gloria sat beside her. "I feel like my breathing is helping Gabby breathe," Gloria said. "I just want to share the air in the room, like maybe my breath will sustain her."

My intimate moments with Gabby were not fully private. There were always people hovering over her—nurses, doctors, aides. For pro-tection, the U.S. Capitol Police were with us twenty-four hours a day. Tucson police were in the hallway. At one point, even the director of the FBI, Robert Mueller, showed up and asked if he could speak to me outside Gabby's room. The FBI wanted to know about any previous threats to Gabby's life, and whether she had enemies. I told him about the political climate in Arizona, and he vowed to use every resource possible to investigate the attack.

Meanwhile, Gabby's sister, Melissa, and our friends signed up on a duty roster to be available, night and day, to sit at Gabby's bedside. Gloria felt, and I agreed, that we didn't want Gabby to be by herself—ever.

As I sat with Gabby, e-mails poured into my BlackBerry from friends, family, colleagues, and just about anyone who had or could get my e-mail address. It never stopped. I didn't know many of those who'd written to us, but I appreciated their concern and support.

I was especially touched that so many astronauts, dating back to the Mercury program, sent heartfelt notes. "We hope you will sense God's strength and presence in Gabrielle's recovery, as well as in your cockpit during your upcoming space adventure," wrote Jack Lousma, the pilot of Skylab 3 in 1973 and later a space shuttle commander.

Neil Armstrong tracked down my e-mail address and wrote: "Dear Mark, We know that you need not be in a combat zone to be in harm's way. But Gabby was just doing the kind of thing that she should be doing." The previous summer, he had gone to Congress to discuss space exploration issues. He wrote that Gabby had been a huge help to him: "Her questions of witnesses were the absolute best." His graciousness extended even to the last line of his e-mail. "Please do not bother to answer this, but know that we are pulling for her—and for you. Most sincerely, Neil Armstrong."

In 2006, when Gabby and I were dating, I'd given her the book *First Man: The Life of Neil Armstrong* as a gift. She loved it. My hero became hers. Three years later, she had changed the channels on the television in the House cloakroom so her colleagues could watch that NASA TV special on the fortieth anniversary of Armstrong's moonwalk. Now, sitting with her in the ICU, I wished I could have tapped Gabby on the shoulder to somehow wake her out of her coma so I could read her his e-mail.

I also wished she could know what was going on outside University Medical Center. It was a remarkable sight. Strangers were leaving thousands of get-well wishes, flowers, gifts, blankets, prayer shawls, candles, and handwritten notes with prayers. The spontaneous memorial was a massive outpouring for the dead and the wounded, and it grew each day. A total of nine hundred stuffed animals were left there and would later be donated to two children's hospitals in Tucson. On the day Gabby was shot, a young soldier from the war in Iraq left his Purple Heart for her, saying she deserved it more than he did. Another Purple Heart was left by a Vietnam veteran who described himself as a conservative Republican. He wanted Gabby to have it because she "had been through a battle."

A World War II veteran wrote a note saying that on October 10, 1944, his twenty-second birthday, he suffered a brain injury. He was hospitalized for a year. He wrote to offer Gabby encouragement. "I went on to graduate from college, get married, have three kids, and work as a sales manager until I retired in 1985. I played softball and volleyball until last year. I'm now eighty-eight and still kicking. Perseverance conquers all."

C. J. Karamargin, Gabby's communications director, handled media interviews outside the hospital, along with Pia. They were touched that the local reporters, having covered Gabby for years, were especially upset by the tragedy. Gabby had a good rapport with journalists, and some of them had tears in their eyes as they asked questions about her condition. One cameraman asked to restart an interview because he was crying and shaking the camera.

I'd sometimes head outside and walk around the displays after dark, just so I could feel the goodwill and positive energy. Wearing a hat so I wouldn't be noticed, I'd pass signs on the front lawn with messages such as: "Fight Gabby Fight!" Gabby would be greatly moved if she knew that so many of her constituents were praying for her. These were the people whose doors she had knocked on over the years. Now they were coming out of their homes to wish her well.

Every night a mariachi band arrived to play on the front lawn of the hospital complex. They came to be part of something special—a spontaneous vigil for those who died and those still recovering. Maybe they knew Gabby was a huge mariachi fan. They weren't expecting that she'd hear them, but their music did make its way up to her hospital room.

The Tucson Girls Chorus also came by to perform, as did Native American singers from the Tohono O'odham Nation. And every morning, in the darkness before sunrise, a lone drummer would arrive outside the hospital and start beating her drum very slowly. She'd keep beating until an hour after the sun had risen. One morning, I spoke with her. "I am doing this out of respect for my congresswoman," she said. "I hope and pray this will help her heal."

To me, it was only a drumbeat. But who knows? Maybe she was playing a role in Gabby's recovery.

* * *

In those earliest days, I determined that the best thing I could do to help Gabby was to become her fiercest advocate. She had several doctors caring for her, including Dr. Rhee, the chief trauma surgeon, Dr. Lemole, her neurosurgeon, and the ophthalmologist Lynn Polonski, who would need to perform ocular surgery.

I was grateful to her doctors—they had saved her life—but I was also insistent. "I want Gabby to have the best possible care," I told Dr. Rhee. "You guys have been great, but I want to get the best people in the country to weigh in on the medical decisions we're making."

Dr. Rhee didn't act on my first or second request. Maybe he didn't fully recognize how serious I was. So in a third conversation, I was more firm. "Let me tell you about my wife," I said. "No matter what she's doing, Gabby is all about putting together the very best team. When she recovers, she's going to ask me what I did to put together a group of doctors who'd give her the best care possible. She'll ask: Did I get the best second opinions I could?"

I was not going to tell her, "Sorry, honey, that didn't occur to me."

So I let Dr. Rhee know that the second opinions were going to happen with or without his help. I told him I'd been speaking to Admiral Mike Mullen, chairman of the Joint Chiefs of Staff, about this very issue. As the senior officer in the military, and a Navy admiral, he was essentially my boss. Dr. Rhee is a retired Navy surgeon, so Admiral Mullen used to be his boss, too. My request to Dr. Rhee finally sank in.

Several hours later, he stopped me in the ICU corridor and said, "I have Geoffrey Ling and Jim Ecklund from Walter Reed on their way here. These guys literally wrote the book on penetrating head injuries and both had experience treating soldiers in Iraq and Afghanistan. Are you happy now?"

"Yes," I told him, and I was.

When Drs. Ecklund and Ling arrived, they spent time reviewing the many CAT scans and pages of medical records, and conferring with Gabby's Tucson doctors. They felt that Gabby had received excellent care from Dr. Lemole, Dr. Rhee, and their teams. They did make recommendations to change some of Gabby's treatment in the ICU. Their advice, and their analysis of the good work being done by the medical teams in Tucson, was very reassuring to me. But there were still a great many medical decisions ahead.

Gabby needed an additional operation to rebuild the upper half of her fractured right eye socket. (Although the gunshot was to the left side of her head, the force of the bullet fractured both orbits. The right side was in worse shape and required additional surgery.) After speaking with Dr. Rhee again about my desire to have second opinions, he invited two Navy ophthalmologists that he knew from San Diego to fly in and examine Gabby. Once they arrived, I asked if I could get them together with the Tucson doctors and residents for a short meeting.

There were eight or nine of us in the room, and the doctors were discussing whether to do the surgery from inside Gabby's eye socket or to do it by cutting through her skull above the eyebrow. I decided to take a moment to tell them what I had learned at NASA about decision-making. I explained that phrase posted on the wall of the conference room used by the Mission Management Team during space shuttle flights: "None of us is as dumb as all of us."

"It means," I said, "that when you get a group of people together to make a critical decision, groupthink can set in. There's all this technical information, a critical decision needs to be made, and everyone starts marching in the same direction. There might be some people who think it's the wrong direction, but they don't say anything. They just remain a part of the group.

"At NASA, we've learned that groups can make stupid decisions that no single individual in the group would make. We had a couple of terrible space shuttle accidents—*Challenger, Columbia*—and when we looked back in hindsight, they may have been preventable. There were individuals who had the right information, or in the case of *Columbia,* had seen the issue before. If people spoke up, perhaps those catastrophes could have been avoided."

I looked around the hospital meeting room. I was searching for the youngest, most inexperienced person, and settled on an ophthalmology resident sitting in the back. She looked to be in her late twenties. I pointed at her. "So yesterday, the plan was to go through the eye socket to approach the fractured area from underneath," I said. "Now, today, everyone is saying that it's better to go through Gabby's forehead and make the repair from above. You've been listening to the whole discussion. I need to know if you think this is the correct approach."

She seemed a little nervous. She never expected me to single her out. She took a breath. "I agree with the plan," she answered.

I thanked her. I thanked all of them. The next day, the doctors made their incision above Gabby's eyebrow and removed a piece of her skull and several bone fragments. Using titanium mesh, screws, and the pieces of bone, they rebuilt the top of her eye socket on a table in the operating room. Then they lifted up the right frontal lobe of her brain, which had been pushing into the orbit, and reinstalled this thing that looked like it was built from a kid's erector set. The surgery couldn't have gone better.

* * *

While Gabby was in a coma in those early days, tens of millions of people who'd never heard of her before were quickly becoming familiar with her. More familiar than she could have imagined. Video clips of her in Congress played all over television. The highlights of her bio and the particulars of her politics were discussed by pundits as if they knew her. And though she had always preferred to be known as Gabrielle in public, within hours of the shooting she had become "Gabby" to the world. It was President Obama who ushered in that instantaneous transition when he gave a three-minute televised statement on the afternoon of January 8.

He started off by referring to her as Gabrielle Giffords. He said she was fighting for her life and he talked soberly about the other victims. Then he got more personal. "Gabby Giffords was a friend of mine," he said. "It's not surprising that today Gabby was doing what she always does—listening to the hopes and concerns of her neighbors. That is the essence of what our democracy is all about. That is why this is more than a tragedy for those involved. It is a tragedy for Arizona and a tragedy for our entire country."

Once the president said "Gabby," the media picked up on it, and it spread from there. People developed affection for Gabby and her nickname. Maybe it helped make her seem more like a regular person. She wasn't some stuffy congresswoman named Gabrielle. She was just Gabby, eager to meet her neighbors, and now struggling to stay alive.

Gabby admired the president, but she wasn't even sure he knew who she was until late 2010 when she came to the White House for a meeting and he said, "I like your new haircut!" She had, indeed, gotten her hair cut that week. His comment made her day because she didn't really like the new hairstyle.

She hadn't backed Obama right away when he ran for president in 2008. During the Democratic primaries, Gabby was torn. As a young female politician, she found that Hillary Clinton's historic candidacy spoke to her. (Gabby has always encouraged women to run for office, believing that if more women serve, compromise on issues will come more easily.) But during that primary season, she was also drawn to

Obama. Knowing she needed to be careful politically, she remained neutral for months.

One day in the spring of 2008, Gabby and I were driving somewhere and the phone rang. It was Senator Clinton, hoping to win Gabby's public support, and her vote as a so-called superdelegate at the upcoming Democratic convention. I heard only Gabby's side of the conversation, but she was very complimentary, telling Clinton how much she respected her. Senator Clinton never came out and directly asked for her vote. She ended the conversation by asking Gabby, "Would it be OK if I called you back sometime?"

"Of course," Gabby said.

When Gabby got off the phone, I asked her what she was going to do. Would she endorse Hillary? "For now, I'll just wait until she calls me back," Gabby said. She knew how to buy time. She believed that it was sometimes best to defer a hard decision. You might make a different choice if you wait.

In the case of Clinton versus Obama, she held off until the very end, when Obama's delegate count proved insurmountable. She was part of that large last wave of Democrats who endorsed him.

Her political instincts were always sharp. Her staffers likened her to a chess player, always thinking three or five moves ahead. She combined strategic thinking with a gut-level understanding of how politics can matter in people's lives. I think that's what made her formidable as a public servant.

Gabby had ambitions to possibly run for the U.S. Senate. But unlike a lot of politicians, she didn't fantasize about her own run for president. She always thought men are more apt to have that ambition, and history certainly has proved that true. "Women don't generally have the ego to think they could be president," Gabby once told me. "And when women lose elections, you rarely see them again. A man loses and he feels the need to come back, to try again, to run for something else."

Gabby thought men often have a harder time facing rejection in the work world. She believed women generally have a greater ability to move on and go in a different direction, or to return to their families with a renewed sense of purpose. If Gabby ever lost her seat in Congress, she figured it would be her last election. She'd do something else. "There are a lot of capable people who can do this job," she'd say. "I don't need a lifetime hold on the office. There are many things I can do with my life, and many other ways I can make a contribution."

Gabby was certainly ambitious. She just resisted being obsessive and unrealistic about it. And she felt a bond with smart, driven women who tried to think the same way.

Four days after Gabby was shot, her friends Senator Kirsten Gillibrand of New York and Representative Debbie Wasserman Schultz of Florida came to the hospital to see her. They were nervous walking into the room. How would they find her?

Gabby was motionless in her bed, nonresponsive. Her eyes hadn't opened since she was shot on January 8. Both women were tearful as they talked to Gabby about the fun they'd have together after she recovered. "You'd better get better!" Debbie said. "We need you!"

I wanted Gabby's friends to be closer to her bedside, so I moved farther back in the room and stood beside Pia, Gloria, and Spencer. (Pia took my cell phone and began shooting video of Gabby and her two friends together.) Nancy Pelosi was there, too. As a leader in Congress, Nancy had come to show her concern and let us know about the outpouring of support on both sides of the aisle on Capitol Hill.

The five of us in the back stood silently as Debbie and Kirsten kept talking to Gabby. Debbie has what she herself has described as a thick "Long Island Jewish" accent. It's very distinctive. Gabby could pick out Debbie's voice across a crowded room.

As Debbie spoke, all of a sudden, Gabby's left eyelid began to flutter. Maybe Gabby was thinking, "I know that voice!" Or maybe it was, as Debbie and Kirsten later put it, "the power of sisterhood." In any case, I pushed myself forward to see this moment. "Open your eyes, Gabby!" I said again and again, my voice rising, urging her on. "Can you see me? Open your eyes!" And then she did just what I asked. All of us in the room, including Gabby's parents, were overcome with emotion.

Gabby really opened just her left eye. The other was covered with a bandage. But it was an amazing moment. At first, her eye was just a slit, but then she opened it wider. "Honey, if you can see me, put your thumb up," I said. We could tell she was using every ounce of energy to comply, and to focus her one eye on those of us in the room.

Her left arm rose from the bed, her thumb pointed toward the ceiling, as we wiped away our tears.

When Dr. Lemole learned what had happened when Gabby's friends visited, he smiled. "We are wise to acknowledge miracles," he said.

*   *   *

That same day, January 12, President Obama and the First Lady also visited Gabby and others who were injured. The president had come to town to speak at a public memorial for the shooting victims, but he first wanted to stop at the hospital.

Before he arrived, a question came into my head. I said to Pia, "If Gabby could talk and was able to ask the president for something, what would it be?"

Pia didn't hesitate. "She'd want the president to visit the border, to see what's really going on down there." Over the years, Gabby had sent numerous letters, first to President Bush and then to President Obama, asking them to see the border crisis in southern Arizona with their own eyes.

Each day in Gabby's district, an average of 660 illegal immigrants are apprehended trying to cross the border. That's 240,000 a year. No one knows exactly how many thousands make it through undetected. Gabby was also troubled by the hundreds of thousands of pounds of drugs confiscated at the border of her district each year. How many pounds got through? "This is an emergency," she'd say.

And so when the president came to visit, I waited for my moment to issue an invitation on Gabby's behalf. He and Mrs. Obama were extremely genuine in the few minutes they spent at Gabby's bedside. She was comatose, but they each had a moment when they took her hand and spoke to her. The president told her that many Americans were wishing her well. He also embraced each of us in the room.

Just as they were getting ready to leave, with Gabby silent in her bed, I said, "Mr. President, Gabby really loves Arizona, and as you know, this community has a crisis on its border."

He was giving me his full attention. I continued. "We've been trying to think what Gabby would want us to say to you today. We think she'd ask you to come back sometime and visit the border, to see for yourself the problems down there.

"So I'm asking you, Mr. President, after Gabby recovers, would you come back to Arizona and let her take you to the border of her district? She'd be so grateful if you'd get a firsthand look at the crisis on the border."

"Absolutely," the president said. "When she's ready, let me know and I'll come back."

(On behalf of Gabby and the people of her district, I hope to hold him to that promise. He and Gabby can ride Warner Glenn's mules out to one of the harshest areas of the United States–Mexico border, and Gabby can show him the problems in her district up close. The Secret Service can follow on their own mules. The president will certainly see the border issues from a new vantage point.)

After visiting Gabby, the president invited me and Gloria to join him and Mrs. Obama for the limo ride over to the University of Arizona's McKale Memorial Center. More than 26,000 people were waiting there, crowded into the main arena and an overflow area.

There were just the four of us in the back of the limo, and though we were all aware of the tragedy that had brought us together, we tried to remain upbeat. Gloria joked about the presidential seal on the two packages of M&M's on the armrest. She asked if the seal meant the candy was for the president only. "No, they're for you," Mrs. Obama said.

When we arrived at the arena, Gabby's staffers and the families of the other victims were waiting for us in private areas, and the president and Mrs. Obama seemed to have a real sense of the pain everyone was feeling. They hugged and kissed them all, one after another. Gloria happened to be standing near the end of the line, and when the president reached her, she said to him, "I already got mine."

The president kissed her anyway. "There are always more hugs and kisses to give out," he told her.

Many people say that the nationally televised speech President Obama gave that day was the highlight of his presidency. He wrote it mostly himself the evening before, and delivered it with his heart. It's often said that people need to turn to their leaders in times of national tragedy, so that's when a president's words have the most power. I thought President Obama's speech rivaled the soaring remarks President Reagan gave after the *Challenger* tragedy in 1986, and the 1995 speech delivered by President Clinton in the wake of the Oklahoma City bombing.

"There is nothing I can say that will fill the sudden hole torn in your hearts," President Obama said to the audience in Tucson. "But know this: The hopes of a nation are here tonight."

He talked about each person murdered, sharing glimpses of their lives. And when he spoke of Gabby, he announced the news we'd told him minutes before, that she had opened her eyes. He shouted it out four times, like a preacher—"Gabby opened her eyes!"—and the crowd's applause truly enveloped those of us who loved her. "She knows we're here," the president said. "And she knows that we are rooting for her through what is undoubtedly going to be a difficult journey."

I was sitting next to Mrs. Obama, and she kept taking my hand while her husband spoke. I appreciated her gesture, as I tried to remain composed.

"Already," the president said, "we've seen a national conversation commence, not only about the motivations behind these killings, but about everything from the merits of gun safety laws to the adequacy of our mental health system. . . . As we discuss these issues, let each of us do so with a good dose of humility. Rather than pointing fingers or assigning blame, let's use this occasion to expand our moral imaginations, to listen to each other more carefully, to sharpen our instincts for empathy."

Toward the end of his speech, the president again paid tribute to those who died.

"The loss of these wonderful people should make every one of us strive to be better—to be better friends and neighbors and coworkers and parents. And if, as has been discussed in recent days, their deaths help usher in more civility in our public discourse, let us remember it is not because a simple lack of civility caused this tragedy—it did not—but rather because only a more civil and honest public discourse can help us face up to the challenges of our nation in a way that would make them proud."

Back in the ICU, Gabby had no idea that the president had stopped by to visit her, or that he'd left her bedside and spoken about her to the world. I returned to her that night and told her about the speech, the crowd, and the hope we all felt in that arena. Her eyes were closed shut and she gave no indication she'd heard me, but I wanted her to know.

* * *

That first week, I tried my best to get away from the hospital to attend the funerals and visitations of those who had died on January 8. I felt a great responsibility to serve as Gabby's representative.

Funerals are tough under any circumstance. I've gone to many of them over my long military and NASA career. Usually the memorial services were for people I knew—whether space shuttle crew members or Navy pilots—who died serving their country, knowing full well that they were putting their lives at risk.

I had never before attended funerals like the ones in that second week of January 2011. Those people died because they chose to visit with my wife. I couldn't help but feel some sort of transferred responsibility for their deaths. It's not that I felt Gabby was responsible. But I did think: If she hadn't worked so hard to win her last election, these people still would be alive. Gabby won the 2010 race by such a narrow margin. It took days until she was finally declared the winner, and then by just four thousand votes. Had she narrowly lost instead of narrowly won, she wouldn't have held a Congress on Your Corner that day.

In some ways, Christina-Taylor Green's funeral was the hardest. New York firefighters had flown in with the large flag that had survived the collapse of the World Trade Center on September 11. They displayed it between two fire trucks, a tribute to the little girl born that day.

When I walked into the church, "Somewhere Over the Rainbow" was playing. I saw the tiny child's casket, and hundreds of children filling the pews. Many were her classmates from Mesa Verde Elementary School. I was teary along with most of the other eighteen hundred people there. For a nine-year-old girl to die because she was passionate about democracy—it was just so unfair.

Suzi Hileman, the family friend who'd brought Christina to meet Gabby, was still hospitalized with three gunshot wounds and a shattered hip. Her husband, Bill, said she was having flashbacks, and at times had been shouting out Christina's name. (When I had visited Suzi in her hospital room, she described to me the moment the shooting began. "Christina and I were holding each other so tightly that we almost broke each other's hands," she said.)

I met with Christina's parents and the rest of her family. "I am very, very sorry," I told them. I didn't know what else to say. During the service, I sat near Senators John McCain and Jon Kyl, and Representative Jeff Flake.

Later, I went to John Roll's funeral, which was a testament to a smart, capable public servant and community leader. He was a faithful Catholic, and it was as if the entire Catholic Church was there. There seemed to be dozens of priests.

I didn't attend the funeral of Phyllis Schneck since it was in New Jersey, her home state (and mine). But I spoke to her daughter about it and, by her account, it was a beautiful service. I was out of town on the day of Dorothy Morris's funeral, so I regretfully had to miss it, but I heard that was very moving, too.

I was able to visit Dorwan Stoddard's family at his home. I found myself thinking about how lucky he and his wife, Mavy, were to have rediscovered each other later in life; two widowed people able to return to being "boyfriend and girlfriend" again after a four-decade break.

Mavy wasn't expected to speak at Dorwan's funeral, but at the end of the service, she asked to talk. She had come in a wheelchair, having been shot three times in her legs. She started by saying that Dorwan made her a better person. "He made me kinder. He made me know there are good men." People at the service noticed that her hand was trembling on the microphone, but then she regained her composure. "He spoiled me rotten, and oh gosh, it was fun!"

Everyone knew that Mavy survived the shooting because Dorwan had protected her with his own body. "He died for me," she said, "and I have to live for him." Her final message: "Hang in there. Hang on to your loved ones. Keep kissing them and hugging them because tomorrow they may not be there."

Gabe Zimmerman's memorial service was held outside. It was one of those warm winter days that explain why people move from elsewhere to the Arizona desert. I looked around at all the people gathered. There were friends, former classmates, congressmen, local military, and almost all of Gabby's Washington, Tucson, and Sierra Vista staffers, past and present. There was even a representative from Speaker John Boehner's office, as Gabe was the only congressional staff member murdered in the line of duty in the history of our country.

I was asked to say a few words at Gabe's service. "Today is a hard day," I began, "and what makes it harder is that Gabby can't be here to share her feelings about Gabe. But she's getting better, and someday, she will get to tell you herself."

I spoke about Gabe's training as a social worker. "His whole mission in life was to take care of other people, to enhance their well-being, and—as the Social Workers' Code of Ethics puts it—'to elevate service to others above self-interest.' Well, losing a person who tried to live his life according to that code can only hurt us all.

"I remember Gabe's ready smile, and his being a big brother to other staffers in the office when they needed help. The interns nicknamed Gabe 'The Constituent Whisperer.' If someone came in angry, Gabe was the person who'd hear them out. He'd try to make a plan to help them solve their problem. It's no wonder that Gabby was drawn to him, and to having him in her office. He was able to calm people down and lift them up.

"Even last Saturday, during the Congress on Your Corner, two people were having a heated argument about politics, and Gabe came over. One was liberal. One was conservative. Gabe calmed them down, got them to listen to one another. Gabe spent his last hour alive doing the thing he loved, using his gift of empathy, warmth, and communication to enhance the well-being of other people."

I ended by addressing Gabe's family and fiancée. "Gabe is loved by everyone gathered here," I said, "and on behalf of Gabby, I thank you for sharing him with the rest of us for thirty years."

When I returned to the hospital that day, there was no way to tell Gabby where I had just been, or that I had been asked to speak because she couldn't. I just sat with her, holding her hand in mine.

CHAPTER SIXTEEN

What Would Gabby Want?

In the early weeks after the shooting, Gabby couldn't speak. People didn't know what she was thinking. At times, it was hard to know if she was thinking at all. And so, several times a day, whenever a decision needed to be made, I'd ask myself the same questions: What would Gabby do? What would she want me to do?

I thought about what Gabby would want at every step in the medical process, and as I planned her long-term care. I thought about how she'd weigh in as I considered the ramifications of her condition on her career—and on mine. In my case, I was set to command the next space shuttle mission in just three months. Should I step down? What would Gabby want me to do?

I wondered what Gabby would want even on more minor issues. Before I agreed to let someone visit her—a friend, a colleague from either party, whomever—I'd ask myself: Would Gabby want to see this person? Would she want this person to see her in such a vulnerable position?

Others closest to Gabby also spent a lot of time wondering what Gabby would want.

After the shooting, Pia led Gabby's congressional staff forward by constantly asking herself: Which of the many issues on Gabby's plate would she want us to prioritize? How would she want responsibilities in the office divided now that she was unavailable? What would Gabby want to do about her apartment and car in Washington? And what exactly should her communications staffers be saying publicly? They were flooded with requests from journalists; one day alone there were nine hundred media inquiries.

To hold on to Gabby's voice in her head, Pia found herself scrolling through old e-mails. She kept coming upon the buoyant all-staff messages Gabby routinely sent out, all of them signed "Gabrielle." It was hard for Pia not to be emotional reading them. They reminded her of Gabby's priorities and principles, her exuberance, and what she wanted from her staff.

The e-mails reiterated for Pia how much Gabby believed in the power of saying thanks.

After the health-care town-hall gatherings of 2009, Gabby sent an e-mail thanking everyone. She was especially grateful to Gabe Zimmerman, who organized the events. His hard work helped draw thousands of attendees. "I will never, ever forget the Tucson event!" Gabby wrote. "Never, ever. The crowd was tremendous but unfortunately extremely rude at times. However we got through it and will live to tell about it. Our staff deserves a medal. Gabe, you are awesome!"

Pia was reminded again and again of the ways in which Gabby encouraged optimism among her twenty-five staffers and interns, especially the younger ones. She began 2010 with a Happy New Year e-mail: "Dear Team: I think January 1 is my favorite day of the year. I love the idea that we can get a fresh start and push the reset button. The endless possibilities for the coming months are glorious. Whatever challenges we meet ahead, on our own or as part of our office, I feel confident that 2010 will be remembered for its positive outcomes. I say this because all of you are especially smart and hard-working, and because you are dedicated to the highest calling, one of service to your country."

To Pia, these e-mails were quintessentially Gabby.

Gabby referred to her constituents as "my peeps." Again and again, she told her staffers, "You rock!" She wrote to them about her travels to the Middle East to visit troops, about a hike she took in Arizona's Sabino Canyon, where she saw "a desert tortoise, eight deer, and a big bushy-tailed skunk," and about her official visit to the Hickman family egg farm in Buckeye, Arizona. "I had no idea what 3.2 million chickens would smell like. Now I know. Don't ask."

On plane trips between Washington and Tucson, Gabby wrote e-mails slugged "Sky Report," and she tried to give them a light touch. An e-mail to staffers on February 27, 2010, ended: "My BlackBerry is about to die, so more next time from somewhere like 19D. Thanks again, Team, from your most moderate member of the AZ delegation."

What would Gabby want? Pia was reminded of the ways in which Gabby wanted to encourage civility.

On March 18, 2010, during the height of the health-care debate, Gabby wrote: "I know the last couple weeks have been hard on everyone—phones ringing incessantly, and angry constituents sometimes behaving badly. It makes me very upset to see any of you treated with rudeness or disrespect. You all have been amazing in your professionalism by demonstrating patience and kindness toward all who contact us. Your compassion reflects well not just on our office, but on our United States government."

On March 23, 2010, after Gabby's Tucson office was vandalized, she wrote to staffers to say how troubled she was. "I never want to put any of you in a situation where you would be harmed or even feel threatened. It has been a hard year and an exhausting few weeks. We all know that nothing worth achieving in life comes easy. Considering how monumental this [health-care] bill is, we have gotten by with relatively few scrapes and bruises."

On Wednesday, January 5, 2011, three days before she was shot, Gabby thanked her staffers for making the swearing-in reception at her office "a smashing success." She mentioned that the Republicans had taken control of the House. "Life will be a bit different in the minority, but we will figure out how we can still be effective and rock our issues hard."

What would Gabby want? She'd want Pia and her staffers to redouble their commitment to those issues. She'd want them to honor Gabe's legacy by passionately serving the needs of her constituents. And she'd want them to take good care of themselves.

On January 9, Gabby's staffers met in Tucson with a counselor employed by the House of Representatives. They were heartbroken, angry, shell-shocked. They spoke of survivor's guilt. They cried together. And then they went back to work.

Gabby's staff opened the office on Monday, January 10, just like their boss would have wanted them to do. They were there for the people of the district—no matter what. They took no days off to grieve. (Magnetic pegs indicated which staffers were "in" or "out" of the office. Gabe was left as "in," and someone added in blue marker "in our hearts forever.")

During the first three weeks after the shooting, while Gabby's staffers were still struggling with their own personal traumas, they tended to nine hundred active requests from constituents seeking assistance. More than one hundred of those were new cases that arrived after January 8. Constituents had issues with Social Security, Medicare, veterans benefits, and student loans. Some were facing foreclosure on their homes and needed help from the federal government's Making Home Affordable Program. Others had problems obtaining visas. Gabby would want those constituents to receive the help they sought.

Gabe was dead. Two other colleagues, Ron Barber and Pam Simon, were seriously injured. And Gabby was fighting for her life. But her staffers said they still considered her to be their North Star. They gave great thought every day to the question "What would Gabby want?" And through their grief, they didn't just soldier on, they rocked.

*　*　*

The first few weeks after the shooting were marked by progress. On January 16, Gabby was taken off the ventilator. She slowly emerged from her medically induced coma, and was able to sit up in bed and dangle her legs. She'd touch her wound with her left hand, and adjust her hospital gown. These were good signs that she was aware of herself, which is not the case with all brain-injury patients. She even reached out at one point and gave me an unexpected backrub, just like she used to do.

On January 19, with the help of nurses, Gabby stood for a few moments by her bedside. She had her challenges, too, including a buildup of cerebrospinal fluid in her brain that required a drainage tube. But mostly, her doctors said they were thrilled that she had taken such positive steps so quickly. They upgraded her condition from "critical" to "serious."

Meanwhile, I had to begin figuring out where Gabby would go for her rehabilitation. What would Gabby want? As a booster of Arizona, she'd want me to consider the facilities there. I knew that. But it quickly became clear that the intensive treatment she needed would be much harder to arrange in Arizona. Though there were great options in Chicago and New Jersey, the closest world-class facility to Tucson was TIRR Memorial Hermann in Houston. Even if I didn't live in Texas, doctors told me, I'd likely want Gabby to be cared for at TIRR, given the rehab hospital's reputation for helping those with severe head injuries.

If Gabby had been able to sit in on the discussions about the rehab options, I believe she would have voted for TIRR also. I made arrangements to have her transferred there as soon as her Tucson medical team determined she was ready.

When it came to such big issues, I think those of us who love Gabby did well in considering what we felt her wishes would be. There were times, however, when we forgot to fully consider "What would Gabby want?" For instance, Gabby would have wanted us to remember to go to her Tucson condo and put food in the fish tank. Everyone was so overwhelmed after January 8 that, for several days, it slipped our minds. The two dozen fish that died in her home ended up being secondary casualties of the shooting.

Often, as I strove to honor Gabby's intent and her wishes, I had flashbacks to our previous life together. When Gabby was shot, her wallet was in her purse. After the wallet was returned to me, I had to smile. I hated that thing. She'd gotten it at a secondhand store in Arizona. It had the word "Cherry" embossed on it, so I always assumed its previous owner was a woman named Cherry.

"You're a member of Congress," I had told her, "and you're walking around with some other person's old wallet?"

But Gabby waved me off. She felt affection for that brown leather wallet with Western stitching. She liked that it was recycled.

Now I held it in my hands. She was carrying $135 in cash on January 8. She also had $10 in coupons for Buffalo Exchange, the secondhand store founded in Tucson that is now a national chain.

Looking through her wallet, I came upon a small folded piece of paper. As I opened it up, an image came into my head of Gabby, on several occasions, taking out that paper to soberly look at it. Then she'd refold it and put it back in her Cherry wallet.

Titled "Iraq/Afghanistan War Deaths Arizona CD8," the paper contained the names of the twenty soldiers in her district who'd lost their lives in those wars. Their ages were listed by their names, along with their date of death. The two youngest were nineteen years old. The oldest was forty-three.

"It's important for me to think about those who died in combat," she told me once, as she held the list in her hand.

Each time a soldier from her district died, a new list would be created. Gabby would take out the old list from her wallet and replace it with the new one.

What would Gabby want me to do with her Cherry wallet? She'd want me to keep it in a safe place. When she was better, I knew, she'd want to take out that list and reflect on it again. And maybe someday, she could go to Buffalo Exchange and use those coupons to buy something old and odd that only she could love.

* * *

Those of us who loved Gabby weren't the only ones weighing in on what Gabby would want. Strangers considered the question, too. TV pundits and Internet bloggers, for instance, speculated about whether Gabby would prefer that I step down from my shuttle mission. "She'd want her husband to remain by her side," some argued, "not off in outer space for two weeks." *The New York Times* asked whether I was "bullheaded to go on such a risky business trip." Readers posted their opinions on the newspaper's website. "The truly courageous and strong thing to do is to be an accessible partner to your disabled wife," one reader wrote. "Just sayin'."

But everyone who knew Gabby well was certain where she'd fall on this issue. I was, too.

"Don't even think of backing out," she would have told me if she could find the words. "Your job is to command that mission, to keep your crew safe. They're relying on you. You can't bail out on these guys at the last minute."

I knew Gabby. She didn't need to say a word. That was her position.

On January 9, I had suggested to my bosses at NASA that they should select a backup commander in case I wasn't able to return. They agreed, naming the veteran astronaut Rick "C.J." Sturckow. C.J. did an outstanding job in a hard and uncertain situation. I'm sure he would have loved to fly on the mission, but he told me he was just my placeholder, that he hoped Gabby would improve and I'd return to training.

"I'm just keeping your seat warm," he said. That was very gracious and honorable of him.

As Gabby's condition stabilized, I gave an interview to the *Houston Chronicle*. It ran on January 25 and began: "Astronaut Mark Kelly, the husband of U.S. Rep. Gabrielle Giffords, said Monday he'll decide within the next two weeks whether to leave his wife's bedside and command NASA's final launch of space shuttle *Endeavour* in April."

One of my managers at NASA took offense to that article. He brought me in to the office and reminded me that the decision wasn't mine to make. NASA would determine if it was appropriate for me to return to the mission.

He started by telling me that it made sense to give me my job back. After all, I'd been training to command this particular mission for almost two years. My crew's ability to work as a team couldn't be replicated with a substitute commander in the short window before liftoff. I knew each crew member's strengths and abilities. They knew what I expected of them, and how I wanted them to approach their duties. They also knew what to expect of me. We had trained together for every possible contingency or eventuality. Sure, we could end up being felled by what astronauts call "the unknown unknown," but on the emergency scenarios we could predict, my crew and I were prepared.

"For mission success and safety, the right decision is for you to be the commander," the director of Flight Crew Operations said. I exhaled, relieved. Then he said, "But I don't know how it will look if you come back. The optics aren't good."

The optics?

He was concerned that the media would think that since I had been through such a harrowing few weeks with Gabby, I wouldn't be able to focus, and the crew and mission would be at greater risk. He was worried that NASA would get criticized.

I couldn't believe it. He had just told me that for safety reasons and mission success, I was the right guy. Now he was concerned about a little criticism? Was he really considering putting my crew at greater risk because of "optics"?

I came very close to saying to him, "I'm going to go outside and dig a hole so you can stick your head in it!"

Instead, I sucked it up. I wanted my job back.

"You know, we're going to get criticized either way," I said. I reminded him that NASA's flight surgeons and psychologists had already interviewed me. Yes, I was dealing with stresses, given my wife's condition. But the doctors determined that I'd have no trouble compartmentalizing my personal responsibilities and my duties in flight. Like so many military men, I'd been doing that my entire career. The NASA doctors gave me 100 percent approval.

I was told by my manager that before he'd make a decision about giving me my job back, I needed to spend a week doing two T-38 check rides and a few evaluations in the shuttle simulator. What did he think? That in the three weeks since Gabby was injured I'd forgotten everything?

I wasn't happy. I saw this evaluation period as unnecessary. It also took me away from Gabby's bedside immediately, when I had planned to have another week to meet with her doctors and get certain affairs in order before going back to work full-time. But I did as I was told because I'd gotten the message from my boss: My return wasn't up to me. It was up to him. And I needed to prove myself. (Fortunately, I had an advocate in Peggy Whitson, the chief astronaut, and that helped.)

Here's the thing about NASA. It is populated by a lot of very nerdy smart people. They are drawn to the science of space exploration. A lot of them don't see inspiration in their job descriptions. Gabby's story had captured the public interest, and as people debated whether I should return to the mission, they were paying more attention to the space shuttle program. That wasn't a bad thing. The American people pay NASA's bills. It was good to have them engaged in what we were doing. But some at NASA considered their interest to be a distraction.

Actually, Gabby and I had become very public examples of an issue facing countless families with injured or ill loved ones: When and how do you return to work? While I was submitting to being retested by NASA, the *Pittsburgh Post-Gazette* actually asked its readers to vote on whether I should return to the mission. By a 2-to-1 margin, they advised me: Fly.

I'm not sure my NASA bosses were following the polls, but they eventually called me in to announce their decision. They said I'd performed well in my week of testing: "We want you back as commander." I thanked them for their confidence in me.

They had issues they wanted to discuss. "We don't think you should be doing any media interviews until the launch," my boss said. "You need to focus on the mission."

I didn't think that would work. "Look, my wife can't speak for herself," I said. "She has become a very public figure. I think I'll occasionally need to give updates on how she's doing—how we're both doing. I'll do it on my own time." They relented, but we were in new territory. My marriage to Gabby would put the upcoming mission under an intense spotlight.

NASA held a press conference to announce my return, but no one knew the behind-the-scenes machinations that had led to it. My bosses were very positive. They explained that having me as commander would reduce the mission risk. They said the decision to reinstate me was unanimous, and went all the way up the chain of command.

At the conference, a reporter asked me if I had received a specific OK from Gabby that she wanted me to fly. "I know my wife very well," I said, "and she would be very comfortable with the decision that I made. She's a big supporter of my career, a big supporter of NASA."

I also told the reporters that Gabby's doctors said it was possible that by launch day, she'd be well enough to attend. What would Gabby want? She'd definitely want to be there.

In the weeks that followed, that became a goal for both of us.

* * *

Gabby's colleagues on both sides of the aisle had their own sense of what Gabby would want—from them. Seventeen days after the shooting, on the night President Obama gave his 2011 State of the Union address, Gabby's colleagues found a way to make a statement about political discourse in America. They agreed to buck the tradition of Democrats and Republicans sitting only with their own party for the president's address. Instead, many lawmakers, as a show of civility and solidarity, sat together in a bipartisan seating arrangement. In the Arizona delegation, one chair was left empty to recognize Gabby's absence.

The representatives and senators wore black and white ribbons.

Tucson residents had been wearing those ribbons since the shooting. The white ribbon represented hope for a peaceful, nonviolent society. The black ribbon paid tribute to those who were killed and injured.

I began watching coverage of the address at Gabby's bedside. She was still quite out of it, but I was nervous about what the president would say and what Gabby might comprehend.

The empty chair in the Arizona delegation was between Jeff Flake, a Republican, and Raul Grijalva, a Democrat. I asked Pia to tell their staffers that what Gabby really wanted was for the two congressmen to hold hands across the empty wooden seat. Gabby, of course, wasn't able to speak or make such a request. But I thought it would be funny to put that bipartisan prospect in these competitors' heads. (Pia was mature enough to resist forwarding my message; she knew it was a prank from me, not a request from Gabby.)

As Gabby and I watched the TV, I did talk to her about what was going on. "Look how they're sitting," I said. "It all feels so different, and it's because of you." I sensed that on some level she understood.

Had she been able to truly focus, she would have agreed with the president's point that bipartisan seating wasn't enough. "What comes of this moment," he said, "will be determined not by whether we can sit together tonight, but whether we can work together tomorrow."

Gabby always knew: Symbols are one thing. Actions are another. If she were to recover her faculties and return to that empty chair, she'd have a great deal to say.

*　*　*

Days after the State of the Union, I was asked to go to Washington to speak briefly at the National Prayer Breakfast. What would Gabby want me to say? I gave great thought to that question as I prepared my remarks. I spoke to her about it, even though she was unable to answer or completely comprehend what I was saying.

Gabby hadn't fully turned to Judaism until she was a young woman, and she knew I was still trying to make sense of my Catholic roots, and my thoughts about God. Gabby would want me to think hard about what fate meant to me in the wake of the shooting. And so when I took the podium that morning, standing before President Obama and clergymen of every denomination, I wanted to be very honest.

"I was telling Gabby just the other night that maybe this event—this terrible event—maybe it was fate," I said. "I hadn't been a big believer in fate until recently. I thought the world just spins and the clock just ticks and things happen for no particular reason.

"But President Lincoln was a big believer in fate. He said, 'The Almighty has his own purposes.' He believed there was a larger plan. I can only hope, as I told Gabby, that maybe it's possible that this is just one small part of that same plan. This event, horrible and tragic, was not merely random. Maybe something good can come from all this. Maybe it's our responsibility to see that something does."

I talked about what I'd seen: "From space you have a different perspective of life on our planet. It's humbling to see the Earth as it was created, in the context of God's vast universe."

I also described the growing memorial outside the hospital in Tucson. People had left all sorts of angels and other religious items on the lawn. "It isn't a formal religious site, but Arizona has turned it into a place of prayer. It's like stepping into a church, a place with heaven itself as a ceiling. That reminded me you don't need a church, temple, or mosque to pray. You don't need a building or walls or an altar. You pray where you are, when God is there in your heart."

I concluded with a short prayer that Gabby's rabbi had said at her bedside days earlier. Then I told the three thousand people in attendance, "Please keep Gabby in your prayers and in your hearts. It is really helping. Thank you."

* * *

When I think back to that first month after the shooting, perhaps the most bittersweet moments were on Friday, January 21. That morning, Gabby left Tucson's University Medical Center to begin rehabilitation at TIRR in Houston.

She had arrived at the hospital in Tucson near death. Now here she was, very much alive, and ready to start the second phase of her recovery.

She left the hospital in an ambulance, accompanied by a large contingent of police and an escort of motorcycle riders from the Veterans of Foreign Wars. This was the same group that Gabby had ridden with in 2009, when they escorted the newly discovered remains of fifty-seven Civil War veterans from Tucson to a cemetery in Sierra Vista, seventy-five miles away.

This time, Gabby was in the ambulance, not on a Harley, but the old vets said she needed an honor guard, and they wanted it to be them.

Hundreds of Gabby's constituents lined the streets, applauding, cheering, blowing kisses, and waving American flags as the motor-cade made its way to Tucson's Davis-Monthan Air Force Base. Gabby couldn't see them, but her ambulance driver rolled down his window so she could hear and feel their emotions. She understood. She cried.

I was in a different vehicle, and I rolled down my window to feel it as well. As I waved to people, I caught glimpses of the signs they were holding, with messages such as "Godspeed Gabby" and "Tucson goes with you. Come home soon!" I deeply appreciated their support and affection for Gabby.

On the flight to Houston—on a twelve-seat Challenger jet—Gabby and I were joined by her mom, Dr. Friese, her staffers Pia and C.J., her intensive-care nurse Tracy Culbert, two flight nurses, two pilots, and Lu Cochran of the Capitol Police. As a precaution, we flew at just 15,000 feet to prevent Gabby's brain from further swelling, which is a risk at higher altitudes. Gabby wore her helmet, decorated with an Arizona flag. There were IV bags hanging from the ceiling, and Gabby was on a stretcher-bed, hooked up to monitors.

Gabby's father, Spencer, stayed behind. He later said that watching the plane depart from Tucson was the loneliest moment of his life.

Gabby couldn't articulate how she was feeling. She mostly slept or gazed out the airplane's window as the clouds went by and the town she loved drifted farther into the distance. For what seemed like the millionth time that month, I thought about that question: What would Gabby want?

I knew the answer because I knew Gabby. Someday up the road, sooner than later, she'd want to find her way back to Tucson, healthy and whole. She'd want to return to the Safeway at the southeast corner of Oracle and Ina. She'd want to set up a table and put out a flag and reach out her hand. She'd want to host a Congress on Your Corner to say thank you to her constituents and to ask them what was on their minds.

CHAPTER SEVENTEEN

The Parameters of a Miracle

When Gabby arrived at the Texas Medical Center two weeks after she was shot, she was first taken to the Neuro Trauma Intensive Care Unit, where doctors evaluated her. Hours later, they told me that the medical team in Tucson was right: Gabby's progress so far had been stunning. "Miraculous" was not an inappropriate description.

The Texas doctors were relieved that the advance word on Gabby's condition was so accurate, and they were pleased to see how alert and aware she seemed to be. Several of the doctors said she was recovering with "lightning speed," but I was quickly learning that when it comes to a brain injury, speed is relative. The doctors were comparing her with others shot in the head, 95 percent of whom die almost immediately, and with the few who survive, most of whom are seriously impaired for life. Some never come out of a coma. Against those markers, Gabby's recovery appeared to be in the top 1 percent. Still, she had a long, excruciating slog ahead of her.

Intellectually, I understood this. I listened carefully to every doctor, trying to interpret the nuances of their word choices. They promised that Gabby would improve, but I wanted answers: By how much? By when? They resisted speculation. I let them know that my goal, and the goal of all of Gabby's loved ones, was clear: We wanted 100 percent recovery.

Doctors and therapists spoke of "the new normal." We spoke of the old Gabby. We wanted her to get all the way back to the woman she was on January 7, 2011.

Gloria, Gabby's mom, was the constant optimist. Spencer, her dad, had great faith, too. Meanwhile, I'd taken on the role of taskmaster. I tried to make sure that all of us—hospital staffers, friends, immediate and extended family—were doing whatever we could to help Gabby fully recover. I wanted no impediments.

From the start, Dr. Gerard Francisco, TIRR's chief medical officer, tried to keep our expectations in check. The good news, he said, was that Gabby had a lot going for her. She was fit and healthy before the shooting, which would help in her recovery. She had already made phenomenal progress in the hours and days after her injury. And given her spirit and tenacity, she'd likely take the lead eventually and chart her own course.

"It's possible that she'll return to herself in every way," Dr. Francisco said. "But at the same time, we all should be realistic. That's my mantra. We need to hope for the best and prepare for the worst. It's always good to have a goal, but as we learn about a patient, we may have to revisit our goals to be successful."

Dr. Francisco, a native of the Philippines, was patient and soft-spoken. We were newcomers to TIRR, and he wanted to help initiate us into the language of brain-injury rehab. He warned us that patients who can't live up to their families' high expectations can feel like they've disappointed them. Patients often get depressed, worrying that they're not trying hard enough. They blame themselves for their inability to recover physically and cognitively at the speed their loved ones want. As a result, some suffer setbacks. To be of help to a brain-injury patient, we were told, families need to find a way to balance pragmatism and optimism.

"It's vital to be positive," said Carl Josehart, the chief executive officer at TIRR. "You have to remain hopeful. You have to push for greater recovery. But it can be problematic if you set expectations beyond what a person is physically capable of achieving."

I had trouble accepting the idea that Gabby might have limitations. But her journey through rehab, and her perseverance, would teach me that recovery is a step-by-step process. Brain-injury patients tend to improve, then they plateau for days or weeks, then they take another step up. None of us, including Gabby, could afford to lose hope during the plateaus. It was possible that the next step would be a very large and exciting one. But we had to recognize that this was a long-term process. It would take months. Maybe years.

None of it would be easy. Gabby had to struggle to overcome her most daunting fears—that she'd end up forever locked inside herself, unable to communicate. And I had to admit to myself that I had my own fears to face: Would my caregiving skills meet all of Gabby's needs? Would our life together be severely diminished for decades to come?

Perhaps the lowest moment at TIRR came in early February, before Gabby had even spoken her first word. One morning, she was in her bathroom and I was in an adjacent room, reading. Gabby's nurse, Kristy Poteet, yelled for me. "Mark, you've got to come here! This isn't good!"

I rushed into Gabby's room and then into the bathroom. She was sitting in her wheelchair, tears running down her face. She was hyperventilating, absolutely panicked.

I saw how scared she was. I got scared, too. Through her tears, Gabby motioned with her left hand, waving it by her mouth. It didn't take me long to figure out what was wrong.

She had tried to speak, and she couldn't. No word came out. She tried again to say something, anything. She was making some sounds, consonants and vowels, but they were few. She was mostly just stuck. It was an extreme version of what we all experience sometimes when we are looking for the right word but can't find it. In her case, she couldn't find any words at all and she knew it.

She was having this panic attack because she had just figured out that she was trapped. Trapped inside herself. Her eyes were as wide open as I'd ever seen them and the look on her face was one of absolute fear. I could tell what she was thinking: that this was what her life would be like from now on, that she'd never be able to communicate even the simplest word.

She cried and I cried with her. All I could do was reassure her. "It'll get better," I said. "I promise you. You're going to get better."

I held her as the tears ran down her face. We were learning the parameters of her "miraculous" survival.

*　*　*

What helped? I found it lifted Gabby's spirits when I talked to her about how far she had come. I'd go over each positive step in her recovery, and she'd nod her head.

She had virtually no memory of her two-week hospitalization in Tucson—the emergency room, the intensive-care unit, the presidential visit. Her only recollection was a faint one, of the day we took her on a gurney to the roof of the hospital so she could breathe some fresh air, get some sunlight, and enjoy the view of Tucson and the Catalina Mountains.

By the time she arrived in Texas, she was more awake and aware. Her health was improving and her mind was clearing.

On her third day at the Texas Medical Center, doctors were able to remove the tube from her head that had been draining excess cerebrospinal fluid. They said the buildup of fluid was no longer dangerous to her. They also arranged to insert a valve into her tracheotomy breathing tube so that when she was ready, she'd be better able to talk. She was capable of breathing on her own, but doctors wanted to wean her off the tube slowly. They also said she could swallow safely, and would soon be able to eat without a feeding tube.

By Wednesday, January 26, Gabby was well enough to be transferred across the hospital complex to TIRR. She'd remain there, in rehab, for the next five months.

Physical therapy began on the very afternoon she arrived at TIRR. Gabby wasn't speaking, but she could follow commands. Her therapists worked with her to improve her conditioning and strength. She was asked to move her good left arm and fingers, to lift her left leg, to turn her head. It was clear that she had almost no ability to move the right side of her body. Doctors called it "weakness" rather than "paralysis," and promised that some of the loss would be recovered over time.

Within a couple of weeks, physical therapists had Gabby walking very slowly in the hallway, leading with her left leg, a brace on her right leg. They held on to her as she moved, and she often moaned in pain as she took each step. But she walked farther every day. Eventually, she'd push a shopping cart up and down the hallways.

Gabby always had to wear her helmet, which she disliked. It was uncomfortable, hot, and awkward, but she needed to have it on her head whenever she wasn't safely in bed or sitting in her wheelchair. Her missing piece of skull—it's called a bone flap—was about the size of a person's hand. Besides the dura mater, the membrane closest to the skull, only a thin layer of skin, stitched together, was protecting Gabby's brain. Though her risk of having a seizure or a blood clot decreased every day, the risk of a fall remained. If she were to hit her head, the impact could set her back—or even kill her. (The skull pieces that had been removed on January 8 were stored in a freezer, but doctors thought they were too damaged to be reinserted. They'd likely have to use a ceramic implant when it was time to surgically replace the missing section of her skull.)

Because of security concerns, Gabby had her own private room at TIRR, with the ever-present Capitol Police outside her door. It was a weird way to live, but over time, we all tried to help make her room feel like home.

Gloria and Gabby's friend Raoul placed a rock from Arizona on the nightstand by her bed. I placed another rock from her district underneath her bed and told her that, in a way, she was in Arizona. She liked that.

Raoul and Gloria decorated the walls with photos that had been blown up into posters—our wedding, a shot of us posing at the Grand Canyon, Gabby and her Chevy Corvair. There were photos displayed of Gabby with her parents and other loved ones. She seemed to recognize every scene. Gloria, meanwhile, began passing the long hours she spent with Gabby painting portraits, in oil, of the hospital staff—doctors, nurses, therapists. It was exciting watching her work—Gabby's bathroom was her art studio—and many of her paintings were displayed in the room. Eventually they were given to her appreciative subjects.

Between 8 a.m. and 5 p.m., I'd head down to NASA to train for my space shuttle mission. Gloria and Spencer remained at the hospital, usually fourteen hours a day, and they reveled in each improvement they noticed in Gabby. On days when Gabby's progress seemed to slow, hospital staffers encouraged her parents to be patient. Gloria said they'd try, but made no promises. "Of course we're impatient," she said. "We want our daughter back!"

* * *

After the shooting, we had decided not to release any photos of Gabby publicly. We wanted to wait until she was looking and feeling better—even if that took months. I was nervous about media reports that the first photo showing the extent of Gabby's injuries might be worth $200,000 to the paparazzi. I asked those who visited her not to bring cameras. For a while, I requested that hospital employees with cell-phone cameras leave them at the door before entering Gabby's room. Everyone understood and complied.

When people came to visit Gabby for the first time, I'd usually talk to them in the hallway. "You don't need to speak loudly," I'd say. "Gabby can hear just fine. And please don't talk down to her." My most important request: "Be positive."

One early visitor was an old friend of Gabby's whom she has known for years and really loves. He's funny, but a bit over the top, and he likes to be thought of as a rebel. Occasionally, I could be sensitive to how people interacted with Gabby. Maybe too sensitive at times, but this particular friend was too much.

Gabby hadn't even said her first word yet, and he seemed set on making sure that the word was "bullshit."

"Hey, Gabby," he said. "If a nurse asks you to do something, you tell her, 'Bullshit!' When doctors talk to you, tell them all the same thing: 'Bullshit!'"

I'm not sure whether he was hoping the media would one day report that Gabby had chosen "bullshit" as her first word. I ignored the request the first time, but after hearing it to the point where I thought his efforts might work, I told him to knock it off and keep his bullshit suggestions to himself.

The media announced that Gabby's first word, uttered on February 7, came at breakfast time. She was eating yogurt and oatmeal and asked for "toast." That update had been supplied by Gabby's congressional office as a word she had said, and the media wrongly assumed it as her first word. Yes, Gabby did say "toast," but a day or so before that she had actually said the word "what"—flatly, as a statement, not a question. She said something that sounded like "whatwhatwhatwhat." It appeared to me that the speech part of her brain was just beginning to boot up and that was the place it picked as a starting point. Gabby's

Gabby and Mark attended Laura and George Bush's Christmas party at the White House in 2008. (Giffords/Kelly Family)

Mark arranged to deliver roses and a note to Gabby a minute after he was safely in space during his 2008 shuttle mission. Gabby's dad, Spencer, watched the launch with her. (Marc Winkelman)

Gabby and Mark rode mules on a visit to the Arizona border. Congresswoman Giffords worked hard to get more federal support for border security. (Office of Congresswoman Gabrielle Giffords)

Gabby and Mark hiked in the Grand Canyon on November 27, 2010, just three weeks after she was elected to a third term in Congress. (Raoul Erickson)

At a community meeting near the border in Douglas, Arizona, Gabby named her top priorities for her second term in Congress as "border security, economic security, national security, and energy security." (© P. K. Weis/www.SouthWestPhotoBank.com)

Gabby talks to Iraqi troops during a 2007 congressional delegation trip. (Office of Congresswoman Gabrielle Giffords)

Gabby visited Davis-Monthan Air Force Base in Tucson during her 2010 campaign. She is seen here climbing into an A-6E Intruder, the same type of aircraft that Mark flew in the Gulf War. (Office of Congresswoman Gabrielle Giffords)

Gabby and Mark attended a Girl Scout event in her district. Gabby wore the pin she'd saved since her own days as a Girl Scout. (© P. K. Weis/www.SouthWestPhotoBank.com)

Gabby and Mark watched the 2010 election returns in a room in the Tucson Marriott University Park with *(from left to right)* friend Marc Winkelman; Gabby's chief of staff, Pia Carusone; her district director, Ron Barber; and staffer Jennifer Cox. (Giffords for Congress)

Standing between Mark and Gabby as she addressed the crowd of supporters on election night 2010 is Rodd McLeod, her longtime campaign manager. (© A. T. Willett/ www.atwillett.com)

The new Speaker of the House John Boehner swore Gabby into her third term on January 5, 2011, three days before she was critically wounded. (AP Photo/Susan Walsh, File)

Gabby's staffers at the start of the 2011 legislative session included *(from left to right)* Ron Barber, the Arizona district director; Gabe Zimmerman, community outreach director; and C. J. Karamargin, communications director. Gabe Zimmerman was killed in the shooting, along with five others. Barber was one of thirteen wounded. (Stephanie Coronado)

Constituent Matthew Laos, an Army Reservist, came to the Congress on Your Corner event on January 8, 2011, to show Gabby his military commendation following his tour of duty in Afghanistan. Seconds later, Gabby and eighteen others were shot. (Office of Congresswoman Gabrielle Giffords)

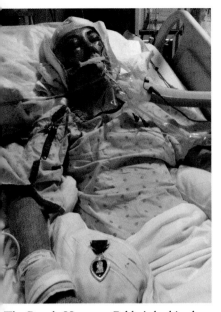

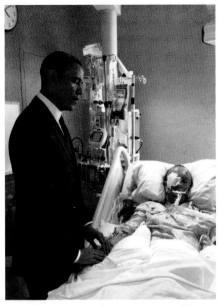

The Purple Heart on Gabby's bed in the ICU at the University Medical Center in Tucson was dropped off at the hospital by an anonymous soldier the day after she was shot. (Mark Kelly)

President Barack Obama visited Gabby in the hospital on January 12, 2011, before the memorial service in Tucson for the victims of the shooting. (Pia Carusone)

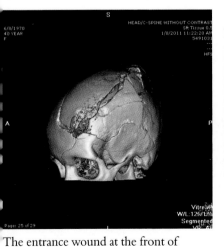

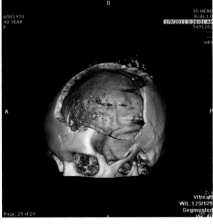

The entrance wound at the front of Gabby's forehead and the exit wound at the back are visible in this 3-D reconstruction from the CAT scan of her skull taken on January 8. (Mark Kelly)

This 3-D reconstruction was made after Gabby's initial neurosurgery. Dr. Mike Lemole removed most of the skull on the left side of her head to reduce the pressure on her brain. (Mark Kelly)

Like Mark, Dr. Peter Rhee, Gabby's lead trauma surgeon, served as a U.S. Navy Captain. (Mark Kelly)

Thousands of people who were grieving and rooting for Gabby left flowers, stuffed animals, candles, and other mementos outside her congressional office in Tucson. (Guy Atchley/azphotoguy.com)

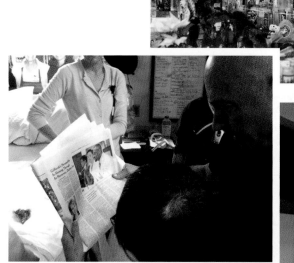

Gabby's chief of staff, Pia Carusone, happened to be taking photos on March 12, 2011, at the moment when Gabby grabbed a newspaper and learned about the other victims of the shooting. (Pia Carusone)

Gabby hugged her Houston neurosurgeon, Dr. Dong Kim, on the day she was discharged from TIRR Memorial Hermann in June 2011. (Gloria Giffords)

Mark drove Gabby to the launchpad in a rented convertible to take a closer look at space shuttle *Endeavour* during the first launch attempt in April 2011. Due to technical issues, it would be nearly a month before Mark got into space. (Gloria Giffords)

On May 16, 2011, Scott, Gabby, Claire, and Claudia watched from the roof of the Launch Control Center as Mark blasted off in *Endeavour*. (Gloria Giffords)

Mark and his fellow STS-134 astronauts and their spouses, without Gabby, gathered for the traditional prelaunch photograph. (NASA)

Mark filmed this video for U2 while aboard the International Space Station. It was used at every concert during their North American tour to introduce the song "Beautiful Day." Mark told the crowd, "I'm looking forward to coming home. Tell my wife I love her very much." (NASA)

"Though Gabby grew up in Arizona, a daughter of the desert, she loves the ocean more than anyone I've ever known," says Mark. This was the memorable moment they had together on the beach on NASA's "space coast" before the first launch attempt. (Pia Carusone)

neurologists said the words that patients seize on initially are impossible to predict, but the repetition of words is very common.

When Gabby said those first early words, it wasn't as if a lightbulb went off in her head: OK, now she'd just start speaking. It was more a case of her willing one word, haltingly, out of her mouth. The next one would need to be willed with equal determination. But soon, she had a few dozen words. Within a couple months, she had perhaps a thousand words she could say. It just took great patience, for her and for the rest of us.

She could mimic a word we said far more easily than she could initiate one herself. Doctors said that was an appropriate first step, and that her ability to repeat our words was an excellent sign of neurological recovery. That meant the area of her brain that controls primary language was working.

By March, Gabby started creating phrases she deemed worth repeating. Sick of being confined in the hospital, she'd say, "Want out of here!"

"Where would you like to go?" Gloria would ask her.

"Tucson, Arizona!" she'd say.

She also started saying, "No more Mr. Nice Guy!" It was her way of announcing that she was going to be more assertive. She wanted to make her own decisions about what she ate, what she wore, how long visitors stayed.

Gabby was good at finishing familiar phrases. I'd say, "Thank God Almighty I am . . ."

"Free at last," she'd say. (This later became her mantra every time she walked out the door at TIRR. "Free at last, free at last. Thank God, I am free at last!")

If I gave her a hint, she could say the amendments to the U.S. Constitution. I told her, "The first amendment is free—"

"Freedom of speech," she'd say.

"What's the second amendment? The right to . . ."

"Arms," Gabby said.

"Yes, the right to bear arms."

"How about this, Gabby. Four score . . ."

"And seven more," she said.

"You're close. It is 'four score and seven years ago.'"

Gabby developed a great ability to sum up hospital food. "What did you have for lunch today?" I asked her one evening.

"Warm juice. Meat salad," she said, and then she burst out laughing.

We saw that Gabby's long-term memory was excellent. Looking at a photo of a certain female politician, Gabby had a recollection she couldn't resist sharing. "Man hands," she said.

* * *

Gloria, Spencer, and I had many consultations with doctors, but they couldn't fully explain the mysteries of the brain. People with serious head injuries all respond in different ways, they said, so it was impossible to fully predict how things would go for Gabby.

A lot of brain-injury patients struggle to understand humor. They may appreciate the slapstick stuff, but anything subtle, including the punch line of a joke, is beyond them.

There are patients who can read but not write. Others can write but they can't read; they could write a letter to a loved one without a problem, but couldn't go back to read what they had written.

Some patients understand perfectly everything said to them, but they will never be able to utter a word. Others are the opposite. They can speak normally, but what they hear is gibberish.

In Gabby's case, as time went on, we saw that her comprehension was nearing 100 percent. She understood jokes, and also found her own ways to be funny, with facial expressions, eye rolls, and a word here or there. She didn't slur her words, which was a great sign. If people with brain injuries slur their words from the start, the slur usually remains throughout their lives.

Another issue: People who survive a gunshot to the right side of their brain often find that their personality changes drastically. They may have trouble interacting with others. They may be depressed. They may act out inappropriately. Gabby, shot on the left side, was able to retain her personality. We all saw that pretty clearly, and were intensely relieved.

Dong Kim, Gabby's neurosurgeon at TIRR, explained that what people consider a part of the human soul is actually a series of distinct brain functions. Depending on where people suffer their head traumas, they may become more or less religious, or more or less empathetic.

"There are great strides coming in brain science," Dr. Kim promised. He compared the breakthroughs ahead to the progress made in cardiology in the late 1950s. We could only hope these advances would come in time to help Gabby.

Gabby's biggest problem, besides the partial paralysis on her right side, was her inability to communicate.

Often, she'd say yes when she meant to say no, or vice versa.

"Gabby, do you want to take a walk?" I'd ask.

"Yes, yes," she'd say, and when I'd stand up to help her, she'd tell me, "No, no, no!"

She knew what she wanted to say. It's just that the wrong words came out—often, the opposite of what she wanted to say. For some reason, "no" was much easier for her to say than "yes."

Carl Josehart, who ran the operation at TIRR, was good at explaining this problem in everyday language. "Think of the brain as a filing cabinet," he said. "Imagine dumping a lot of the files on the floor and then randomly putting them all back in the cabinet. That is what Gabby is dealing with. When she reaches to say a word, it might be in the wrong folder. She may not even realize right away that she has used the wrong word. But even if she does realize it, she can't help herself and correct it. She still says the wrong word. And it's common to get hooked on one word, and to say it over and over again."

One day, Gabby was saying "no" in response to every question. Her well-meaning father took it upon himself to talk to her about it. "Let me give you some ideas about when you'd use the word 'yes,'" Spencer said to Gabby, and then he began rattling off situations in which answering "yes" would be appropriate. "For instance, if I asked you if the sky is blue, you'd say 'yes.'"

Spencer gave her about a dozen examples. "No, no, no," Gabby said. I could see she was getting upset.

"Not 'no,'" Spencer said. "You'd use the word 'yes.'"

Gabby knew exactly when you're supposed to say "yes" versus "no." After all, she comprehended almost everything. It's just that, for some reason, she wasn't able to deliver the word "yes." Her father's heart was in the right place, but he just wasn't seeing the faulty circuits in his daughter's brain.

"No, no, no, no, no . . . !" Gabby said the word about twenty times until Spencer backed off. I'd never seen her that angry with him. Gabby and her father always had a special bond, which had gotten ever stronger after she came home to run El Campo. Who could have imagined that they'd one day be at odds over the definitions of "yes" and "no"?

One day, a while later, Gabby and I were alone and she said to me, "Voice in my head."

"Whose voice?" I asked her. She didn't answer. She was struggling to find the words to explain herself, but couldn't.

"Is it someone else's voice?" I asked.

"No, no, no," she said.

"Is it your voice?"

"Yes," she said. "Hear my voice."

"So you can hear your voice, but you can't get your voice out. Is that what you're trying to say?"

"Yes," she answered. "Very frustrating."

To ease her frustration, I tried my hardest to interpret what she meant when she used a wrong word or phrase.

"Room for pillow," she said one night when we were in her hospital bed together. She was waving her hand over her head.

"Gabby, you have your pillow," I said. In fact, there were multiple pillows and plenty of space for them on her bed. "Room for pillow!" she said several more times.

I was at a loss to figure out what she wanted, and she was growing more agitated about it. It went on for fifteen minutes of her saying "room for pillow" and me trying to guess what that could possibly mean.

Finally, it hit me. She wanted the head of her bed tilted backward. She couldn't come up with the word "tilt." I showed her the button to use to move her bed up and down, and then I blamed myself. "Gabby, it's not you," I said. "It's me. I'm a moron."

"Yes," she said. "Moron."

Because I knew Gabby so well, I didn't always have to ask her to explain things. One day early in her hospitalization, I was home and needed to take a look at her online bank statement to make sure her mortgage was being paid. But I had a problem. I didn't know her password and she wasn't well enough yet to tell me. To get a new password, the bank's website prompted me to reply to a few questions that Gabby had answered when she set up the account.

Question #1: "What is your favorite flower?"

What would Gabby have answered? I typed in "tulip." That was correct.

Question #2: "Who is your best friend?"

"Raoul," I typed. Correct again.

I was given a new password and breezed into Gabby's records.

I later told her how easily I'd cracked her code. "You don't have to tell me what's in your head," I said. "A lot of times, sweetie, I just know."

*   *   *

Gabby's doctors and nurses were patient in trying to help us understand brain science. They explained that some babies are born with half a brain and they grow up relatively normal. That's because either side of our brain is capable of doing pretty much everything. The problem for adults is that it's difficult to rewire a brain later in life. It's doable, but it takes a lot more time. The brain's ability to change itself is called "plasticity of the brain." In Gabby's case, the right side of her brain would need to pick up some functions that for forty years had been performed by the left. Her brain literally had to rewire itself, and that's a slow, inexact, not-always-successful process.

Like many brain-injury patients, Gabby was often exhausted. An hour of speech or physical therapy took a lot out of her. Doctors explained that sleep helps the brain heal, and Gabby took seriously her need to rest. She slept thirteen or fourteen hours a day, then woke up ready for therapy. "Work, work, work," she'd say.

There isn't a lot of shiny, expensive equipment used to rehabilitate brain-trauma patients. In Gabby's case, physical therapy often involved some white PVC piping and an Ace bandage. Her right hand would be tied with the bandage to contraptions built from the piping. The contraptions were designed so that as Gabby moved her left hand, her damaged right hand would follow suit. The purpose of this was to try to train her brain to start giving signals to her right hand, just as it did to her left. By moving her hands in tandem, the hope was that the brain might begin rewiring itself to better acknowledge her right hand.

Later in the day, Gabby's speech therapist would arrive with a box of cards featuring pictures of objects, or she'd bring the objects themselves. Sometimes they'd play tic-tac-toe. They'd also leaf through *People* magazine, discussing what the celebrities were wearing and doing. This was sometimes an exercise in futility because, even before Gabby was shot, she couldn't tell you anything about celebrities and what they were up to. She didn't pay attention to celebrity culture. So why would she know now? Still, it was helpful if Gabby looked at clothing, objects, and scenery, and tried to identify the names of things.

Often, Gabby and her speech therapist would just talk. Sometimes they would sing. "American Pie" was a favorite.

Music therapy may seem like an idle entertainment to help patients pass the time, but it's a crucial and fascinating part of healing. Singing familiar lyrics, a right-brain activity, helps those injured on the left side of their brain. Stimulating a part of the brain that wasn't damaged can help rebuild a patient's broken circuitry. When a patient undergoes an MRI while singing, many different areas of the brain light up. "Singing," the doctors told us, "is a pathway to language. It's great exercise for the brain."

Because lyrics to well-known songs are imprinted in people's minds, those with brain injuries often find it easier to access lyrics than spoken conversation. Many can sing in sentences before they can speak in sentences. In Gabby's case, music therapy also helped her with physical issues. Sometimes, while she walked the hall, a certain rhythm was played, and the cadence helped her improve her gait. And, of course, there were also emotional connections when she sang, such as the memories evoked when she and her mom shared duets of "Tomorrow."

Gabby's parents sat through countless hours of therapy, and they appreciated seeing it all unfold. In those months, they were staying at a friend's home in Houston, but they were reluctant to leave the hospital at night. "I'm afraid if I go, I'll miss something," Gloria told me. Sometimes she'd return to the hospital at 5 a.m. She couldn't stay away. "I realize that even while Gabby is sleeping, bits and pieces of her brain are rebooting and coming on line," she said. "I want to be there when things happen. I want to watch her get better."

* * *

Sometimes, Gabby would repeat the same sing-song phrase: "Wondering what's happening to me." She wasn't exactly singing it, but almost. Her delivery was mischievous, as if she were really saying, "There's something you guys aren't telling me."

"Wonder what's happening to me," she'd say again, her inflection rising.

I'd respond in my own sing-song voice: "You're getting better. That's what's happening to you."

Gabby often used the word "hazy" to describe her memory. And then one night she couldn't think of the name of Longworth, her office building in Washington. "What I know I can't remember," she said.

For a while, she also repeatedly said, "I've been beaten." I didn't like hearing that. Did she mean her injury had beaten her? That she was down for the count?

"You haven't been beaten," I told her. "You've just been beaten up."

She'd pump her fist when I said that. "Yes," she'd say, and give me a half smile.

Sometimes, I'd ask her what she missed about the life she left behind. "The office," she said. She was referring to her congressional office. And then she said: "The people are important." She hadn't forgotten her constituents, either.

Pia, Gabby's chief of staff, spent a lot of time in Houston, and often gave Gabby updates on legislation and issues in her district. Gabby listened intently, though she couldn't formulate questions.

I didn't want Gabby to forget that she was a formidable politician. In early April, Speaker John Boehner came to Houston to attend the NCAA Final Four tournament. Considering that she was a member of Congress and he was the highest-ranking member, we thought he'd ask to visit Gabby, or at least give a call to see how she was doing. Our only contact with him had been a simple get-well card he'd sent a few days after Gabby was injured.

When he came to town for the basketball games and we didn't hear from him, I told Gabby that maybe she had scared him off. "Remember before the 2010 election, when we saw him in that restaurant?" I said to her. Gabby remembered.

We had been at a restaurant in Washington and spotted Boehner, then the House minority leader, at another table. He was wearing a white shirt and a crisp tie, and was dining with ten other middle-aged men, all in white shirts and similar ties. Gabby wasn't intimidated. As we were leaving the restaurant, she stopped by their table—a young female Democrat unafraid to stand before a group of older male Republicans and speak her mind.

"Hey, Leader Boehner, how are you doing? How's everything going?" she said. He knew who she was. He nodded politely.

She got right to the point. "You stay out of my district," Gabby said to him, a big smile on her face. "OK? Remember. Stay out of my district!" She was trying to be funny, but she was also giving him notice. She didn't want him using the Republican war chest in the campaign against her. And she didn't want him coming to Tucson to do fund-raisers for her opponent.

To my eyes, Boehner had an uncomfortable look on his face as Gabby spoke. He barely said hello, and no one else said a word.

"Well, good seeing you," Gabby said to him, still smiling. Then she turned and waved, and we walked toward the door.

Now, less than a year later, Gabby was no longer able to deliver such self-assured patter. So much had changed since that night in Washington. But I wanted Gabby to know she still had it all in her. "Maybe Boehner doesn't want to see you because he's worried you'll tell him to stay out of your district," I said.

She smiled at me, and I could see the same twinkle in her eye that had carried her through that Washington restaurant.

Gabby still had a long way to go. I saw that. But in so many vital ways, she remained the person she always was. Her daily journey had been difficult and painful, but she had blossomed in this rehabilitation hospital. And it was exciting to contemplate the progress to come.

Sometimes, I felt almost elated. The parameters of a miracle were widening.

CHAPTER EIGHTEEN

STS-134

The launch of my mission on space shuttle *Endeavour,* postponed several times, was finally slated for April 29, 2011, a Friday afternoon. In the weeks leading up to it, doctors repeatedly said they could envision Gabby being well enough to travel to Florida to see me and my crew off. They didn't commit to giving their blessings, but they thought it was appropriate for Gabby to make that a goal of her rehabilitation.

"See the launch," she'd say repeatedly.

In mid-April, she went on a secret practice run to the airfield she'd fly out of, so the logistics of her departure could be ironed out. A special chair was brought along to get her up the stairs of the jet. Gabby vowed that on the day she actually traveled, she'd walk up the stairs if she could.

On April 24, we got the final OK from her medical team. Gabby was good to go. In their words she was "medically able." It was a milestone. "Awesome!" was Gabby's response when she learned the news.

Her doctors looked at it as a kind of field trip. Patients often left TIRR to attend special events or family functions, to help reacclimate them into their former lives. In Gabby's case, her life before she was injured included her role as an astronaut's wife. This would be a nice coming-out for her, and maybe helpful to her recovery.

By then, I had already begun serving seven days of quarantine at NASA's Johnson Space Center. My crew and I were being kept away from other people and their germs so we'd remain healthy before the mission. Being quarantined at NASA, twenty-five miles southeast of TIRR, was hard for me. I didn't like the separation from Gabby. Her mom and Pia could tell me how Gabby's days were going, but I wanted to see with my own eyes.

I was able to call Gabby and ask her questions, but she couldn't really answer or initiate much. Mostly it was me talking. But then, on the night of April 26, Gabby and I were on the phone and during a pause in the conversation, she said, "I miss you." It took me by surprise. Until then, Gabby was almost never able to deliver a line like that unless someone else said it first. This was a new sentence, delivered all on her own, and it was a sentiment that went straight from her heart to mine.

TV networks and newspapers that day were full of stories about Great Britain's Prince William and Kate Middleton, who would be getting married on the very morning of our scheduled launch. The royal wedding was gearing up with unprecedented pageantry. It was the biggest love story of the year, with satellite feeds to a billion people.

Yet on this day, I was reminded that love can also be small and simple. I was alone in quarantine. Gabby was stuck in the hospital and in her own mind. All we had was a phone line. And all it took was three words: "I miss you."

* * *

This was the second-to-last space shuttle mission, so those days in April were a bittersweet time for all of us in the space program. Thousands of workers at NASA and its contractors, including many people I knew and admired, would be losing their jobs after the thirty-year shuttle program wound down. I was impressed and moved to see the dedication and professionalism of the space-program workforce—engineers, technicians, flight controllers, factory workers, simulator instructors—given that the end of the road was nearing for many of them.

This would be the 134th space shuttle launch. At NASA, we referred to our mission as STS-134; STS stands for Space Transportation System.

Endeavour, our spacecraft, took almost four years to build. Congress authorized its construction in August 1987, to replace *Challenger,* which had exploded eighteen months earlier. It was largely built from a collection of spare parts left over from the construction of *Discovery* and *Atlantis.*

In a national competition involving seventy thousand students, NASA selected *Endeavour* as the spacecraft's name. *Endeavour* was a ship captained by explorer James Cook that sailed the South Pacific in

1768. Cook, an amateur astronomer, had brought along ninety-three crewmen, including eleven scientists and artists. They came to Tahiti to observe Venus as it traveled between the Sun and the Earth. That helped them estimate the distance from our planet to the Sun. Those *Endeavour* crew members from 1768 were groundbreakers. It was an honor to continue their efforts.

As a space shuttle, *Endeavour* was designed for one hundred missions. Before STS-134, it flew twenty-four flights, traveling 103,149,636 miles. There were many successes. *Endeavour*'s astronauts replaced the rocket motor on a nonfunctioning communications satellite in 1992; they were the first to service the Hubble Space Telescope in 1993; they delivered the first American component of the International Space Station in 1998.

Our mission's highlight would be the delivery to the space station of the $2 billion Alpha Magnetic Spectrometer, a cosmic particle detector, which would help researchers study how the universe was formed. It was designed by Samuel Ting, a Nobel Prize–winning physicist, and built by six hundred scientists and technicians from sixteen countries.

Once installed, the Spectrometer would help scientists understand complex high-energy particles, potentially solving mysteries of the universe such as the existence of antimatter and the nature of dark matter and dark energy. (Antimatter is defined as any substance that, after combining with an equal portion of matter, leads the entire substance to convert into energy.) Is there naturally occurring antimatter in the universe? Where is it? Are distant stars and galaxies, visible to astronomers, made of antimatter? If we got the 15,251-pound device installed correctly, we'd have answers. It could be historic.

I wasn't exactly nervous, but I was very aware of the stakes. As the commander, I had to make sure every part of the multibillion-dollar mission went exactly as planned. I knew I'd be under a microscope. A lot of people—in the media, at NASA, in the general public—would be watching to see if my dual responsibilities to Gabby and to STS-134 would result in stresses that would compromise any part of the mission. Knowing this, I wanted to perform well beyond expectations. That was a pact I'd made with myself.

As an astronaut, you have to become one with a mighty machine.

I wanted to help make sure that *Endeavour* carried me and my crew safely into space, that it allowed us to complete our complicated mission without any major problems, and that it brought us safely home.

After our mission, *Endeavour* would be retired. A museum in Los Angeles, the California Science Center, was waiting for it. I was determined to get it there without a scratch.

* * *

While in quarantine, before heading down to Florida, there was one particularly difficult astronaut ritual I had to attend to: the writing of the "contingency" letters.

Many astronauts feel the need to write these goodbye letters to their loved ones in case they draw the ace of spades and don't come home. This was my fourth mission, so I'd already penned such letters three previous times. They're not easy to write, and I hate doing it. But given the risks, the letters can help wives, children, parents, and siblings grieve after a tragedy.

The legendary astronaut Story Musgrave has described the space shuttle poetically and perfectly as "very unsafe, very fragile. It's a butterfly bolted onto a bullet." The shuttle doesn't fly very well. It's this vehicle with stubby wings, launched at the front end of a giant ball of fire, which then becomes a glider for the ride home. It is an awesome spaceship. It's also a miracle that it ever makes it back to the runway at the end of a mission. Our families know all this, though we don't talk about it a lot. The letters, delivered only if we don't survive, address what is often unspoken.

On April 26, alone in quarantine, I began writing four letters to be left behind in my backpack in crew quarters. If I died, my brother, Scott, would know to look there. His job would be to take out the letters, open the one addressed to him, and then deliver the other three.

The letter I wrote to him wasn't too emotional. He and I know the drill. Between us, there's not much to say. I mostly scribbled out some financial concerns and details of my trust for my daughters. I had already left my will and detailed bank account information in an envelope at the front office. Scott knew to find that stuff there. In my letter to him, I covered other nuts-and-bolts issues, such as giving him the name of a specific financial advisor I wanted him to use when investing my money. Since this letter wasn't notarized, I put my thumbprint on it. How legal was that? I had no idea, but I was getting ready to fly into space and out of time. I needed to do something.

Next, I wrote to Claudia and Claire. My letter to Claire began: "If you are reading this, things didn't turn out as we expected, and I will not be with you anymore." I told her I loved her more than she'll ever know, that she's my "little buddy," and that Uncle Scott would be there for her in my place. I reminded her I'd always be proud of her, and that she's smart, loving, and beautiful. I also wrote: "Please try to stay connected with your stepmom. Gabby loves you very much and needs you in her life. You need her, too. She will get better. Please help her with that."

I told Claudia: "I will always be with you in spirit. I will be there with you when you are at graduation and at all those big events in your life—just not in person." I asked her to look after her younger sister, and to stay connected to Gabby. "I am very proud of how you put your previous feelings aside after January 8 and made changes. Gabby loves you very much and will be there for you as best as she can."

It was hard for me to imagine the girls opening and reading those letters after receiving news of my death. I tried not to think about it.

My final letter was to Gabby. I'd written to her before previous launches, of course, but this time, given what we'd been through together, my emotions couldn't have been more intense. On the outside of her envelope I wrote, "Open in 134 contingency only." Inside was the letter:

Dearest Gabby,

I am so sorry. If you are reading this, it has certainly been a tougher year than either of us could have ever imagined. It is odd how things turn around so quickly. As you recently said, "Life is strange."

Maybe things happen for a reason or maybe this is just a random world we live in. I hope it is the former. I certainly believe that what happened January 8th was fate. My mishap, on the other hand, can be chalked up to flying a vehicle that is very dangerous. It really stinks that we won't be together, but no matter how awful this is, you will persevere. You are tough! The toughest person I know.

You will get better, recover and move on and do great things. Please try to meet someone else and fall in love again. You deserve that. Please know that I will always love you madly.

We are still a team—in spirit.

I love you and will miss you always.

MK

*   *   *

On April 27, 109 days after the shooting, Gabby arrived at Houston's Ellington Airport to fly to Florida for the launch. She made a willful decision that her coming-out would be a statement, to herself and those around her, that she was on her way back to self-sufficiency. She got out of her wheelchair and slowly climbed the stairs onto the NASA jet. A news helicopter captured long-range video of the moment, which aired all over television that day. It was the first glimpse the public had gotten of Gabby since January 8.

Gabby landed at Florida's Patrick Air Force Base, thirty miles from the Kennedy Space Center. She then was checked into the barracks there along with her mom, Pia, her nurses, her security detail, and the astronaut Piers Sellers, who was serving as Gabby's NASA liaison. I was in crew quarters, preparing for the launch, but I got several e-mails from Gloria about the "bleak" accommodations: an old table and chairs, industrial-grade carpeting, "a stiff little sofa," a discolored pastoral landscape on the wall. The place was on a sand lot dotted with crabgrass. "It's like living in a motel at the end of the universe," Gloria wrote.

Gabby had spent six months with the Mennonites. She knew what it's like to live austerely, so I figured she'd be OK with the barracks. I was wrong. When I called to ask her about the accommodations, she registered her dissatisfaction. "Awful," she said.

Maybe living in a hospital for months had her longing for something less sterile. In any case, it was nice to see she was taking over her life to some extent, and asserting herself. She wanted new accommodations, calls were made, and we were able to get everyone set up at the local Residence Inn.

"It's amusing," Gloria told Gabby, "that a brain-injured woman had to take matters into her own hands to finally get us adequate lodging."

In the early pages of this book, I described Gabby's arrival at the NASA beach house on April 28, the day before our scheduled launch, when I was able to take her down to the water's edge. That may have been our happiest moment since the shooting.

Later, Gloria told me that when Gabby left the beach house and got into the car, she seemed exhilarated and almost carefree. As they drove off, "Don't Stop Believin'" by Journey was playing on the car radio, and Gabby surprised everyone by happily singing along. I was sorry I missed that.

Gabby's four days in Florida were not without incident. One night while she was returning from a NASA function, Gabby needed to use a restroom. It can be pretty desolate around the Kennedy Space Center, and her support team couldn't find one in time. "Gabby was mortified and started to cry," Gloria wrote to me in an e-mail. "Darlene and I both comforted her. It's in these times when I almost lose it to grief over Gabby's humiliation and current helplessness."

There were fifteen hundred requests for media credentials at the launch, in large part because of Gabby's presence. Journalists kept asking Gabby's congressional staffers how she was doing. Their answers were true: She was extremely excited to be there. Just the fact that she was able to make it to the launch was an uplifting story. But those feel-good stories were only part of the picture. They couldn't possibly convey all the emotions Gabby was experiencing—that her excitement at times was tinged with sadness, and even despair.

Those escorting Gabby to and from various events around the Kennedy Space Center learned to make sure there were predetermined restroom breaks. One stop was at a police station in Cocoa Beach. Gloria told me that what seemed like the entire force came out to say hi to Gabby. Gloria wrote in an e-mail: "As we were leaving, a new face appeared—a bike cop. While Darlene and I have differing opinions on what color his eyes were, we both noticed his physique. He said hello to Gabby, and she responded, 'Hot Daddy!' He really was a hottie."

I read that e-mail, alone in my quarters. It would be an interesting wrinkle in our story if I returned from my sixteen days in space and Gabby had run off with a bike cop.

* * *

Before each shuttle mission, there typically would be a barbecue for the entire crew and a small group of family and friends. (All attendees first had a physical to make sure they were healthy.) For the STS-134 barbecue, each of us got to bring five guests. I brought Gabby, Gloria, Claudia, Claire, and Pia.

As commander, I emceed the evening. I invited everyone to stand up and introduce themselves. At previous missions, Gabby liked to ask people to talk about the first concert they attended. "I won't make you all do that," I said, and Gabby laughed.

We toasted all our loved ones who had supported us. We toasted for a safe flight. Then, as the get-together was ending, I asked Gabby, "What do you think? Do you want to go see the shuttle on the launch-pad?"

"Yes!" she said.

"OK, it's a good thing your hair is now short, because we're taking my convertible," I said.

By tradition, NASA rented convertibles for astronauts to drive around Kennedy Space Center in the days before their flights. NASA got a good government rate, and it was nice for us to have a car available. For this mission, NASA got us all matching silver Chrysler Sebring convertibles. (In the glory days of the space program, back in the 1960s and 1970s, astronauts were able to lease Corvettes for a dollar a year because Chevy dealers liked having them on the road, showing off their products. Those days are long gone.)

Gabby's nurse helped her into the front seat of the car. Gloria and the Capitol Police supervisor, Lu Cochran, hopped in the back. (Like Gabby, they'd been given medical clearance to be with me.) We took off, fast, with Aerosmith's "Dream On" on the car radio and *Endeavour* and its launchpad tower rising ahead of us.

When we showed up at the gate, the security officer was surprised to see me. "You can't drive all the way up to the pad," he said. I told him I'd just do a loop or two around the inside perimeter. He let me through.

It was a blast as we sped around the shuttle with the wind in our faces. Gabby's close-cropped hair was undisturbed, and she loved looking up at *Endeavour,* just hanging there off the side of the big orange external fuel tank and the solid rocket boosters. Seeing the space shuttle up close at the pad is always an awe-inspiring experience.

Later, I got a call from one of my managers at NASA. She had heard I was driving around the launchpad and wanted to know why. That was a time when technicians were fueling the orbital maneuvering engines, and it was considered a hazardous operation. Unessential vehicles weren't supposed to be out there.

"The security guard let me in," I said. "I wanted to let my wife have a look."

"You were speeding on your way to the pad, too," she said. The speed limit on the beach road behind the launchpad is thirty-five.

"Well, I always speed when I'm out there before a launch," I said. "How fast was I going? A hundred?"

"You were clocked at seventy-five," she said.

"Seventy-five?" I answered. "I was trying to go a hundred! I ran out of room."

She didn't like my attitude and I didn't like her phone call. One hundred and thirty-three space shuttle crews before this one had sped all over the Kennedy Space Center and now it was an issue? My manager was making a point. "I want to make sure I made the right decision in assigning you to this flight," she said.

I understood she had a job to do. But to me, it was classic NASA Astronaut Office management bullshit: Try to track down people's little misdemeanors and then rag on them over them.

"OK," I told my manager. "I'll try not to speed in the space shuttle."

* * *

The day before the scheduled launch, astronaut Dan Tani, who'd been a crew member on my first mission, had the job of giving more than a hundred people from our extended families a presentation about STS-134. They all gathered in an auditorium at the Kennedy Space Center. Dan was the man for the job. My crew and I weren't there, but we heard he put together a great slide show.

"OK, let's look at the key players tomorrow," he said, and then he showed a slide of Prince William and Kate Middleton, with their ranks: prince and commoner. "Let me show you the vehicle which will be used tomorrow," Dan said. Instead of a photo of the shuttle, he flashed a slide of the 1902 State Landau carriage, which would transport the bride and groom. "It's a six-horsepower carriage. Top speed: 5.4 miles per hour. At NASA, we call that Mach 0.007105."

When his royal-wedding jokes ended, Dan showed slides of me and my crew in training, and our loved ones cheered each photo. It was like a pep rally. He told them about our mission. "You have to bring every spare part with you," he said. "You don't have FedEx to bring more parts." He talked about why we wear those bulky orange suits. "The suits have a pressurized environment, in case they have to bail out at a high altitude." And he used the phrase PEU to describe how the shuttle stood on the launchpad. "That's 'Pointy End Up,'" he said, explaining that astronauts have to get their bearings when they enter it. "It's like turning your house on its side. You wouldn't recognize it."

Dan said it was good that Gabby's story had brought more media to the launch. "Because of all the attention this mission is getting," he said, "we can show the world the capabilities of this magnificent machine and crew."

When Dan was finished, buses were waiting to take our family members several miles away to the launchpad, where my crew and I would show up to meet them. It's another NASA tradition—the extended family farewell.

Everyone stood behind a rope line, facing the launchpad. On my earlier flights, we stood with a ditch separating the crew from the guests, so the ritual came to be called "the wave across the ditch." This time, the six of us drove up in our convertibles, got out, and stood together on the other side of the rope. Because we were still in quarantine, we couldn't get too close to anyone. I always feel like a circus animal as everyone takes photos at the wave across the ditch.

Because the crew's wives had been given physicals and deemed healthy, they were allowed to join us for photos. Gabby had been in these photos during my past missions, but since she was still not up to being seen publicly, she wasn't there for this one. So it was just me, my five crew members, and their five wives. We were all lined up and everyone was clicking away. I smiled through it, but I was thinking of how the sixth wife belonged in those photos.

Twice in the history of the shuttle program—the final launches of

Challenger and *Columbia*—the wave across the ditch was the last time astronauts' loved ones saw them alive. Everyone on both sides of the rope—astronauts, wives, siblings, cousins, parents—was aware of that.

Claudia and Claire were allowed to cross the rope line and give me a hug goodbye. Those were long hugs. Then it fell to me to end the goodbye ceremony.

"OK," I said to my crew. "Time to go."

We all got back into our convertibles, waved goodbye, and sped away to crew quarters.

*   *   *

That night, alone in our quarters, my crew and I watched *The Patriot,* starring Mel Gibson. Gabby doesn't like Mel anymore, since his infamous anti-Semitic remarks a few years back. I understood that. But I had watched *The Patriot* on the evening before my first launch in 2001, and that mission went well. I thought it would be good luck to rewatch the movie.

A lot of astronauts are prone to superstition and ritual. My brother in 2010 flew into space aboard a Russian Soyuz rocket. He talks about the half-century-old tradition in which cosmonauts urinate on the right rear wheel of the bus used to take them to the launch site. They do this because Yuri Gagarin, the first man in space, did that before his first flight—and lived. Some female cosmonauts have tossed a cup of their urine on the right rear wheel. (Scott joined his comrades by the back wheel of the bus before his mission, but he couldn't go.)

By the time I woke up on the morning of launch day, I wasn't thinking superstitiously. I was thinking pragmatically.

While Prince William and his new wife, Kate Middleton, were parading through the streets of London, I put a chair on my bed. Then I got into the bed, on my back, and put my feet on the chair for a while. I'd always do this before a mission. I was trying to get the fluid to shift so my kidneys could get rid of some of the urine that otherwise would soak my diaper during the launch, scheduled for 3:47 p.m. I didn't want a wet sock like I had at the Terminal Countdown Test.

All I had to do after that was jump in the shower, shave, and then it was off to the races.

As it turned out, the race never got started. Just before noon, my crew and I were all suited up and set to depart for the launchpad when we got word that there was an electrical problem. It was a glitch affecting the hydraulic power system that would move the shuttle's engines and flight controls during ascent and reentry. We still boarded the astrovan and headed for the pad, but halfway there, the mission was scrubbed. We were disappointed, as were an estimated 700,000 people who were already lining the beaches or were on their way to viewing sites.

While we were making the U-turn to return to crew quarters, President Obama was in Alabama, visiting areas devastated by tornadoes. He and his family had planned to fly from there to Cape Canaveral. Even though the launch had been postponed, they decided to come anyway.

When the president arrived at the Kennedy Space Center, I joked with him. "I bet you were hoping to see a rocket launch today," I said.

He said he'd come to see me, my crew, and Gabby.

Because we were still in quarantine—it was still possible the launch would go ahead three days later—the NASA physician Joe Dervay had to make a request. "Mr. President, is it OK if I examine both you and your wife?"

"Absolutely," the president said. "We don't want the astronauts getting sick."

Joe took their temperatures, looked down their throats, looked in their ears, and listened with a stethoscope. They were healthy.

Before the president and First Lady entered the room where Gabby was waiting, I prepped them. "Gabby is going to feel like she wants to say a lot, but she won't be able to," I said. "She'll be a little nervous. She might say things more than once. She might repeat what you say to stay engaged."

The president thanked me for the heads-up.

When the Obamas entered the room to see Gabby, she was sitting. She thought it appropriate to get to her feet, but she stood up so quickly that she almost fell. My brother, Scott, had to reach over and grab her. It was lucky she didn't hit the ground because she wasn't wearing her helmet. (She had asked to leave it off when the president visited, and for that special moment, her nurse had said it would be OK.)

Once Gabby was steady on her feet, the president hugged her and told her she looked great. The last time he'd seen her was in the hospital in Tucson, several days after the shooting, and she had been comatose. The time before that was at the White House, when he noticed her new haircut.

"How are you feeling, Gabby?" the president asked.

"Fine, how are you?" she answered. She had mastered that simple exchange.

President Obama told her that the country was wishing her well, that he was proud of her, and that she needed to get back to Washington. It would have been more intimate if they could have sat together. Everyone standing there was a little awkward. But Gabby wanted to stand to show respect to the president and to show she could do it.

The Obamas stayed about ten minutes. "Thank you for coming," Gabby said as they were leaving.

After that, the president met my crew and toured the facilities with his family. He was in good spirits, relaxed and friendly. None of us knew it at the time, but that very morning, he had made one of the most important decisions of his presidency. He had secretly authorized the military operation that would lead, two days later, to the death of Osama bin Laden. Looking back, the president's poker face was perfect. He's obviously a man who can compartmentalize things.

His daughters, Malia and Sasha, spent some time that afternoon with Claudia and Claire. I later texted Claudia, asking what it was like meeting them. She texted back: "One tall. One short. Both nice."

Gabby later said she was "bummed" the launch was scrubbed, but we both agreed that, despite the disappointments, it had been an exciting day. I was confident that NASA technicians would figure out the electrical issues, and soon enough, my crew and I would be on our way.

Gabby's recovery had taught me a few things about patience, so I wasn't too antsy about this flight delay. I knew it was a decision made for safety. As the shuttle-launch director, Mike Leinbach, said that afternoon, "I'd rather be on the ground wishing I was flying than be in the air wishing I was on the ground."

* * *

The mission was delayed another seventeen days. So I was able to spend time with Gabby at TIRR, before heading back into another week of quarantine.

After we returned to Houston, Gabby and I went out publicly for the first time, joining our friends Tilman and Paige Fertitta at one of Tilman's restaurants, the Grotto. We drove Gabby over from TIRR, and when patrons in the restaurant saw her, they nodded politely and didn't disturb us. News did get out, however.

Later, Gabby and I were back at the hospital watching *The Office* on TV. A promo came on for the 10 p.m. news, with the big story of the day: "Gabrielle Giffords was seen out for the first time at a Houston restaurant . . ."

Gabby looked at me with this what-the-hell expression on her face, as if she and I had just arrived in an alternate universe.

Gabby was also able to go on an outing for Mother's Day, May 8, at another one of Tilman's restaurants, Landry's, down in Kemah. I'd bought her an orchid to give to her mom, and had her sign a card with her left hand. My girls came to the dinner, too, and for the first time ever, they gave her a Mother's Day card and a gift, a nice plant. Their gesture meant a lot to Gabby.

Still, I saw that Gabby had been feeling down that entire day. I didn't want to bring her down further by talking about it, but I thought she was depressed because Mother's Day had her thinking about her future. She'd likely never have children of her own. I held her hand at dinner, and she was mostly quiet and subdued.

The next day, May 9, I had to say goodbye to Gabby yet again and head back into quarantine. This stay in quarantine was harder. The launch was set for May 16 at 8:56 a.m., meaning my crew and I would have to wake up at 11:30 the night before to start getting ready. It was important for us to begin "sleep-shifting," adjusting our internal clocks, so by week's end we were sleeping from 4:00 to 11:30 p.m. Eastern Time, a schedule that would continue during the mission. It's not easy to change sleep patterns. It has to be done gradually, over days.

Luckily, there were no new mission delays, and we flew to Cape Canaveral on May 12. Gabby came three days later. The traditional family events this time were very limited since we'd already been through them before the scrubbed launch. But Gabby and I did meet again at the beach house, where we exchanged our wedding rings. Mine was too big for her to wear, so she decided to put it on a chain. "I'll see you in two weeks," I told her. "Call if you need me."

On the morning of the launch, a team of firemen helped carry Gabby, in her litter chair, up an external flight of stairs to the roof of NASA's Launch Control Center. She was joined there by Gloria, Claudia, Claire, Pia, my brother, Scott, and Piers Sellers. My crew members' wives and kids were there, too. It was a nice place to privately view the launch.

This time, everything went flawlessly.

My crew and I arrived at the launchpad three hours before liftoff. As I went about my many duties in the orbiter, I was able to take a few glances at the mirror on the glare shield. I could look back to where Gabby was on that rooftop, and think about improvements she might make over the next two weeks, while I was gone. She was scheduled to have surgery in the days ahead to reinsert the missing piece of her skull. Her head would have to be shaved again, of course, but the good news was that when a patient's skull is reattached, her cognition and ability to speak often improves. I wondered how I'd find Gabby on my return.

Just before liftoff, strapped into the commander's seat, I said a few words that were broadcast publicly. "On this final flight of space shuttle *Endeavour,*" I said, "we want to thank all the tens of thousands of dedicated employees who have put their hands on this incredible ship, and dedicated their lives to the space shuttle program.

"As Americans, we endeavor to build a better life than the generation before, and we endeavor to be a united nation. In those efforts we are often tested. This mission represents the power of teamwork, commitment, and exploration. It is in the DNA of our great country to reach for the stars and explore. We must not stop . . ."

Mike Leinbach, the launch director, replied, "Thank you, sir. And to do that, you are clear to launch *Endeavour.*"

"Copy that," I said. "Thank you."

After that, we were off, in an earthshaking rumble through heavy cloud cover, burning fuel at the rate of one thousand gallons per second.

I was told that Gabby smiled through the launch but she didn't say much. Claudia and Claire had shouted out the final ten seconds of the countdown, and then there were a lot of smiles and tears. Everyone felt relieved that we'd made it safely into orbit.

Part of the bond that Claudia and Claire have with Scott's kids, Samantha and Charlotte, is rooted in a shared understanding of what it's like to watch a father go off into space. STS-134's liftoff inspired Claire to later send me a beautiful e-mail about her feelings at all four of my launches. "When I hear the roar of the engines," she wrote, "tears start streaming down my face. Am I happy or am I sad? I watch you turn into a little white dot high in the sky, until I can't see you any longer. I'm not sure what state of mind I'm in. I just can't stop crying. I can't say whether I'm nervous, scared, excited, proud. It's everything bundled up and shaken up together. It's an emotion with no name."

Gabby knows well that nameless emotion. And, since January 8 especially, she knew well the inability to describe it. Minutes after the launch, searching for words, she said, "Good stuff."

Maybe that's as good a description as any.

After the shuttle was safely in space, my brother presented each of my girls with a single rose. He gave Gabby red tulips and a note from me reminding her how much I love her. On her neck, she was wearing my wedding ring on a silver chain. She vowed to wear it until my return.

By then, I was already in zero gravity, hurtling through space at 17,500 miles an hour. Gabby's wedding ring, on a leather string around my neck, was soon floating in front of me. It would float like that, a nice reminder of my marriage, for the entire mission.

CHAPTER NINETEEN

From a Distance

Thirty-two minutes after we were safely in space, traveling at a speed of five miles per second, my crew and I changed the shuttle's orbit by firing maneuvering engines. We had to get on the right path to meet the International Space Station two days later. Meanwhile, on the ground, Gabby would soon head to the airport for her return to Houston. Two days later, she'd be undergoing surgery to replace the missing piece of her skull. We both had a big week ahead of us.

As I settled in on the shuttle, I received my first e-mail from Gabby since January 8. She had painstakingly typed it out herself, with a nurse at her side. It read: "Hi Mark, Sweetie Pie. Feel fine. Proud. Tulips, thank you. KISSES. GABBY." I also found a handwritten letter from her packed with my belongings: "Come back soon and don't forget to bring me a star. Thanks for all you do. Love, Gabby." I knew Gabby hadn't come up with that line herself; a nurse had helped her compose the letter. And because Gabby was writing with her left hand, the letter looked like it was penned by a first grader. Still, it reminded me of how hard she was trying to communicate with everyone, and especially with me.

I didn't have time to dwell on any of this, of course. It was time to get to work.

For astronauts, the first day in space always felt tenuous. We were trying to adjust to weightlessness, and there was a long list of duties to address. Space shuttle missions were incredibly complex and very busy. It was easy to get behind schedule. I got my crew in the habit of saying, "If you're not early, you're late." We tried to stay ahead of the timeline, constantly working to build up some padding in the day's schedule for when things went wrong.

I admired each member of my crew, a talented group of veteran astronauts, and it meant a lot to me that they were wearing "Gabby" bracelets. The rubberized wristbands, sold to benefit a scholarship fund in memory of Gabe Zimmerman, had come to be called "Peace-Love-Gabby" bracelets. I didn't need my crew asking all the time about how Gabby was doing. Their wristbands let me know that they, too, had her in their hearts on the mission.

Each crew member had taken his own circuitous route into space and onto STS-134. But for all of us, our yearnings to be astronauts began in childhood.

Mission specialist Greg Chamitoff had been in Florida on a family vacation in July 1969 and actually saw the liftoff of Neil Armstrong's *Apollo 11*. Then six years old, he announced he wanted to be an astronaut and never wavered, getting a PhD in aeronautics and astronautics. He spent ten years applying for the astronaut program before being accepted. (The title of "mission specialist" is given to astronauts who are not the commander or the pilot. NASA wanted to give them a title, and that's what they settled on.)

Pilot Greg "Box" Johnson was also inspired to be an astronaut by *Apollo 11*. As a seven-year-old in 1969, he watched the launch on a black-and-white TV at his grandparents' home in Michigan. Box became a U.S. Air Force colonel, and like me, served in Desert Storm. He was one of the astronauts on the team that investigated the cause of the *Columbia* accident in 2003.

Mission specialist Mike Fincke loved watching spacewalking astronauts as a boy. "That's it!" he'd say. "That's what I want to do with my life." On STS-134, Mike would break the record for most time spent in space by an American astronaut—382 days. (A Russian cosmonaut holds the world record at 803 days.)

When lead spacewalker Drew Feustel was young, he assumed that most humans would be astronauts in the future, and he'd be one of them. He thought, mistakenly, that space-faring would be common-place. He grew up wanting to study rocks, especially moon rocks, and eventually got a PhD in geology. (A spacewalker is the astronaut who ventures outside the spacecraft. The technical term is an EVA astronaut. EVA stands for "extra-vehicular activity," which is one of many examples of how NASA uses technical acronyms to make the most amazing activities sound boring.)

Mission specialist Roberto Vittori landed a seat on STS-134 through the European Space Agency. A colonel in the Italian Air Force, Vittori was one of my students at the U.S. Naval Test Pilot School at Patuxent River, Maryland. His space dreams also began when he was young, but he figured, "I'm an Italian. How will I ever be able to go?" Lucky for him, the Italian Space Agency was established in 1988. He is now one of five Italians to have flown in space.

The six of us, all adventurers, our boyhood dreams achieved, had now grown into men on a mission. We needed to find our way to the International Space Station, an outpost the size of a football field, but a mere dot in the universe.

We approached the space station on Wednesday, May 18. While I would be manually flying the later parts of the approach and docking, the rendezvous required a meticulously choreographed effort by the entire crew. It was a six-hour process that required tremendous focus, attention to detail, and coordination between the crew and the team in the mission control center. It's a high-risk event to bring one spacecraft together with another spacecraft, when both are moving at 17,500 miles per hour. Though I knew Gabby was in surgery, I had to set aside my worries about her for those hours, so we could complete this procedure safely. It wasn't easy. A few times I had to say to myself: "Gabby will be fine. The doctors know what they're doing. She has people looking out for her. Focus, focus, focus."

I'd long ago learned to compartmentalize. More than one hundred times in my career as a naval aviator, I had to land on aircraft carriers in the dark of night. Doing that, you figure out fast that you can't let thoughts about the rest of your life interfere. Distractions could be deadly.

So it was on the space shuttle that day. During the rendezvous, I remained hyper-focused.

We performed multiple firings of our orbital maneuvering engines and used smaller jets to change our orbit and close in on the space station. For navigation, we started with a rough idea of the position of the space shuttle relative to the space station. Over time, we updated this geometry by improving our "state vector"—a calculation of position, speed, direction, and time—with sensors we had on board *Endeavour*. To dock with another spacecraft, you must have a really good idea of where you are and where the target spacecraft is. So we used a "star tracker" that optically tracked the space station to improve our state vector. (A star tracker determines a spacecraft's position by tracking stars. It's similar to how seafarers would use a sextant.)

Later in the approach, we tracked the space station with our Ku-band radar, which illuminated the target with electromagnetic radiation to determine its position and relative velocity. As we got closer still, we used a laser trajectory control system to give us an accurate picture of our position and closure on the space station. This system is similar to the laser devices police officers use to detect the speed of cars on a highway.

Using these systems, we were able to precisely place the orbiter about two thousand feet below the space station. At that point, it fell to me to take over manually and fly the shuttle for the final hour or so, sometimes looking out the window through an optical sight, which is similar to the sight of a gun. It is positioned in the shuttle's window.

The final few feet, as always, were stressful. We had practiced this many times in the simulator, but that can't replicate the thrill, tension, and difficulty of closing in on one million pounds of International Space Station with the planet Earth hovering below. As my crew completed the final items on the checklist, I inched closer, closing in at just one-tenth of a foot per second. At just two inches away, I commanded additional thrusters to fire to give us one final push, and then, with a heavy metallic *clunk,* we were docked.

We were about two hundred miles above the planet, somewhere over Chile, but I didn't know it at the time. I was just thankful that the rendezvous and docking went well. Our lead flight director, Gary Horlacher, called it "really silky smooth." I took a second to think of Gabby and then I went over the approach in my mind. The goal, as always, was to accomplish the docking as efficiently as possible, without mistakes or too much energy expended. At first, I didn't regret a single pulse of the jets I had made. (Looking back, maybe there's one pulse I might have skipped, but I'm still thinking about it.)

As the shuttle commander, I was the first of my crew members to go aboard the space station. It was my fourth visit. "It's good to be back," I said, greeting the six current residents on the station: three Russians, an Italian, and two Americans, including Ron Garan, one of my crew members from my previous flight on *Discovery*. My crew followed behind me and there were handshakes and hugs all around. During the six hours it took to rendezvous and dock, I was way too busy to check e-mail. It was a moot point anyway, because we were using the Ku-band antenna as our rendezvous radar. That antenna is also how we get data, including e-mail, up from and down to the ground. There was no way to access e-mail until after we docked and the ground crew had time to sync our mailboxes.

Once we settled in at the space station and completed all the work for the day, I finally opened up one of our shuttle laptops. I knew there would be e-mails stacked up—from Gloria, Pia, my brother, Gabby's doctors, the astronaut/family liaison Piers Sellers—with reports of the surgery. Floating on the flight deck of *Endeavour,* behind my pilot's seat, I waited for them to load, hoping for good news.

*   *   *

Before each mission, NASA would send out a memo to astronauts' loved ones, going over e-mail rules. Families were asked not to burden us with issues that could wait until we returned. They didn't want us distracted by reports that our kids were bickering or that we forgot to pay the power bill. If it wasn't urgent, NASA asked, hold the news.

At the same time, NASA would ask astronauts for a clear picture of how we'd want tragic events in our lives handled while we were in space. For STS-134, this was addressed in a short conversation with our flight surgeon, Joe Dervay. Each crew member had to decide what he wanted to know about the death, sickness, or injury of a loved one. What if one of our parents were to die? What if it was one of our children?

Dan Tani, my former crew member who'd given the presentation to astronauts' families before STS-134's launch, experienced just such a tragedy while aboard the International Space Station in 2007. His mother was killed by an oncoming train as she drove across a railroad track in a Chicago suburb. A NASA flight surgeon and Dan's wife informed him of his mom's death in a videoconference call. He had no choice but to remain in space for two more months.

In my case, before STS-134, Joe had asked me flat-out, "What do you want to be told if Gabby has a seizure, a bad fall, a blood clot, or if she dies? Do you want to know immediately? Do you want to know at all?"

On my three previous missions, I kept these conversations short and answered them in just three words: "Ask my brother." I figured he'd know what would be a major distraction for me, what I should be told immediately, and what should wait. This time it was different. On STS-134, I wanted all of the unvarnished details from Earth as soon as possible, no matter what. It had been a roller coaster of a ride over the previous months and I had been the primary decision-maker for my wife. I wasn't able to completely give that up.

I had authorized Gloria to have medical power of attorney in my absence, overseeing decisions regarding Gabby's care if I was unable to be contacted in space. I'm not a big hugger, but when I had said goodbye to Gloria at Cape Canaveral, I hugged her and kissed her on the cheek, thanking her for being the go-to person for Gabby while I was gone. "You don't have to thank someone for loving someone else," she said.

I knew I'd left Gabby in good hands, and as I imagined, Gloria's e-mails were direct. She told me whatever she knew when she knew it, and she didn't hold back on details when Gabby was in pain during recovery.

"Gabby seemed subdued while Dr. Kim shaved her head," Gloria wrote in one early e-mail to me. She was at Gabby's side for the shaving, along with Pia, Gabby's operations director, Jen Cox, and family friend Suzy Gershman. "We all applauded when her head was finished being shaved," Gloria wrote, "and though we all offered to get our heads shaved in solidarity, Gabby nixed the idea."

I had thought I would be with Gabby for this cranioplasty surgery. But given the repeated delays in the launch of the shuttle, the procedure needed to go on without me. It was important that Gabby have the piece of skull replaced at the optimal time for her recovery. Doctors advised against waiting for me to return from space. She was ready.

The surgery, led by Dr. Dong Kim at Memorial Hermann Hospital, was not terribly complicated for brain surgeons, and they assured us it was low-risk. Gabby was actually pretty upbeat about it because once her missing pieces of skull were replaced, she'd no longer have to wear that dreaded helmet. (Gabby's nurse, Kristy Poteet, wrote "5-17-11" on top of the helmet, so Gabby could be reminded of the last day she'd have to wear it.)

Pieces of Gabby's skull had been removed on January 8 to reduce the impact of her brain swelling. Those pieces were frozen and preserved, but the passing bullet had shattered much of the removed skull and contaminated the bone with germs. The doctors could have attempted to piece together the bigger parts like a jigsaw puzzle, but it wouldn't have been as smooth, strong, or clean as the ceramic implant they ended up using. The implant's structure and dimensions were computer-generated to exactly match the missing section of Gabby's skull, which was about the size of a person's hand with his fingers spread apart. (After her implant was in place, Gabby's Tucson neurosurgeon, Michael Lemole, successfully screwed together some of the larger pieces of Gabby's taupe-colored real skull, which showed the bullet's entry and exit holes. It now sits in a Tupperware container in our freezer.)

Gabby suffered from excessive buildup of cerebral spinal fluid after the shooting, and the doctors decided that it would require a permanent drain. So during the three-and-a-half-hour surgery to replace her skull with the implant, they added a tiny tube about the diameter and thickness of the cords used to charge cell phones. The tube snaked its way from Gabby's brain, down her neck, and through her chest to her abdomen. This cerebral shunt would permit drainage of the excess fluid. The doctors inserted the tube so it was barely noticeable, running it down the left side of her neck just under her skin.

I talked to my brother and Gloria after the surgery, and also got reports from a press conference in which Dr. Kim said that everything had come together nicely—bone, plate, and skin. He explained that Gabby had developed mild hydrocephalus, which means "water in the head" in Latin. "It's a condition that develops in many patients who have a brain injury," he said. Every day, all of us produce about six ounces of clear cerebral spinal fluid that bathes our brain. That fluid is continually reabsorbed in our bodies. "When there is an injury," Dr. Kim said, "that reabsorption can become partially clogged, just like having a partially clogged drain. When that happens, the fluid can build up, and that's something that can be treated with a shunt. You can have it for the rest of your life and it doesn't impede anything."

The reattached skull and the shunt would allow Gabby to have a more vigorous rehabilitation. Without the fluid pressure, it was possible she'd concentrate better and think more clearly. Without the helmet, she'd feel more confident that she was getting closer to her previous life.

Dr. Kim said he viewed skull restoration as "the end of a journey," with the next eventual step being outpatient therapy. He expected that Gabby, like other patients, would soon feel a renewed "sense of wholeness" and improved morale. The side of her head had been swollen after the shooting, and then it was sunken in. Now she'd look more like herself. "I started calling her 'Gorgeous Gabby' today," Dr. Kim said at the press conference.

It was reassuring to me, being so far away, to hear Dr. Kim's new nickname for Gabby, and to get an e-mail from him. "Everything is going well," he wrote. "Hope you are enjoying your ride. I will take good care of Gabby."

I thought back to the days before I went into space, when I got into several discussions with Dr. Kim about the possibility of doing the surgery without shaving Gabby's head. Occasionally, neurosurgeons will do this at the request of patients or their families. Gabby had just spent four months regrowing her hair, and I wanted her to have the opportunity to keep it if she wanted.

After Dr. Kim and I talked, I presented Gabby with the data. "Gabby," I said, "if we leave your hair as is during this surgery, you'll have about a three percent increased risk of infection."

I didn't need to go any further. "Shave it off!" she said.

That was the end of the discussion. It was nice to see that Gabby was taking charge of her own recovery.

* * *

The hours and days after surgery were not easy for Gabby, who left the operating room with her head wrapped in bandages. "She's back in her room with a yellow turban on her head, asleep," Gloria wrote in an e-mail. "They may give her blood. Her color is a bit sallow."

Gloria continued to give me news without sugarcoating it. "Gabby is in a lot of pain and became nauseous when they did a CAT scan," she wrote in one e-mail. In another, she explained three attempts to insert an IV line. "It was extremely painful for Gabby, even with some painkillers first." In a third e-mail, Gloria wrote: "She has a headache and some swelling on the left side. Perfectly normal, say her doctors. I have the NASA channel on so Gabby can hear your voice while she sleeps." (While I was in space, Gabby asked that NASA TV be left on in her room twenty-four hours a day.)

On Thursday, May 19, as e-mails updating me on Gabby's condition continued arriving in my inbox, my crew undertook the most crucial part of our mission: the installation of the seven-ton Alpha Magnetic Spectrometer. We began at 12:56 a.m. Houston time, when Drew and Roberto used the shuttle's robotic arm to extract this giant cosmic ray detector from *Endeavour*'s cargo hold. Then it was handed off to the space station's robotic arm, controlled by Box and Greg, who began the process of attaching it to the space station's exterior metal truss. By 5 a.m., the job was done, and a couple hours after that, the machine began sending data about the high-energy particles in cosmic rays back to a team of scientists on Earth. The scientists planned to monitor the particles passing through the device—via data collected twenty-five thousand times a second—twenty-four hours a day for at least ten years.

"We're seeing an enormous amount of data coming down," Dr. Ting, the lead scientist, said. "We're very pleased."

I was incredibly relieved as the Spectrometer was latched into place. Six hundred physicists, engineers, and technicians built this machine at a cost of $2 billion, and it was up to us to get it attached to the space station. "Whew, that's a relief!" I said to my crew when they were done. "You guys did a really great job!"

Before launching, I had visions of us dropping the thing and it floating off into space. Or we'd get it installed and it wouldn't work, making it a very expensive hood ornament for the space station. All bad outcomes. At the end of flight day four, we had completed our primary mission objective. There would be dozens of others, including four dangerous spacewalks by three of my crew members to maintain and upgrade the space station. During one eight-hour spacewalk, they connected hoses to transfer ammonia to the station's cooling system. During another, they inspected and lubricated a joint for the station solar arrays, which generate the station's electricity.

Every day was full and challenging. But so far, so good.

* * *

Gabby kept improving after her surgery. The shunt was working well, and the fluid between her skull and brain had started to get back to normal. "Stop the presses!" Gloria e-mailed me, two days after the surgery. "Gabby just said, 'I am optimistic!'"

Gloria was always reading books aloud to Gabby, and the latest was *Learning to Breathe* by photojournalist Alison Wright. The book traces the author's spiritual and physical recovery after almost dying in a bus crash in Laos in 2000. Gabby and Gloria found it very inspirational.

Gloria told me that as she read, Gabby liked to close her eyes. "Are you still awake?" Gloria would ask. "Do you want me to keep reading?"

"Yes, yes," Gabby whispered, still weak from the surgery.

A week after the cranioplasty, Gloria sent me an e-mail: "Tonight, Gabby was wide awake through the reading, and she nodded when the text told of the author's determination to heal and never give up. She's getting there, Mark."

Those were tough days for Gloria. Spencer had to have surgery on his back, so Gloria found herself shuttling back and forth between wings of Memorial Hermann Hospital, visiting her daughter and then her husband. Sometimes she'd take Gabby in a wheelchair to see Spencer.

I tried to phone Gabby every day when she was awake, I wasn't working, and we had a phone link to the ground. I got through on most days. Then one day, Gloria sent me an e-mail: "When I told Gabby you were trying to call her, her heart rate went up three points." She said it reminded her of the popular Valentine line: "My heart beats for you." She also e-mailed me a photo of Gabby, still wearing my wedding ring on her necklace.

When I could, I tried to send Gabby short updates on how the mission was going. One problem early on was a "wardrobe malfunction." Before the launch, when I was so busy with Gabby's care and my mission training, there were things that I just didn't have time for: inconsequential stuff, like trying on the pants I'd wear in flight. On the second day of the flight, I put on my first pair of pants and realized that there had been a mistake. All of my pants were made for someone who was way taller than six feet. The pants weren't even close to my size. Fortunately, my brother had left pants on the space station, which I found and used for the rest of the flight. It was only one pair, but it was better than freakishly long, giant pants.

As the sixteen-day mission continued, my crew and I were given some time in our schedule for special appearances, what the media sometimes refers to as a "cosmic call." One highlight was an eighteen-minute videoconference with Pope Benedict XVI, the first-ever call to space by a pope. "Welcome aboard, your holiness," I said.

I was touched that Pope Benedict mentioned Gabby, who was able to watch our encounter on NASA TV. Speaking to those of us on the space station, the pontiff said, "It must be obvious to you how we all live together on one Earth, and how absurd it is that we fight and kill each other. I know that Mark Kelly's wife was a victim of a serious attack, and I hope her health continues to improve."

We were grateful to receive a blessing for our safety from the Pope, and I got a kick out of the e-mail I received afterward from Gloria. She told me that Gabby was intrigued by the Renaissance painting of Jesus that was behind the Pope as he spoke.

Another conference call that we found very meaningful hit closer to home. One morning in space—a Sunday night in the United States— Mike Fincke and I fielded questions via a live video feed from four hundred students at Mesa Verde Elementary School in Tucson. Many of the students were classmates or friends of Christina-Taylor Green, the nine-year-old girl killed on January 8.

The kids, their teachers, those of us in space—we all knew the subtext. But I tried hard to be upbeat, like a friendly adult brought in for show-and-tell. I wore a red Arizona T-shirt, and when the Earth-to-space link was established, I said with enthusiasm: "Mesa Verde Elementary School, how do you hear?"

The kids cheered wildly, and then, one by one, stepped up to the microphone. Their questions—and questions I later received from students at Tucson's Gridley Middle School—were familiar to me. When Claudia and Claire were younger, I often spoke to their classes about life as an astronaut. I'd also given talks to other groups of students many times.

One of the students from Tucson asked how I adjusted to zero gravity.

"The first time you fly, it takes a while to get used to it," I answered. "There's no up and down anymore, and the fluids in your body shift. You don't feel so well. But this is my fourth flight, and it seems like my body remembers what this is all about. I can adjust more quickly."

"How do you sleep in space?" another student asked.

"You could sleep floating around," I said, "but you'd bump into other people and wake them up. We sleep in sleeping bags with a bunch of straps and hooks. Sometimes, people sleep on the ceiling. It takes a while to get used to. My first night in space I got in my sleeping bag and rolled over on my side, like I would in bed. That was dumb. There is no side, or up or down. You might as well stay in the position you're in."

The next question: "How do you shower in space?"

"We don't have a shower," I said. "We take a bath like someone would in a hospital bed, with a towel, water, and soap. You rub soap on and wipe it off later. It's not the greatest, but it works for two weeks."

Another student asked what inspired me to be an astronaut. I thought this was a good chance to mention Christina, and how she'd been a dreamer.

"Over the last four months," I said, "I've come to admire your classmate, Christina Green, very much. I've learned a lot about her.

"When I was Christina's age, that's when Apollo astronauts were walking on the moon. I remember watching that on TV and thinking if I worked really hard in school and really, really concentrated, maybe someday I would have the opportunity to fly in space." I didn't exactly tell the kids the full story—that I was a late bloomer on the academic front. I figured it was better to just encourage them to start early.

As the session ended, I had a surprise for the Mesa Verde kids. "Since my wife, Congresswoman Giffords, is from Tucson, I spend a lot of time there," I said. I showed them the Mesa Verde Mountain Lions 2010–2011 yearbook I had brought with me into space. I held it up in front of the camera. "I'll get a picture of this with the Earth in the background, and I'll bring it back and hand it over to your school," I promised. "I'm opening up to the pages here honoring Christina. It's a very nice yearbook. Mike and I just signed it, and I'll get my other crew members to sign it."

I twirled the yearbook and it floated like a spinning top in front of me as I waved goodbye to Christina's friends and classmates.

*　*　*

Gabby had selected U2's "Beautiful Day" as my crew's wake-up song during my 2006 mission, back when we were dating. Bono, the band's lead singer, once explained that the song is about someone who has suffered great losses in his life, yet finds joy in what he still has. That had meaning for Gabby, long before she was injured.

Gabby once said to me, "Mark, I really love you, but there is one person on the planet I'd leave you for."

"Who's that?" I asked.

"Bono," she said.

"Well, I like Bono, too," I told her. But I'd never give up without a fight.

Before the launch of STS-134, by coincidence, I received a surprise e-mail from Bono. He had an idea he wanted to discuss with me and asked if we could speak by phone. His idea turned out to be a creative one. He wanted me to send greetings from space to every city on his current tour, while letting some of the lyrics to "Beautiful Day" float in front of me.

I thought that sounded kind of cool, and told him that if NASA approved, I was game. NASA would likely let me get the video done during some of my free time on the mission.

Bono then told me that after Gabby was shot and he saw her picture on TV, he had a feeling he had met her before. He had someone look at the photos he had taken once with members of Congress. He located the picture. Gabby has that same photo framed and on her desk.

I told Bono about Gabby's crush on him, and that I was sure she'd get a kick out of our plan, too.

On our first morning in space on this mission, Claudia and Claire selected "Beautiful Day" for our wake-up music because they knew Gabby would appreciate it. Later in the mission, with NASA's approval,

I taped the short video clips for about thirty cities on the U2 tour. "Hello, Chicago, from the International Space Station . . ." "Hello, Montreal . . ." "Hello, Seattle . . ." "Hello, Moncton . . ." How the hell do you pronounce "Moncton"? And where is Moncton, anyway? (The answer is New Brunswick, Canada, but at the time I had no idea.)

I floated the words in front of me but they kept drifting too far away. It took more than a few takes to get it right.

It all looked pretty terrific in concert. Each night from the stage, Bono would say, "This next song is dedicated to a woman who serves her country and nearly lost her life in that service." Then Bono looked up at the giant screen. "Imagine a man looking down on us from two hundred miles up, looking down on our beautiful crowded planet, where borders disappear and cities connect into a beautiful web of lights, where the conflicts of the world are silent. What would he say to us? What words would be in his mind?"

As he spoke, I was shown floating the words: "Seven Billion. One nation. Imagination. It's a Beautiful Day."

"What's on your mind, Commander Kelly?" Bono asked.

"I'm looking forward to coming home," I said, floating closer to the camera, and then away. "Tell my wife I love her very much. She knows." (That's a line from David Bowie's "Space Oddity.")

As the crowd cheered each night and I flickered off the screen, U2 would begin the opening notes of "Beautiful Day."

In an e-mail thanking me, Bono explained how the video is received in concert. "It's quite a special moment," he wrote, "as it slowly dawns on people what you're doing with the weightless word puzzle. What's interesting to me is the level of love and support in the crowd for Gabby. The crowd roars."

Gabby was invited to see the moment live in concert, but given her rehab schedule and her difficulty traveling, it never happened. Like thousands of other people, Gabby watched the video—"NASA Commander Mark Kelly appears at U2 360"—on YouTube. Bono is quite charming in it, but she vowed to stay with me.

*   *   *

On May 30, the day the stitches were removed from Gabby's head, we undocked from the International Space Station. On June 1, it was time to come home. The landing was set for the early morning hours on the runway at Cape Canaveral, and I knew it would be tough for Gabby to return to see it. I told her I'd get to Houston as fast as I could.

Our flight directors said the mission had so far gone "absolutely flawlessly," but I wanted to finish with a flawless landing, too. It was my job to bring *Endeavour* safely to the runway, and I didn't want anyone saying I was distracted by the issues swirling in my personal life.

Shuttle commanders worked very hard to make sure that our landings were as close to perfect as possible. We practice this thousands of times in the shuttle training aircraft—a modified Gulfstream—and in the shuttle simulator. After sixteen days in space, however, it was not an easy thing to do. We'd be dehydrated during reentry because when fluids shift in zero G, astronauts end up passing a significant amount of urine. At the same time, our neurovestibular systems were not quite right. It was not uncommon to be dizzy and tired. Then there was the added pressure of knowing that every detail of the approach and landing are highly scrutinized by NASA's engineers, the flight control team, and your own colleagues in the astronaut office. It was a lot of pressure, and this landing was at night, which added another level of difficulty.

At 1:29 a.m., we initiated the de-orbit burn. We entered the Earth's atmosphere at 2:03 a.m., like a glider, with no engines. As the orbiter hits the atmosphere at such a high speed, an incredible amount of friction is generated. This friction strips the atmosphere of some electrons, creating plasma, which is a state of matter that has some properties of a gas but can flow like a liquid. It doesn't take long for the wings and fuselage to heat up to thousands of degrees, and you are literally flying in the middle of a giant fireball of plasma. There is a bright orange, eerie glow outside. You can't help but think of the crew of *Columbia*.

I'd been in the fireball three other times, but this would be my second landing at the controls. The space shuttle was never known to be a great flying machine in the atmosphere. It is actually a lousy airplane with some pretty objectionable flying qualities. It flies about as well as a Coke machine. Imagine throwing one of those out the back of an airplane. The space shuttle didn't fly much better.

I had wanted the shuttle's wheels to cross the edge of the runway— called the threshold—at an altitude of thirty-two feet. I was at thirty-two feet. At our landing weight, our ideal touch-down speed would be 195 knots. I touched down at 191. You want to touch down at a descent rate of no greater than three feet per second. I touched down at less than one foot per second. I wanted to start braking at 120 knots. I got on the brakes at 119.

I was really happy with the approach, the landing, and the numbers, which I knew would be closely analyzed.

I had spent the sixteen-day mission vowing not to screw up, not to let anyone say I shouldn't have flown. Now, at 2:35 a.m., here we were back on Earth and I was feeling tired, proud—and relieved.

As the commander, I was the last one out of the ship on the runway. I ducked my head to exit the hatch, then turned around and went back inside for one more look.

There was an impromptu ceremony on the runway, recognizing the legacy of *Endeavour,* which would never fly again. It was bittersweet as we stood there. I knew that, like the shuttle behind me, I'd never again return to space.

The space shuttle program was about to end, and I didn't think I was suited for a desk job in the astronaut office. I wouldn't be too enthusiastic about telling other astronauts not to drive so fast at the Kennedy Space Center. Besides, there wouldn't be too many astronauts in Florida for the foreseeable future. NASA's next launch vehicle was many years away from being ready to fly.

I didn't say it that night, but I pretty much knew I'd soon be retiring from the Navy—and from NASA. That would be my last flight as an astronaut and my last as a naval aviator after twenty-five years of service. Still, it felt like the moment was right. Best of all, I'd be able to have more time with Gabby.

* * *

I e-mailed Gloria to say I'd landed, but it was too late to call Gabby. She was sleeping. I was able to phone her in the morning, and she was so excited to learn I'd returned safely. She told me she loved me three times.

Because we landed so late after a very long day, we weren't able to head home until Thursday, June 2. There was a quick press conference when we arrived in Houston, and then I went north to TIRR.

I walked into Gabby's room at about 5 p.m., earlier than she expected, and found her still putting on her lipstick. It was just the third time she'd worn makeup since January 8. Though her head was wrapped from surgery, she'd dressed up for me, wearing jeans and a black camisole.

After we hugged and kissed and hugged again, we sat down together. I was still getting used to gravity, so it was nice to sit in one place, peacefully. "I've got your wedding ring," I said to Gabby. "Would you like it back?"

I gave it to her, and she took my ring from the chain on her neck and put it on my finger. We remained in her room, contentedly, for a couple of hours, just holding hands, both relieved that we were together.

CHAPTER TWENTY

Great Signs of Progress

For most of our relationship, Gabby was never overly sentimental about her birthday. A card, a cake, good wishes—that was enough. We were in separate cities sometimes on her birthday, and on mine. We both understood.

Still, I had to muster up some courage to tell Gabby that I'd be out of town, in London, on Wednesday, June 8, her forty-first birthday. I felt bad that I'd be leaving her, especially since I already had been gone for so long in quarantine and then in space.

At first, Gabby didn't register any objection when I said I'd be away. She listened as I explained that I had agreed, before the launch of STS-134, to join British businessman Richard Branson at a gathering of colleagues and entrepreneurs he was hosting at his home. One of Branson's companies, Virgin Galactic, is working to launch space science missions as well as suborbital space-tourism flights. As I contemplated what my post-NASA life might look like, I thought it was important to meet a creative thinker like Branson. Maybe there was a way to be involved somehow in his space exploration efforts.

"I might not get another opportunity like this to spend time with him," I told Gabby, adding that our friend Tilman was going to fly over with me. We'd be gone just four days. Gabby listened and said OK.

She remembered that I had come through for her on her fortieth birthday, helping her friends throw a surprise party with a mariachi band. This forty-first birthday was a milestone, I knew. She almost didn't live to see it. But she didn't seem especially upset by the idea that I'd be away.

On the Saturday night before Gabby's birthday, Tilman and Paige hosted a lovely party for her at their house. She had been spending some weekends away from TIRR, staying with me at their guesthouse.

About fifty people came to the party. We invited family members, doctors, hospital staffers, astronauts, and a few friends from Tucson. Despite all she had been through, Gabby looked beautiful. She wore a gold chain with replicas of various patches from my space shuttle missions as medallions. Her hair was just starting to grow in from the cranioplasty, and the shunt under her scalp and down her neck was barely visible. The lines of incisions from her surgery were pronounced, but Gabby chose not to cover her head with a scarf or wig. Gloria described Gabby's attitude: "The scars are there. You might as well all take a look."

The party was noisy, which at that stage in Gabby's recovery made for too much stimulation. At one point, a friend who hadn't seen her since she was injured came over to talk to her. Holding her hand, he soon became emotional. Then Gabby started crying, too. The evening sort of fell apart from there.

At about 8 p.m., Gabby said she wanted to call it a night and excused herself. "Wiped out," she said. "Wiped out." She returned to the guesthouse with her nurse Vivian Lim and got ready for bed while the party continued without her. In Gabby's honor, Brad Holland, her friend and neighbor from Tucson, sat down at the piano. He played "Tomorrow," the song from *Annie,* and Gloria sang along with him. I wasn't sure if Gabby, in bed over in the guesthouse, could hear it. Everyone wished she were still there. When I came back later to check on her, she was sound asleep.

Tilman and I headed overseas two days later. We met Richard Branson at his home, which wasn't a place I'd expect a billionaire to live in. It was kind of ordinary, in a typical British suburb. Richard asked me to give a short, impromptu speech about my space flight and how Gabby was doing to those in attendance, five hundred successful entrepreneurs and other associates, mostly from the United Kingdom. I wasn't sure what, if anything, would come of the visit, but I enjoyed seeing how engaged Branson was in the future of space exploration. I sat next to him at dinner, and I was inspired listening to his ambitious goals. We spoke of how a revolutionary rocket system could be built to deliver a passenger from New York to Europe in thirty minutes. We'd do that in the space shuttle. His goal was to privatize that capability.

Given the stresses in my life the past six months—Gabby's injury, the mission—Tilman suggested that before we returned to the States we could spend one day relaxing on his boat, which was docked in Monaco. "You could use the break," he said.

Many people had told me that as a caregiver, I'd need a respite once in a while. I didn't think it was such a terrible idea to spend a day on Tilman's boat.

But I soon realized that my whole trip wasn't sitting well with Gabby. She was mad at me for going, and blamed Tilman as a co-conspirator. I called Gabby the night before her birthday and she hardly spoke to me. She handed the phone to Gloria.

"She's pissed at you," Gloria said.

On June 8, Gabby had her usual six-hour regimen of physical, occupational, and speech therapy. A portion of the physical therapy was done in a pool. After that, hospital staffers, her parents, and some friends shared cake and cupcakes. Her staffers phoned in from their offices in Washington, Tucson, and Sierra Vista and sang "Happy Birthday." When I called her that day, I could feel her cold shoulder through the phone. She accepted my birthday wishes and then she was done with me.

I returned to Houston on Thursday night, June 9, and when I came into Gabby's room, she wouldn't talk to me or look at me. Finally, she spoke.

"I am mad at me!" she said.

She wasn't the type of woman who'd blame herself when it was really the man in her life who'd screwed up. I knew that. "I think you mean you're mad at *me*," I replied.

"Yes," Gabby snapped, and now the words came perfectly. "Yes, Mark, I am mad at you!"

She didn't have much else to say to me for the rest of the night. In all our time together, she'd never been that upset with me.

Part of it was that, since the shooting, her emotions often seemed magnified. When she was happy, she was really happy. When she was sad, she could get very sad. But in this case, I knew I was at fault. I shouldn't have been gone on her birthday. I shouldn't have taken that one day in Monaco.

I came into Gabby's room the next morning and she rolled her wheelchair around so that her back was to me. I asked Kristy, the nurse, if she'd give us some private time.

After Kristy left the room, I moved my chair around and went to hold Gabby's right hand. Using her good left hand, she lifted my hand off of hers and plopped it back in my lap.

I tried to explain myself. "Sweetie, we talked about my trip ahead of time," I said. "You told me it was OK. I was only gone four days. And it was a pretty important opportunity."

Gabby glared at me. Then she rolled her wheelchair out of the room.

I ended up talking to Carl Josehart, the chief executive officer at TIRR, who used to be a marriage counselor. He sat down with both of us to help iron things out. He started by asking Gabby to express her feelings.

"Mad," she said. "I'm mad."

"Well, that's understandable," Carl said. "Mark was away for several weeks, then he came home for a few days and then he was gone again. A lot of wives wouldn't like that."

Carl asked me to tell Gabby how I was feeling.

I wanted to explain myself. "Honey, you know I'm in this with you for the long haul," I said. "This is a lifelong marathon that you and I are on together. I'm not going anywhere. But early on, after you were injured, people gave me advice. They said I'd need a life outside of caring for you or I'd get burned out. I'll need my own time sometimes."

That said, I knew I needed to admit that, in the case of her birthday, I had made a mistake. "I thought I could sneak away for four or five days. Boy, was I wrong. I wish I could undo all this and make a different decision. But I can't. I just hope you'll forgive me."

Gabby is a very smart woman. She understood my commitment to her, and appreciated my willingness to admit to screwing up. She accepted my apology, reached over, and gave me a kiss.

"Could you forgive Tilman, too?" I asked.

She smiled. "Yes, Tilman, too."

* * *

Given Gabby's continuous improvement, physically and cognitively, her doctors at TIRR set her release date for June 15. She was walking better. Her ability to comprehend what people were saying was at 99 percent or better. The thin scar on her forehead was fading. After five months, she was ready to go.

Once she was released, she'd become an outpatient, returning to one of TIRR's satellite facilities for daily rehab. "Gabby is on the verge of complete sentences," said Angie, her speech therapist, who expected great progress in the weeks and months to come.

Tilman and Paige invited us to move into their guesthouse, closer to downtown. "Stay three years if you want," said Tilman, whose generosity seemed to know no limit. But Gabby felt she'd be more comfortable at my home, twenty-five miles south in League City, even though that meant she'd be spending a lot more time in the car being driven to daily rehab.

As her departure date approached, Gabby got sentimental about TIRR.

She had almost no memory of anything she experienced between January 8 and her arrival in Houston on January 21. TIRR was the place where she pretty much woke up and became aware after the shooting. In a lot of ways, the rehab hospital was now a comfortable and safe place for her. It was home.

Sure, she had complained about being there. Especially in March and April, she often said "Gotta get out of here" or "Get me out of here!" But as she got closer to leaving, Gabby was having separation anxiety. She didn't say she wanted to stay, but she stopped saying she wanted to leave.

Gabby oversaw the packing up of her belongings. She pointed out which items should be loaded into boxes bound for Tucson, for storage, or for my house. All the posters—of Tucson, the Grand Canyon, me and Gabby—were taken down from the walls, and her mom's artwork was parceled out to the doctors and nurses whose portraits she had painted.

On the day she said goodbye to Dr. Kim, he asked her how she felt. "Emotional," she answered.

As a going-away present, nurses on the night shift gave Gabby a journal they'd been writing in after she went to sleep. Their entries, often unsigned, were addressed to Gabby, chronicling her progress at TIRR. The nurses hoped she'd someday be able to read what they'd written, and be proud of how far she'd come.

The journal's first entry was from January 26, the night Gabby arrived at the rehab center, barely aware of her surroundings. "A somewhat restless night," a nurse wrote, "but a magic tonic is discovered. You love to have your feet massaged."

January 30: "You gave your first thumbs-up as a sign for yes!"

February 9: "We all feel privileged to be part of your miraculous recovery. In my twelve years here, I've never seen a more dramatic healing process."

February 14: "You were asleep until the pain started in your right leg. You cried. While I rubbed your leg, you said 'Superman' three times. Then you concentrated for a moment, and said, 'Super nurse.'"

February 25: "You went outside again today. Your enthusiasm and joy at being outside is wonderful. You wave and greet anyone we pass. (I'm sure those people would vote for you if they could!)"

March 2: "After dozing off, you woke up and I read the *Wall Street Journal* to you. Your face lit up as we toured Libya, Egypt, China, Russia, and finally, Wisconsin. So much to catch up on!"

June 10: "Last night may have been the last time I got to take care of you, if you are discharged as planned. I'm sad! You've been a delight. I can only hope to have the same optimistic outlook that you have. I do hope to see you again under better circumstances!"

Gloria read some of the entries aloud to Gabby. She talked to Gabby about what beautiful care she had received, and what a lovely gesture the journal was. Gabby agreed.

Gabby was lucky that her workers' compensation coverage as a federal employee allowed her to stay at TIRR for so long—more than five months. "Gabby's rehab was once the norm, but it's not anymore," Dr. Francisco told me. In his early days at TIRR, in the mid-1990s, patients with severe brain injuries often stayed for half a year. Now, given changes in reimbursements, some insurance plans allow such patients to stay only one month.

"Think of rehab as an antibiotic," Dr. Francisco explained. "If you have a bladder infection, you have to use the right antibiotic and the right dose. The same is true for rehab. You need the right rehab program for the right length of time and the right frequency each day.

"Here's a crude analogy. If you go into McDonald's and you only have ninety-nine cents, don't expect to buy the Big Mac. Gabby was able to get the Big Mac of rehab because she had insurance coverage that allowed it. I wish every patient had the same opportunities."

As a health-food proponent, Gabby would find it amusing that her doctor chose McDonald's to make his analogy. Still, Dr. Francisco's words resonated with Gabby, and with all of us in her family and on her staff. We read about brain-injured soldiers who weren't getting the best possible care, and we saw other brain-injured patients at TIRR whose insurance coverage was limited. Some of TIRR's patients would return to the facility each year for one month, year after year, because that was all their health-care providers would allow.

Learning all of this, Gabby's office took the lead on several fronts. Her staffers called on Health and Human Services Secretary Kathleen Sebelius to ensure that all Americans with traumatic brain injuries have access to high-quality, comprehensive care. They asked her to end the "treatment gap" by defining rehabilitation care as part of the essential benefits package in the federal Patient Protection and Affordable Care Act. More than 1.7 million Americans sustain traumatic brain injuries each year.

Gabby's staffers also proposed initiatives to a defense-spending bill that would create better guidelines for the rehab treatment of brain-injured soldiers. A staggering 115,000 U.S. soldiers experienced traumatic brain injuries in Iraq and Afghanistan, often from roadside bombs. After the House Armed Services Committee approved the bill, Pia didn't mince words in the statement she released as chief of staff:

"Congresswoman Giffords is receiving excellent medical treatment. She was injured while she was on the job and her rehabilitation is covered by workers' compensation under the Federal Employees' Compensation Act. The members of the military who step forward to serve our nation deserve no less if they suffer a traumatic brain injury."

After Gabby left TIRR, the doctors, nurses, therapists, and patients she left behind had high hopes that she'd continue to recover her voice, and that she'd use her voice for a high purpose.

"Gabby, you can become a national advocate for why rehabilitation is important," Carl Josehart, TIRR's chief executive officer, suggested.

From early on in rehab, Gabby had been upset to learn that the treatment she received was out of reach for many brain-injury patients. And she was heartened to think that all the attention to her traumatic brain injury might have a direct, positive effect on members of the armed services. I have no doubt that when she gets back to work, righting this wrong will be a new priority for her.

* * *

During her early months at TIRR, Gabby would often say "Tucson, Arizona." Sometimes she said it wistfully, sometimes with determination. Eventually, she was able to say exactly what she was feeling: "I miss Tucson." Those of us who love her knew how badly she longed to return, so as soon as she was released from the rehab facility, we made the trip. It was Father's Day weekend.

Gabby was excited to be returning home, but she was visibly nervous, too. On the way there, I asked her, "How do you feel?"

"Mixed emotions," she said.

Tilman had again graciously lent us his plane, which enabled us to fly low over the wildfires that had been raging in Arizona, including in her district, near Sierra Vista. Gabby had been keeping tabs on the fires in the newspaper, and she wanted to see the devastation with her own eyes. As she looked out the window of the plane, she was transfixed. She was every bit the congresswoman, surveying the scene.

We landed at Davis-Monthan Air Force Base on Friday evening, and Gabby walked down the stairs to the tarmac. She headed straight for Air Force Brigadier Gen. Jon Norman, who was waiting for her along with the base commander Colonel John Cherrey.

"Congresswoman Giffords, so nice to have you back," the general said.

"Thank you very much," Gabby answered. "Nice to be back." It was as if she had fallen right back into her congressional persona.

We drove south to Gabby's parents' house, which is in an isolated spot deep in the desert. It is so remote that you spend twenty minutes on a dirt road and drive through two creeks to get there.

Gloria and Spencer hosted a dinner for friends and family, and everyone said Gabby looked great and seemed to be doing well. Ron Barber, her district director, saw Gabby for the first time since they both were injured on January 8. It was an emotional experience for both of them. Gabby stroked the new dimple in his cheek where one bullet had passed, and she examined the scars on his leg from another bullet. Gabby showed him her scars from the bullet and her surgeries, and they compared the progress each of them had made in walking again. They held hands as they ate dinner.

There had been news reports that we were returning to Tucson for a private family visit, so locals knew we were there. The next day, Saturday, we drove downtown and passed the Rialto Theater. Gabby read aloud from the marquee, "We love you, Gabby," and then she got a little teary. I'd been ready for this weekend, with tissues in my pocket. I handed them to her.

Later we stopped by her condo. Gabby hadn't been there since the morning of January 8. Her friend Brad Holland had kindly replaced the fish that died after the shooting, and he'd been coming to the condo to feed the fish tank's new residents.

"Beautiful fish," Gabby said when she saw them.

Gabby went around her condo, looking at the artwork, mostly Latin American folk art, remembering what she liked about each piece. She also went "shopping" in her closet. I had packed a couple of suitcases for her when we departed Tucson in January, but I'd left a lot behind. Gabby was happy to find outfits she'd been missing and, with her nurse Kristy's help, she stuffed them in her suitcase.

Gabby was also able to nap in her own bed. I napped, too.

That afternoon, Gabby visited her new district office, which was bigger and in a more secure location. It was a weekend, so there were few staffers there, but she walked around trying to figure out who occupied each desk or office.

Later in the evening, we attended a dinner for Gabby and her staff at the home of her district office manager, Joni Jones, and Joni's husband, Gary. It was encouraging to see that Gabby didn't have an issue remembering anyone's name, even a new staffer she'd met only a couple of times. Gabby gave each of them a hug and thanked them for their continued hard work. It was exhilarating and emotional for everyone.

Gabby still was unaware that Gabe Zimmerman was one of those killed on January 8, and no one told her. I had prepped the staff in advance: Until she could ask questions herself, we'd been advised by doctors not to give her the full details of the tragedy.

Even though her staffers saw that her communication skills were still compromised, they were uniformly impressed by Gabby. She was sharp the entire weekend. When the Capitol Police officer driving us made a wrong turn on a Tucson street, she'd point him in the right direction. When I couldn't find her rental property that I'd been to several times, she showed the way.

The two-day visit was much too short, however. After an early Father's Day breakfast with Gabby's parents, we headed for the Air Force base. When we arrived, Gabby saw a group of officers about fifty yards from the plane. She walked toward them, shook all their hands, and gave them each a hug. "Gabrielle Giffords," she said. "Nice to meet you. Thank you." Then she turned and boarded the plane. She needed to get back to Houston for therapy in the morning.

* * *

Once she was home with me in League City, Gabby settled in very nicely and pretty happily. She was soon able to walk around the house unassisted. We'd also walk slowly around the neighborhood, and Gabby made it her mission to bend over and pick up every speck of trash she came upon. She was used to trying to make a difference in the world. Though her abilities were now limited, she was doing what she could.

Gabby was eager to contribute to the housework, too, by washing dishes, watering the plants, and doing the laundry. She strove to be self-sufficient.

One day, Kristy was the home nurse on duty and she saw Gabby struggling to fold laundry with her left hand. Gabby's right hand, as usual, sat limp.

"Let me help," Kristy offered.

At first Gabby rebuffed her, but then Gabby said, "Kristy, left hand."

Kristy agreed to use only her left hand to fold the laundry. And so that's how it went, the two of them using two hands between them to get the laundry folded.

Gabby didn't mind that the piece of her bullet-scarred skull was in the freezer. In fact, when we'd have friends over, she'd sometimes walk to the freezer, pull it out, and show them. Some visitors were intrigued. Others were squeamish; one nearly fainted. Gabby got a kick out of seeing people's reactions. (Hospital staffers in Tucson had also given me Gabby's bloody hair, which was shaved off on January 8. The hair was in my backpack for a couple of days, but it was soaked with blood and started to smell. I threw it in a trash can in Tucson and it is now somewhere in an Arizona landfill.)

All of us in Gabby's life kept getting indications that she understood pretty much everything and that her long-term memory was clear. Traveling in the car one day with Leslie, one of Gabby's nurses, and two Capitol Police officers, we listened to the radio and played "Name That Tune." We heard three songs, and Gabby got them all right. The first was AC/DC's "Back in Black." The second was "Only the Good Die Young" by Billy Joel. She was the only person in the car able to identify the band that performed the third song, "Amanda." The band was Boston.

Such positive signs of Gabby's cognitive strengths and sharp recall were tempered, however, by the frustrating moments between us, when she struggled to express herself. Sometimes, Gabby would try to communicate with me, saying the same word repeatedly, and I wouldn't understand her point. She'd try again, and I'd still be lost. A few times, she was so discouraged that she put her head down on the table. On one especially frustrating day, I had to leave for an appointment. As I headed for the door I promised Gabby: "Listen, I'm going to think about what you were saying to me all day, and we'll get back to it when I get home tonight. We'll figure it out."

Sometimes, Gabby was able to find her way to the right word on her own. One morning I said to Gabby, "What would you like to do today?"

She responded, "Hospital."

I was surprised. "Why would you want to go to the hospital?"

She closed her eyes and thought for a long time, trying to pull out the appropriate word, and then she said, "Nursing home."

She wanted to see my ninety-five-year-old grandmother in the nursing home where she lives, not far from our house. Whenever Gabby visited Houston, she had always tried to see my grandmother. So we got in the car and headed over there. My grandmother, who has some dementia, did most of the talking, and Gabby was happy to listen.

Sometimes, the communication failures between Gabby and me would last for hours, but then we'd finally figure it out and it was as if we'd struck gold. We felt like screaming "Eureka!"

One day, for instance, Gabby kept saying to me, "Block of time."

I didn't know what she was trying to tell me. "Block of time," she said again. It went on like that for thirty minutes and I never understood her. Eventually, we had to give up.

Then, the next day, I said to her, "Hey, Gabby, I'm going to go to the gym to get some exercise."

"Block of time!" she exclaimed, gesturing with her left hand for emphasis.

And then I understood. She recognized that as a caregiver, it was important that I take time for myself. She wanted me to have a "block of time" to work out at the gym.

"OK, Gabby," I said, "I'm going to take a block of time at the gym and then I'll come home."

From such small exchanges, our ability to understand each other blossomed.

* * *

When we had first settled into my home in League City, I was a little concerned that the press might stake out the house, trying to get videos and photos of Gabby. But the media turned out to be generally very respectful of Gabby's privacy, as they'd been since January 8. (With the exception of the two news helicopters and the ten cameramen and reporters who showed up the first day Gabby was home, we didn't see much of the media in the neighborhood.)

We knew, of course, that people wanted an update on how Gabby was doing and what she looked like now. For that reason, a few days before Gabby left TIRR, her office released two photos of her. Taken by Gabby's friend P. K. Weis, one of the photos was a simple portrait of Gabby wearing glasses, her hair darker and shorter than people remembered. The other photo showed Gabby and Gloria together, both of them smiling. Except for that grainy footage taken of Gabby boarding the stairs onto that NASA jet in April, this was the first time since the shooting that the world got to see Gabby. We heard from countless friends and strangers telling Gabby she looked great. She was buoyed by their good wishes.

Though Gabby kept improving, it was sometimes dispiriting for her to go to outpatient group therapy, where many of those with brain injuries weren't as far along as she was. In her "group communication" sessions, there were eight men and Gabby, no other women. Only one of the men could speak at all. Gabby came home at night and would tell me about it. "Scary," she said.

I hadn't been in favor of Gabby joining group therapy until Jimmy Hatch, a friend of Gabby's, visited us. Jimmy is a Navy SEAL, and in 2010 Gabby had helped him through bouts of depression related to injuries he'd received in Afghanistan. He'd been in group therapy for service-related head trauma. "Gabby ought to try it," he told me when he came to Houston. "She may find comfort seeing other folks with similar problems. It could motivate her to improve." Gabby had helped Jimmy. Now he had come to help her.

Gabby did well in group therapy, but it was hard to watch others who struggled there.

Kristy drove with Gabby to rehab, and she'd sometimes peek through the window of the therapy room to see what was going on. Most of the patients were silent, slumped over, not too alert. "Gabby sits there, singing away," Kristy told me.

It was sad to hear about these other patients, and it only made us more grateful for Gabby's progress.

* * *

Gabby began venturing out into public more. One day, for occupational therapy, she went shopping at a drugstore for an hour, reading labels and filling her cart. She bought various toiletries, including toothpaste for me. I had asked her to get Aquafresh, which I normally use. But she bought me Tom's natural toothpaste, because it had fewer chemicals. She always had that stuff in Tucson, and even though I told her it tasted horrible, that's what she got me.

It was a surreal scene at the drugstore, with two Capitol Police officers wearing their suits and strolling the store with empty carts. Everyone in the store had to know they weren't shoppers; it was obvious they were there for Gabby's protection.

Gabby's first public appearance before a large group came on June 27 at a NASA awards ceremony. I wasn't sure she should attend; her previous outings had been subject to detailed advanced planning. This outing would be impromptu. But Gabby insisted she wanted to be there. I had announced my retirement from NASA and the Navy a few days earlier, and Gabby knew this was her last chance to see me get a NASA award.

My *Endeavour* crew and I were set to receive the NASA Space Flight Medal for our work on STS-134, and six hundred people had gathered in the IMAX Theater at the Johnson Space Center's visitor center for the ceremony. Many in the audience worked for the space program or were the friends or family of astronauts, but a lot of people from the general public were there, too.

When Gabby entered the auditorium in her wheelchair unannounced, we could hear the crowd murmuring as people realized she was there. Within a minute, the entire audience had risen for a prolonged standing ovation for Gabby. She smiled and waved. Hundreds of cameras seemed to be flashing at once, and Gabby was genuinely grateful for the crowd's affectionate welcome.

When I received my medal, Gabby stood up, and I walked over to hug and kiss her. The crowd liked that. After the ceremony, my crew and I narrated a PowerPoint presentation of photos taken during our flight. Then a fourteen-minute video of mission highlights was shown on the giant IMAX screen, with "Beautiful Day" as part of the soundtrack.

Gabby and I made eye contact as the song played. We were both smiling, but I figured she was thinking the same thing I was—about all that had transpired in the five years since she first played that song for me as a wake-up call in space.

We had both learned so much. What defines a beautiful day? Sometimes, something as simple as a sentence with a question mark at the end of it.

* * *

If people can't ask questions, it's not always easy to have a conversation with them. You don't realize that until you spend your life with some-one unable to ask a question.

Gabby's inquisitiveness used to define her. She was full of great questions. I loved that about her, and I missed it. As the months went by, I knew she must have had a lot of questions piling up in her head. I continued trying to coax them out of her, with no success. I would frequently just answer those unasked questions for her. That resulted in a lot of one-sided conversations. In time, things improved.

People would always ask Gabby, "How are you?" Eventually, she was able to easily answer, "I'm fine, how are you?" But that was sort of a rote response. She was repeating what she'd just heard. It was very practiced.

Meanwhile, I kept waiting and hoping for a real question.

On July 6, two days before the six-month anniversary of the shoot-ing, the breakthrough came. Gabby and I were alone together at home, eating dinner. "What did you do today?" I asked her.

"Therapy," she answered.

"How did it go?"

"Worn out," she said. "Really tired. This is hard. I'm trying."

We continued eating our salad and spaghetti. Then Gabby turned to me. "Your day?" she said.

From her inflection, I completely felt the question mark at the end of the sentence.

"Gabby, was that a question? Are you asking me how my day was?"

She was sensing the power of the moment, too. "Yes!" she said.

Her entire face lit up with a big smile. She spoke more confidently: "Yes, how was your day?"

I was momentarily shocked. "Gabby, this is a big deal!" I said. "I've been trying to get you to ask me a question for months, and now you've done it. This is the first time you've asked me anything!"

Gabby smiled. I was actually emotional. It's not that I was going to cry. I was just very happy. Almost overwhelmed.

"Your day?" Gabby said again. In my excitement, I couldn't even remember my day at all. I took out my BlackBerry and scrolled through e-mails to jog my memory.

"Let's see, I went to lunch with Claudia." I continued scrolling down. "I went into my office at NASA to pack up some things and go through everything on my computer . . ."

Gabby listened intently. "Oh," I said, "I also went to Dillard's to return your clothing."

She smiled. She definitely considered that to be a necessary errand. I had gone shopping days earlier and bought Gabby a pair of shorts that were too big and a pair of white jeans. She hated the jeans. She actually had a negative physical reaction to them. She shuddered. I'd never gone clothes shopping for her before and I apparently wasn't very good at it. How was I to know that Gabby wouldn't like white jeans?

In any case, after I finished answering Gabby's question, I told her how happy I was to hear it. "You've finally asked a question, a real one. And it's something you wanted to know. It's really great."

Gabby and I were both grinning.

"Now," I said, "you just have to come up with another one."

CHAPTER TWENTY-ONE

Inch by Inch

Once Gabby had moved home with me, I began taping *Meet the Press* every Sunday on my digital video recorder. Gabby liked the show. It kept her abreast of issues in Washington. We developed a little ritual of watching it together later in the day.

One Sunday afternoon in July, as Gabby headed for the bathroom, I told her I'd meet her in the living room so we could watch the show. I sat down on the couch, but she never showed up. After ten minutes, I went looking for her.

I found her in the bedroom. "Sit down," she said. "Shut the door."

It occurred to me that she should have told me to shut the door and then sit down, but I didn't correct her. I saw by the expression on her face that she was serious. I closed the door. I sat down.

"Shot," she said.

"Yes, you were shot in the head," I said. She knew that, of course, but sometimes it helped a conversation if I provided a sentence to get started.

"Questions and answers," she said, very seriously.

I could sense what was coming. It had been more than six months since her injury, but now she was ready to find out.

"Who died?" she asked.

This was only the fourth or fifth question she'd asked me since the "Your day?" breakthrough a few weeks earlier.

I'd spent months considering exactly how I'd deliver the news when asked this question. But now that the moment was here, I needed to take a step back. Our friends Marc and Suzanne Winkelman, and their daughter, Eli, were driving in from Austin for a visit. They'd be arriving in forty minutes. I didn't want to give Gabby all the terrible details, knowing she'd then have to be upbeat and social for visitors. I explained that to Gabby.

"I'm glad you've asked me this," I told her. "You know, after you were injured, there was a lot of debate about how much to tell you about the shooting. Doctors said it was best to wait to tell you all the names until you were able to ask questions yourself. That made sense to me. And now that you've asked, I'm going to tell you. But I know it's going to upset you. So let's wait until tonight, after the Winkelmans leave. I promise I'll talk to you about who died and show you their photos."

Gabby understood that the news would likely leave her distraught. She'd waited this long. Could she wait a few more hours? "Yes," she said.

We had a great time with the Winkelmans. Gabby was very engaged and interacted with them easily. When they left, and Gabby had gotten into bed, I came and sat beside her.

"OK," I said. "I'm going to tell you who died on January eighth. It's going to be really hard because you knew two of the people."

Gabby waited for me to continue.

"One of the people killed was on your staff," I said. "It was Gabe. Gabe Zimmerman."

She started half-crying, half-moaning. She was overwhelmed with grief. I gave her a hug and then I continued. I wanted to get it all out.

"And do you remember John Roll, the federal judge?" I asked.

"Yes," she said.

"Well, he was standing very close to you when the shooting started. He was near Ron Barber. You know that Ron survived, but Judge Roll, he didn't make it. He died."

I then told Gabby about the four people killed whom she didn't know. I spoke about Phyllis Schneck, the seventy-nine-year-old widow from New Jersey who was devoted to her church, loved to read, and had come to the Congress on Your Corner event to talk about border security. I let Gabby know about Dorothy Morris, the seventy-six-year-old retired secretary whose husband, a retired airline pilot, had tried to save her by covering her with his own body. Shot in the shoulder, he survived.

I told Gabby about Dorwan Stoddard, the retired road-grader who died while protecting his wife and childhood sweetheart. His wife was shot in the legs but lived. Finally, I spoke about Christina-Taylor Green, the nine-year-old girl with a passionate interest in government.

About three months earlier, a nurse at TIRR had inadvertently told Gabby that a young girl had died in the shooting. So Gabby was aware of Christina's death. But she'd never seen photos of Christina or the other victims until I showed them to her that night on my computer.

I held on to Gabby as she digested the news and cried. She didn't ask questions; she had a hard time saying anything. So I just continued talking to her.

I told her about the funerals I had attended, and she listened. "At Gabe's funeral, his brother spoke, along with his dad and C.J. from your office. I said a few words on your behalf."

I tried to give Gabby a sense of what I had said at the funeral—about how Gabe was a great young man who wanted to help people. I told her about the bipartisan resolution to name a meeting room at the U.S. Capitol's Visitor Center in Gabe's memory. Gabby knew Ross Zimmerman, Gabe's father, because he sometimes came in to the office. "Would you like to call Ross one of these days?" I asked her.

"Yes," she said, and we made plans to do that.

Before she went to sleep, I asked Gabby how she was feeling.

"I'm sad," she said. "Sad, sad, sad."

I was sad, too. The rest of us already had six months to grieve for those who died. For Gabby, the grief would be fresh and raw. Still, it was a relief that she finally asked the question we'd all been waiting for. She needed to know who was lost on January 8. Now she did.

* * *

It was remarkable, really, that despite everything, Gabby kept soldiering on, giving her all in therapy.

To me, it seemed she was making excellent progress, day by day, but I wanted to better understand the extent of her cognitive abilities, and how all of us could help her continue to improve. I heard good things from several people in the brain-injury field about Dr. Nancy Estabrooks, an expert in neurological communication disorders at Western

Carolina University. I invited her to spend the day with us, getting to know Gabby and testing her.

At age seventy, Nancy had studied brain trauma and recovery for decades. Her insights were very helpful. She explained that most people with aphasia—an impairment of language ability—are the victims of strokes or they have head injuries from falls or car accidents or, among soldiers, from IEDs. As I knew, those with brain injuries from bullets rarely live, and if they do, their prognosis is often very bad. Gabby was very much an outlier.

Nancy explained that during World Wars I and II, a large number of soldiers survived being shot in the head, and so there was useful research on the treatment of "traumatic aphasia" based on their cases. Many of these soldiers made a relatively good recovery from aphasia. Some recovered fully. In more recent wars, however, the caliber and velocity of bullets increased. Advances in battlefield medicine have kept more soldiers alive with devastating injuries, but for the few who survive being shot in the head, the gravity of their brain damage tends to be more pronounced. They often have a tougher time recovering than those injured in past wars, which is yet another burden for the health-care system, and their families.

In Nancy's many decades working with aphasia patients, she'd seen more than one thousand cases of stroke-related aphasia, but only a handful of cases involving shooting victims. As a result, she said, in order to treat the rare survivors like Gabby, aphasiologists still turn to research done in the 1940s, with World War II vets who were shot in the head.

Nancy explained that Gabby appeared to have a form of "nonfluent aphasia," which meant she had good auditory verbal comprehension but had trouble saying complete sentences. Nancy got up to speed on Gabby's progress: the "zombie" she was early on, the repetition of the word "chicken," the great strides she had made since then, both physically and verbally.

Nancy sat with Gabby at the kitchen table from 10 a.m. to 6 p.m., with just a break for lunch and a short afternoon nap for Gabby. Gloria was there for most of the testing, and I was also around for a lot of it.

Gabby was eager to perform well, and hopeful that Nancy would find ways to help her. Gloria thought Gabby was very much Congresswoman Gabrielle Giffords that day—alert, serious, with good posture, her eyes focused on Nancy's face during her opening remarks about her qualifications and her plans for the day.

Nancy noticed quickly that Gabby never wavered in her attention or ability to stay on task, that she could understand subtle directions, and that she was able to concentrate despite distractions in the house, including me walking around doing chores. "These facts alone are a very positive sign for Gabby's recovery," Nancy said.

Gabby did well on almost all of Nancy's tests. Nancy laid out photos of various U.S. presidents in random order. Without being asked, Gabby began arranging them, left to right, chronologically. She eliminated the "ringer," Ben Franklin, knowing he didn't belong. She held up the photo of Franklin and said, "Wonderful. Electricity."

Nancy scribbled in her notes: "For FDR, she spontaneously commented, 'Roosevelt,' 'wheelchair,' 'braces.' For Jimmy Carter, she said, 'Habitat for Humanity.'"

Gabby earned a perfect score while arranging and identifying photos of other famous people, including First Ladies and politicians from other countries. She had no trouble identifying the face that didn't belong in a particular group, and made appropriate comments without being asked. She called Margaret Thatcher "Iron Lady."

Nancy was also impressed to see that Gabby was up on the news. Gabby looked at Arnold Schwarzenegger's photo and said, "Messin' around. Babies.'" When she looked at a photo of Michele Bachmann, she said "Tea Party" and "Running for president."

Nancy gave Gabby a set of cards with photos that told a story, and asked her to put them in order. In Gabby's early months at TIRR , this sort of exercise was beyond her, but now she aced it every time.

One set of illustrations was set at a gambling casino. Gabby easily put the cards in the correct order: (1) A man sits at a slot machine. (2) He looks frustrated; he's obviously losing. (3) He abandons the machine. (4) Just then a woman appears and sits down at the machine. (5) The man watches her pull the lever. (6) The woman wins a jackpot.

Nancy wrote on a dry-erase board: Scotland, Ireland, Holland, England. "Which doesn't belong?" she asked Gabby.

"Holland," Gabby said, correctly.

Then Nancy wrote: "Cake, cookies, bread, pie."

Gabby looked at the words. Nancy expected her to choose bread as the item that didn't belong, since the other three words referred to desserts. But Gabby picked "cookies" instead. When we told her that "bread" was the correct answer, Gabby pointed to the "s" in cookies and then erased it. That was impressive, too. Gabby noticed that "cake," "pie," and "bread" were singular nouns. "Cookies" was a plural noun. It showed a high level of thinking.

"Gabby is paying better attention to everything than we are," Nancy said.

She and Gabby also worked with money. She gave Gabby four twenties, eight fives, and three ones. Gabby put all the money in order of value and arranged the bills with all the faces in the same direction. Gabby had a difficult time making change for a twenty-dollar bill. But when it came time to give me back the bills I'd lent them from my wallet, Gabby knew exactly how much needed to be returned to me.

Nancy pulled no punches in her time with Gabby. She wanted to determine Gabby's emotional and psychological state, and so she asked a question no one had asked since January 8. "Given all that has happened since the shooting," Nancy said, "the tough times you've had, all the pain and sadness, are you glad you survived?"

"Yes, yes, yes!" Gabby said. Nancy was struck by her lack of hesitation.

Nancy's question was surprising. We might assume that shooting victims who are in a vegetative state may wish they had died. But Gabby? She was so highly functional. Why would Nancy ask that?

"A lot of stroke patients with aphasia are highly depressed," Nancy explained, "and they haven't been through as much as Gabby has. You could imagine Gabby being very depressed, because she was at the top of her game—a young congresswoman, a new marriage. If you consider how much she had going for her, and how it all stopped so abruptly, it's not hard to imagine someone in that situation feeling suicidal, or losing the will to live."

Nancy was impressed by Gabby on other fronts: her optimism, her performance, her stamina, her memory. "If you don't have memory, therapy is so much harder," Nancy said, "because you can't build on anything. Gabby's memory is great."

Nancy said she was ready for a more intensive aphasia therapy program to supplement her three to five hours a day of outpatient work at TIRR. On Nancy's recommendation, I started interviewing speech language pathologists to work with Gabby every afternoon for two to three more hours. We also planned a fall visit to Nancy's office in Asheville, North Carolina, so Nancy and her colleagues could work with Gabby intensely for twelve days.

When Nancy was leaving my house, I asked her: "So what do you think? Will Gabby eventually be able to return to Congress?"

"Yes," she answered. "I think Gabby will be able to do whatever she wants, and I think she has good judgment. Whether she should return to Congress, whether she should run again, when the time comes, she'll know."

Nancy said that Gabby would certainly have difficulties in future debates; her remarks will come more slowly. She might not have the easy glibness that politicians often rely on. But quick retorts aren't the essence of public service. Could Gabby return to work and be an effective lawmaker? "Absolutely," Nancy said.

"But for now," she advised, "like a lot of people with health problems, she needs to take things one day at a time. Give her each day, one at a time."

* * *

In the history of our country, Gabby appears to be the only female elected official to be wounded in an assassination attempt. She endured this horrific injury on the job, while serving her constituents. From the day she was shot, I believed that she deserved time to recover before she decided whether she was capable of returning to her seat.

As her health and abilities improved, Gabby often articulated that she wanted to get back to work. At times in July, she seemed to be just a breath away from full sentences, and just a step away from being ready to resume her duties. Her urge to return, and these steady improvements, only cemented my feeling that she should be given the time she needed to heal. Thousands of Americans are injured on the job each year, and their positions are held for them while they recover. So it was with Gabby.

Gabby's doctors repeatedly told us that those with traumatic brain injuries often continue to make large strides for a year to eighteen months after they are hurt. Beyond that, they said, Gabby would continue to improve throughout her lifetime.

Considering the doctors' input, and Gabby's resolve, I believed she deserved a year or longer to make her decision. So far, it had been just over six months. How much more progress would she make? Maybe a lot. Maybe she'd get almost all the way back. Doctors said it was unlikely that she'd ever use her right hand again to, say, play the piano, but she never did play the piano anyway. As she improved, she might be able to use it for some tasks. And she'd definitely keep making leaps forward in her language skills. So the signs were encouraging.

Against my better judgment, I'd occasionally read the anonymous comments at the bottom of stories about Gabby on media websites. Many people wished Gabby well and rooted her on. It was nice to read those postings. But from the start, there were some people calling for Gabby's immediate resignation. They said she wasn't able to represent her constituents in Washington, so she should step down. They ignored how hard her staffers were working to deal with every issue brought to them.

Some of those calling for Gabby's resignation had online names I recognized from the roughest rhetoric of past campaigns. It's ironic. They were the same people who disagreed with Gabby's votes and decisions while she was in office. You'd think they'd be happy if she missed votes, since they wouldn't like how she voted anyway.

Both Gabby and I understood why her inability to work would be a matter of public discussion. If she knew for sure she wouldn't progress well enough to do her job, she would step down. But we just didn't know yet.

So what was our timetable?

In May of 2012, by state law, Gabby would need to file for reelection. Certainly, a decision would need to be made by then, which would be sixteen months after the shooting. It was possible Gabby would be able to decide earlier. But that was the time frame we were looking at.

As I saw how hard Gabby was working to get back to her job, how hard her staff was working, I didn't think it was fair to anyone—including all the people who had elected Gabby to that seat, and wanted her to represent them—to rush the decision.

As I told Gabby, "The time will come when you'll know what the right decision is. It'll be clear to you. Until then, you just keep getting better."

* * *

People who had recovered well from brain injuries often wrote to Gabby, or offered to visit so they could give her pep talks. A cellist with the Houston Symphony suffered a traumatic brain injury in a 2009 motorcycle accident, but was able to return to the orchestra after eleven months. He said he'd be happy to give us a private concert to inspire us. We thanked him, and said that maybe some night up the road, we'd be honored to take him up on his kind offer.

We also heard from Mike Segal, a social worker in Houston who counsels brain-injury patients. He offered to come over and tell Gabby his story.

On February 18, 1981, when Mike was a nineteen-year-old pre-med student at the University of Texas at Austin, he spent the evening studying organic chemistry with his girlfriend. As he drove her back to her dorm, he saw he was low on gas, so he pulled into a convenience store parking lot.

Mike entered the store to pay for the gas, and walked into a robbery in progress. The store clerk, hiding in the restroom, heard the three robbers say they planned to "waste all witnesses." They took Mike, the only customer, into the store's cooler, told him to get down on his knees, and shot him, execution-style, in the back of his head. They assumed they'd left him dead.

Mike was not expected to survive, and if he did, doctors said he'd never walk or talk again. For months, he couldn't speak at all. He couldn't move the right side of his body. (Like Gabby, he was shot in the left side of his head.) He considered killing himself, but couldn't figure out a way to do it.

Through a tremendous amount of hard, painful therapy, and the faith of family and friends, Mike was able to reclaim himself. His parents had to reteach him the alphabet. They helped him learn to count. Eighteen months later, he returned to college. He graduated with honors, and went on to get a master's degree in social work. He married his girlfriend and they had a child. Some disabilities still remain—he has breathing issues, he can't move his right arm much, he speaks a bit more slowly—but Mike's cognitive comeback is remarkable and complete. He wanted Gabby to see him. Thirty years down the road, at age forty-nine, he was thriving.

Mike told Gabby that he doesn't think about the three men who tried to kill him, two of whom are now out of prison. He doesn't think about the fact that he used to be able to do five hundred things well, and now he's down to two hundred. He thinks about all the things he can do. "I've come to see that everyone in life has obstacles," he said. "I believe that's the definition of being human. These are our obstacles, Gabby, and we just have to deal with them."

He talked about how his father, a rabbi, had pushed him to work hard in therapy, and how he resented his father's efforts. Now, of course, he's grateful. He told us, "My dad had this corny saying, but it was true: 'Mile by mile, it's a trial; yard by yard, it's hard; but inch by inch, it's a cinch.'"

Gabby knew that even the inches are no cinch, but she listened very intently as Mike spoke. She had been a little down in the days before he arrived, and his visit lifted her out of her funk. "I can't help people with their broken bones," he told Gabby, "but I can help them with their broken spirit."

Mike had a nice way about him. He told Gabby how well she was doing compared with where he was six months into his recovery. Gabby could see how far he had come. "My parents were praying I'd say a few words," he said. "Now they pray I'll shut up!"

He and Gabby laughed together over that line, which he had surely used before.

Mike stayed about an hour and Gabby hugged him before he left. They were two people, left for dead, who were both very much alive. He gave her a T-shirt. Written on the front: "Got hope?" On the back it said: "I do."

* * *

After Mike's visit, Gabby was in physical therapy and had a breakthrough. Her therapist placed two tennis balls on the table in front of her. She asked Gabby to pick up one tennis ball with her strong left hand and the other with her floppy right hand. Gabby firmly grasped the ball in her left hand. Her grip on the ball in her right hand was weak, but she was able to wrap her fingers around it.

"OK," her therapist said. "As you slowly lift your left hand, I want you to try to make the exact same movements with your right hand." Gabby's brain was able to give clear signals to her left hand. The hope was that if she could move both hands simultaneously, the left guiding the right, Gabby might be able to retrain her brain.

Gabby concentrated, lifting her left and right hands in tandem. She actually willed her right hand to lift that tennis ball. One inch. Two inches. Three inches. She lifted the ball four inches into the air. It was a triumph.

When she and her nurse Kristy came home that afternoon, Gabby was grinning, eager to tell me. I was very proud of her. I had a real sense of the future: There'd be better days ahead for that limp noodle of an arm.

It was great to see Gabby's progress on other fronts, too. She was asking more questions: "What time is it?" "Where is my brace?"

I thought it would be helpful if, when she wanted to know something, she began by saying: "Mark, I have a question." Or: "Kristy, I have a question."

She started saying that line regularly, and it helped her thought processes. Though her questions didn't always begin with the words "what," "who," or "when," they were definitely questions: "Having for dinner?" "Go for a walk?"

Meanwhile, I was constantly impressed by Gabby's work ethic in rehab. She had a singular focus. She knew that success in therapy was her ticket back into the world.

One day, Kristy was telling Gabby about the items on her bucket list—the things she still needed to get to in her life. "I want to play the piano again," Kristy said. "I want to visit South America. I want to go on an African safari."

Then Kristy turned to Gabby. "So how about you?" she asked. "What's on your bucket list?"

Gabby could have mentioned that having a child had been at the top of her bucket list. After all, two frozen embryos of ours remained in storage at the Walter Reed Naval Medical Center in Bethesda, Maryland. It was still possible for us to have a child together, though given Gabby's injuries, we'd probably need to go through a surrogate.

But Gabby knew she had to put such dreams aside. Kristy asked her again: "What's on your bucket list, Gabby?"

Gabby had just one answer: "Get better."

* * *

As the hot Houston summer continued, I noticed Gabby paying even closer attention to the news. She was more and more engaged in all the issues that had driven her work as a public servant. She was also more in tune with tragedies in the news.

On July 22, when a political extremist in Norway killed seventy-seven people, mostly teenagers, it was natural for all of us to think about the gunman in Tucson. I couldn't help myself. I had to say something. "There's a special place in hell for those two dudes," I said.

"Yes," Gabby said. "Yes."

We didn't talk about the Tucson gunman too much, though Gabby did look at a photo of him online. She stared at his smirking face, but had no comment. She was aware of the questions about his mental stability, his fitness to stand trial. Given her advocacy throughout her career for mental-health care, she understood that these were issues that needed to be sorted through. Still, she didn't see a need to contain her own personal feelings about this man, which were understandably visceral.

"What would you like to see happen to him?" I asked her.

"Rot," she said.

I found it interesting that this woman, with a limited ability to communicate, could sum things up in just one syllable.

* * *

As Gabby's life settled into a predictable pattern of weekday therapy and more-relaxed weekends at home, she was better able to get back to one of her favorite roles, that of the concerned wife.

One day she said to me, "Brief. Brief."

I thought she was talking about a briefcase or a pair of underwear. Maybe I was telling her stories that were too long.

"Brief," she said again.

Then it hit me. She wanted me to work on my "debrief" for a meeting I was scheduled to have at NASA, debriefing my managers on the particulars of STS-134.

I did as Gabby said, prepared well for the meeting, and afterward, I couldn't wait to get home to tell her about it. She was a good listener.

I told her how there were ten of us, seven men and three women, gathered in the conference room—my crew, the people from flight-crew operations, several of our managers. We talked about the mission in detail, the successes and the challenges. I thanked my managers for their support when Gabby was injured. But I also wanted to bring up the matter of a recent e-mail I'd received from another manager about astronaut evaluations of my crew.

The e-mail asked me to say something negative about each member of my crew. "They were calling it constructive feedback," I told Gabby, "but to me, it's like they want to make sure they have some negative evidence they can point to if they want to deny someone a flight assignment or a specific position or role. I didn't like it, and I told them I refused to do it. I said, 'I don't think you manage people well through negativism. They're in space, they're risking their lives, and it's a tough job. I'd rather focus on what's positive.'"

"Yes," Gabby said, nodding her head. That sounded right to her.

I continued to vent. I told Gabby that during sixteen days in space, we hadn't received one single positive or supportive e-mail from our office. This was my fourth space shuttle flight, and I'd never before seen stinginess with praise. We had completed all of our objectives. We didn't hurt anyone or break anything. The flight directors and the space shuttle and station program offices were extremely happy with our performance. But from our management? Nothing. How hard was it to type "good job" and press "send"?

"I pointed all of this out at the meeting," I said to Gabby. Then I told her what happened next. One of our managers stood up and said, "I've been here thirty years, and in thirty years I've never seen anything like this! There are four thousand people being laid off around here, and you guys are worried about constructive criticism and no positive feedback? You guys are a bunch of pussies!"

Gabby's eyes widened as I spoke. "Oh no, oh no!" she said.

"He was pretty upset, but I was really surprised that he chose that word," I told her. "We'd had this very challenging mission that was one hundred percent successful. We just risked our lives serving our country, and he was calling us 'pussies' in front of three women, one of whom was his boss." I'd been dealing with Gabby having a difficult time finding the right word. Apparently this boss of mine had the same problem.

"Terrible," Gabby said.

"So I figured I'd better smooth things over. I said to them, 'Well, I didn't expect things to go this way. I was just trying to make the point that the culture within the astronaut office had become rather negative over the last several years.'"

When I finished telling Gabby my story, I felt kind of bad. Here she was, reacquainting herself with language, and I was using an inappropriate word. She'd heard it before, of course. Now she'd heard it again.

We ended up laughing together about it. Since I was retiring as an astronaut, I didn't feel a great need to follow orders and force myself to conjure up unnecessary negative comments about my crew.

"Maybe that makes me a . . ." I didn't say it, and Gabby just laughed.

* * *

Gabby and I would sometimes play a game called "How did you vote?" We did it partly for the sense of nostalgia, and partly because it got Gabby to think hard and engage her recollections.

Our game worked like this. I'd bring up an issue that came before Congress during her time in office, and she'd recall how she voted.

"The climate change bill?" I asked. That was the 2009 bill aiming to reduce greenhouse gas emissions by 17 percent by 2020.

"Voted yes," Gabby said. Yes, she did.

"Cash for clunkers?" I asked. That bill provided federal vouchers for up to $4,500 for people to trade in their old cars for new ones that got better mileage.

"Voted no," Gabby said. She was right.

I also quizzed her on her stand on positions. "Do you support *Roe v. Wade?*" I asked.

Gabby shook her head back and forth, but she said, "Yes."

"That's the perfect answer for a politician!" I said, and she instantly realized she was moving her head the wrong way. She nodded up and down. Yes, she supported *Roe v. Wade.*

Gabby got every question right. She knew how she voted. She knew where she stood.

By late July, Gabby was closely following the debate in Washington over raising the debt ceiling. If Democrats and Republicans couldn't reach a compromise, the government would default. The partisan bickering was upsetting to Gabby. She had always vowed to reach across the aisle, to work out a compromise. Every day, she waited for signs that her colleagues back in Washington had found solutions. The whole mess saddened her.

Then, on July 31, President Obama announced that an agreement finally had been forged. Speaker Boehner's office issued a statement outlining the terms. There were still representatives in both parties, however, who were unhappy with the deal, and vowed to vote it down.

And so Gabby wondered: What if it all came down to one vote? What if her vote could make a difference and get the bill passed?

"The right thing," she said to me. That's what she wanted to do, if she could.

I saw her mind at work. She recognized that the country was teetering on the brink of default. Trillions of dollars would evaporate out of the world economy overnight. She wouldn't feel right if she remained on the sidelines, allowing that to happen.

Certainly, she knew that she'd be safer on the sidelines. Taking a stand on a controversial vote will always come back to haunt a politician. Gabby set that possibility aside. She'd survived so much in the seven months since January 8, the risk of political fallout was survivable, too.

I texted her friend Representative Debbie Wasserman Schultz, chairwoman of the Democratic National Committee, who is close to the legislative leadership. Debbie was tallying how many "yes" votes could be counted on in her own party. She also had some sense of the Republican support.

"You got the votes?" I texted.

She texted back, "Unclear at this point. It may be close."

I went into the bedroom, where Gabby was getting ready to go to sleep. "They might need your vote in Washington tomorrow," I said. "What do you think?"

"I'll go," she answered.

CHAPTER TWENTY-TWO

Back to Work

On Monday morning, August 1, Gabby got into tennis shoes and a comfortable sweat suit, ready for her regimen of therapy. "This may be just an ordinary, demanding day of rehab," I told her before she left. "Then again, it may turn out to be very crazy. If you're needed in D.C., are you sure you want to go?"

"Yes," she said. She was resolute.

Gabby and her nurse on duty, Kay, headed out of the house at 8 a.m. I called after them, "I might be seeing you soon!" Gabby smiled at me and waved goodbye.

By then, the phone was already ringing, and my BlackBerry was buzzing with e-mails from Gabby's advisors—Pia, Ron Barber, Rodd McLeod, and several consultants. They were all weighing the pros and cons of Gabby casting a vote.

The debt-ceiling bill—raising the debt limit by at least $2.1 trillion while cutting federal spending by $2.4 trillion—was an uninspiring, unpopular, concession-packed agreement; it would be safer if Gabby skipped it. She understood that voting "yes" would displease many of her constituents. She certainly recognized the complaints of Tea Party Republicans, who wanted to further rein in spending, and of liberal Democrats, who were unhappy with cuts to social-service programs. But she believed that this bill, however flawed, would need to be passed to save Social Security, Medicare, and Medicaid from immediate cuts. If it didn't pass, many companies would immediately stop hiring. Investors would flee stocks and U.S. Treasuries. The economy could collapse.

For Gabby's aides, however, the question wasn't just whether she should vote "yes" on this controversial bill. The question was should she be voting at all. They feared that pundits or political adversaries would start asking: If Gabby could show up for this vote, why wasn't she showing up for other votes? The honest answer, of course, was that this vote was by far the most critical one of the term. Though Gabby was still very much in recovery, she felt a responsibility to be there.

"Even if we explain that," Pia said, "there still could be a lot of fallout from this. I'm not sure she should do it."

I understood the trepidation of Gabby's advisors and why they were looking at the decision from all angles. They'd helped Gabby every step of her career by making smart, rational choices. But Gabby was leaning toward trusting her gut. She knew the bill was flawed but necessary. She wanted to do what she could to help the country avoid a monumental crisis. She thought she should go to Washington, and I agreed.

Before she got on the plane, though, we had to consider another question: Was her vote truly needed?

That morning, no one seemed to know for sure if the bill had enough supporters to pass it. The Democrats were going to caucus at noon Eastern Time, the Republicans at 1 p.m. By then, it would be clearer how everyone was lining up, but it would be too late for Gabby to make it to Washington for a late-afternoon or early-evening vote.

I told Pia: "Whether or not she walks onto the floor and votes, I think she needs to head to Washington. She can always hang out in her office, see how the vote is going, and then make a decision about whether to vote. But if she doesn't fly in, she won't have that option."

Pia saw the wisdom in that. "OK," she said. "How fast can Gabby get here?"

A mad scramble ensued. I quickly packed my bag and Gabby's. Then I sped around the house trying to guess what else she would want me to bring. I contacted the Capitol Police and made arrangements to get Gabby out of therapy so she could go directly to the airport. We needed a day nurse and a night nurse to join us, and I was relieved when Kristy and Kay said they could make it. There was so much to do in just a few minutes. Jen Cox, Gabby's operations director, worked her magic on the phone, coordinating airline reservations. Pia coordinated the rest. As for me, I was so busy I felt like I was in the space shuttle simulator.

I remembered to pack Gabby's official House of Representatives voting card. It's the size of a credit card with her photo on it, and without it, she wouldn't be able to use the voting station on the House floor. Luckily, the FBI had gotten it back to me; it had been in her wallet on January 8. I also brought her "112th Congress" pin, which identifies her as a member and allows her on the House floor. About the size of a quarter, Gabby was wearing it on her red suit jacket the day she was shot.

There was also the urgent matter of what Gabby would wear. All of her suits were way too big on her now. Since January 8, she had dropped from 128 pounds to 115, from a size four down to almost a size zero. If she was going to appear on the House floor, she needed something appropriate to wear. So I charged Jen with finding some clothes in D.C. Just in case, I packed for Gabby as well as I could. (If you think flying the space shuttle is dangerous, try packing for your wife.)

As Gabby and I headed to the airport—I was coming from home, she was coming from TIRR's outpatient facility—her deputy press secretary, Ashley Nash-Hahn, offered to help. Over her lunch break, she ran into a Washington mall to buy black pants and three blazers for Gabby to choose from. Ashley selected one teal blazer, another houndstooth, and a third in basic black. She found pants with a wide leg opening to accommodate the brace Gabby now wore on her right leg.

Ashley also needed to find shoes for Gabby, and buying those was a complicated task. Gabby had worn only sneakers since January 8. And because the brace on her right leg went from her knee to the tips of her toes, she needed a size 8 shoe for her left foot and a size 10 for her right. To give Gabby a few choices, and to make sure she could cobble together a pair of shoes in both sizes, Ashley came back from her shopping expedition with six boxes of shoes. She'd return whatever didn't work or fit.

As Gabby and I were heading for the airport in separate cars, my phone rang. It was Kay, the nurse, making sure I had brought Gabby's medications. I had assumed that Gabby's meds were in the bag she took to rehab each day, but I was wrong. I had to turn the car around.

Even with that mix-up, Gabby and I were able to make a 12:51 p.m. Continental Airlines flight from Houston to Washington, boarding last so we wouldn't be too conspicuous. It was Gabby's first time flying commercial since January 8, and though some passengers may have recognized her, they just nodded politely. Gabby was still in the sweatpants and sweatshirt she'd worn to rehab.

I had printed out the eight-page, section-by-section summary of the debt-ceiling bill before leaving the house, and brought it on the plane for Gabby. She studied it, line by line, and it was actually not so hard to follow. She understood the major points, and so did I. Among them: The bill saved $1 trillion over ten years, balanced between cuts to defense and non-defense spending, by capping discretionary spending. It also established a bipartisan "super committee" to achieve an additional $1.5 trillion in deficit reduction.

Gabby and I were able to watch CNN on the plane's television, and Gabby paid close attention to the speculation about whether the measure would pass. No one was sure what time the House would vote, and it was possible that Gabby would miss it while we were still on the plane.

We landed at Reagan National Airport just after 5 p.m., and voting hadn't yet begun. In case Gabby decided not to vote, almost no one knew we were coming to town. But given the magnitude of the day politically, the airport was crowded with lawmakers, House staffers, journalists. We decided Pia would quickly push Gabby through the airport, and I'd follow a couple minutes later. One of us might not be noticed. But the combination of the astronaut people had seen on TV and the short-haired woman in a wheelchair was a give-away. They'd figure out who we were and our cover would be blown.

Representative Steve Cohen, a Democrat from Tennessee, was the first person at the airport to recognize Gabby. "Gabby!" he called out.

"Steve!" she said.

He wanted Pia to stop the wheelchair so they could chat, but she told him, "Congressman Cohen. We're trying to be discreet here." He lowered his voice and they all got on the elevator together, where he and Gabby had a more private reunion.

The Capitol Police had a car waiting for us. Ashley was there, too, with the three outfits she'd bought and the six pairs of shoes, in case Gabby needed to change in the car on her way to the Capitol. When we learned that we had over an hour until the vote, we went to our hotel.

A final decision had to be made. From the hotel room, Pia led a teleconference with Gabby's trusted advisors from Tucson, Rodd and Ron, and we all went over the pros and cons of Gabby casting this vote. It now looked as if the bill would pass easily. So we looked at the long-term implications of taking a stand on a very unpopular vote. The discussion lasted a half hour. "My advice is don't do it," said Rodd. We all knew Gabby wasn't the type to take the safe or easy way out, but the general feeling was the same as Rodd's: she shouldn't do this.

Finally, with time running out, Gabby reviewed the recommendations of her staff. "It's up to you," I said finally. "You tell us what you want to do."

"Vote," Gabby said. She gave her now trademark fist pump, then added: "Let's go."

Though she couldn't fully articulate her reasoning, I knew Gabby. She'd traveled all this way. She knew her vote would have meaning beyond the final tally because people would recognize the effort she had made to come. It was her way of showing that the mechanics of government, while messy, are still vital, and that it is an honor and a responsibility to cast a vote in Congress. She thought maybe her coming to vote could be a statement about the need to break the gridlock, to resist knee-jerk partisanship, and to remember the high calling that is statesmanship. Her presence could speak to the idea of not avoiding difficult choices.

"OK," I said. "That's Gabby's decision. We're on!"

Gabby had gone through her clothing choices and selected the teal "wrap blazer" with a ruffle and a belt to tie it up. The bright color was more her style. She had two blouse options, one in turquoise and one in purple, and she chose the more modest purple one. Ashley smartly had bought loafers with traction on the soles, but Gabby looked at the shoes and wasn't sure if they'd work. She opted for the white sneakers she'd been wearing since morning rehab.

Jen, her operations director, helped put makeup on Gabby. Kristy, her nurse, used hairspray to fluff up Gabby's short hair.

Kristy thought Gabby seemed contemplative and serious. It was understandable that Gabby would be nervous, thinking about stepping into that giant room filled with more than four hundred of her colleagues. She knew they'd be measuring her progress and her ability to speak. But she also knew they'd be very welcoming and thrilled to see her. She was excited to see how everything would unfold.

We drove the two miles to the Capitol, and when we pulled up, voting had already begun. It would last only fifteen minutes total, so we needed to get moving. Gabby almost fell getting out of the car; I had to grab her arm. It was the excitement, the anticipation, the rush to get inside. I worried about how things would go for her once she got on the floor. It would be crowded. People would be approaching her. Could she stay steady on her feet?

Gabby's friends Debbie Wasserman Schultz and Adam Smith, a congressman from Washington State, were waiting for us on the curb. We all got into an elevator and headed up one floor. Standing right there when the door opened was Bill Livingood, sergeant at arms of the House.

"Livingood!" Gabby called out, with a smile, and then hugged him. (Bill would later say that there are long-standing members of Congress who don't even know his name. For Gabby to greet him so affectionately and by name was very meaningful to him.)

John Boehner was also in the hallway, and he was gracious. "Welcome back, Gabby," he said. She hugged him, too, and wisely refrained from telling him, "Stay out of my district!"

It would fall to Pia and Debbie to escort Gabby into the chamber—without a floor pass, I'd have to watch the proceedings from the Democrats' cloakroom—and I squeezed Gabby's hand goodbye and wished her luck.

Within seconds, at about 7:02 p.m., they made their way through the door and onto the floor. "Oh my God, it's Gabby Giffords!" someone said. The murmuring started at the door and then spread quickly throughout the room. Pia noticed dozens of people, Republicans and Democrats, with tears in their eyes. Within ninety seconds, the entire room was cheering, applauding, and moving in her direction.

A crowd of people surrounded Gabby. She greeted some by name. To others she said, "Good to see you" or "I missed you." She was completely poised. It was an electric moment, but Pia knew that all the good wishes and embracing would have to wait. The clock was ticking. Before the voting period ended in about four and a half minutes, Gabby would need to make her way to one of the forty-six voting stations scattered throughout the chamber.

The closest machine was about five steps away, but a mob of House members was in the way. Pia and Debbie held Gabby's arms and helped navigate. "Let Gabby through!" Debbie said in that Long Island train-conductor accent of hers. Given the crowd, it took two minutes to walk those five steps.

When Gabby reached the machine, she knew exactly what she had to do. She steadied her left hand on the voting box, which is about two inches wide and four inches long, and stuck her card into the slot. A blue button was supposed to light up, indicating the voting station was activated. The light didn't work. Before anyone could say anything, Gabby pulled out her card and tried again. This time, she got the blue-light signal to proceed.

For the next step, Gabby needed to negotiate the three other colored buttons on the box. The green button would indicate a "yea" vote, the red button "nay," and the amber button "present." Members were reaching out to lend Gabby a hand, and Debbie told them, "Back away! She can do it!" Of course she could. Gabby had voted here hundreds of times. She pressed the green button, and her "yea" vote was reported with all the others above the Speaker's dais. A moment that seemed impossible on January 8 was now a reality.

The voting continued but attention in the room was laser-focused on Gabby. Members crowded around her, everyone speaking at once. Vice President Joe Biden approached her and was very affable. "I rushed over as soon as I heard you might be here," he said.

The civil rights legend John Lewis, whom Gabby had voted for in early January to be Speaker of the House, made his way to her side. Pia saw that Gabby was thrilled by his attention. Gabby responded to him so respectfully, mindful that she was a junior member of Congress and he was a civil rights pioneer with twenty-four years of service in the House. She knew he'd been beaten almost to death during several protest marches, and that his skull had been fractured when he marched in Selma in 1965. As always, she was honored to be in his presence.

"God bless you, child," he said to her, and kissed her forehead. She put her left hand up to his cheek. When he said goodbye and turned away, he broke down crying.

Gabby was on the floor for about fifteen minutes. Then she was back in the car, headed for the hotel. She seemed completely happy on the ride, but the whole experience had drained her. "Wiped out," she said.

We all told her how proud of her we were, and she smiled.

"Gabby, you were brave to walk into that mob," I said. "I didn't expect that wave of people coming at you, but you held your own, you didn't get knocked down, and you voted! Great job, sweetie!"

"Thank you," she said. "Whew, I'm tired."

Back at the hotel, we watched the news coverage of the vote, which passed, 269 to 161. Sixty-six Republicans and ninety-five Democrats voted against it. Gabby was moved by all the attention to her appearance on the floor. Her friend Debbie Wasserman Schultz gave an interview to CNN. "All our hearts were so full," she said. "You had grizzled, hardened members with very hardened hearts, and everybody just melted when Gabby walked in the chamber. It was so incredible." Debbie spoke of jaws dropping, of tears flowing, of how partisan bickering fell away at the sight of their injured colleague.

Gabby worked the TV remote, surveying the coverage. She was pleased with what she had accomplished. "Proud of me," she said.

Then she excused herself, went into the bedroom, and napped for an hour. I went out to get us a pizza.

Photos of Gabby in the House chamber made the front page of newspapers across the nation the next morning. There were scores of editorials written about her, and Gabby's office sent me links to some of them via e-mail. One of my favorites came from *The Record,* a newspaper in northern New Jersey. I was moved while reading it to Gabby, and so was she.

The editorial began: "Finally, nobility. After months of rancor and pettiness, one small woman brought Washington to its feet. Her 'yes' vote did not affect the outcome; the bill passed by a wide margin. But for a few minutes, it changed the tenor of the debate. For that, America should be grateful."

The editorial continued: "Giffords' physical rehabilitation is far from complete. . . . We do not know how much more progress she will make or whether she will ever return to full-time duty in the House. But on Monday, she did return. Without speaking and without fiery rhetoric, she brought all of us to the same conclusion: This nation is worthy of personal sacrifice . . . We can compromise on how we fund America; we cannot compromise on how we define America. That definition does not require words. Just look at Gabrielle Giffords."

* * *

By tradition, presidents often thank astronauts for their service after a successful flight. Coincidentally, the crew of STS-134 had been invited to meet with President Obama at the White House the day after the debt-ceiling vote. Members of my crew were bringing their spouses, and naturally, I wanted Gabby to come, too. The president would be glad to see her, and I knew he'd be impressed by her progress.

"No," Gabby said. "Back to work."

What did she mean? "In Congress?" I asked.

"No, no," she said. "Rehab."

I was surprised. Given the option of visiting the president in the Oval Office and spending five hours in rehab, you'd think the choice would be obvious.

"Sweetie, you can miss one day of therapy," I said. "Your therapists will understand."

"No," Gabby said again. "Fly back for therapy."

I saw from the look on her face that she was adamant about this. Her job was to commit herself to every facet of rehab, and to get better. Improving her speech, using her arm, returning to Congress—so much hinged on that hard work. That was her foremost responsibility.

I knew there was no arguing it. "I'll tell the president that you say hello," I said, "and that you didn't want to miss rehab. He'll understand."

Gabby met with her Capitol Hill staff in the hotel conference room, and then she and Jen, along with the two nurses and her security detail, headed to the airport. I went to the White House without her.

Jen later told me about the plane ride back to Houston. Gabby watched CNN for a while and smiled whenever the news crawl at the bottom of the screen announced: "Giffords returns to House."

At one point, Gabby turned to Jen and said, "I am optimistic."

* * *

The next morning, I was at NASA headquarters in Washington, and I got an e-mail from Jen. She had accompanied Gabby to the outpatient rehab facility. She wanted me to know about an encounter Gabby had minutes earlier.

Gabby was in the waiting room before going in for rehab. She was wearing the orange zip-up that she'd worn on her last bike ride with Raoul, the night before she was shot. She didn't look like the congresswoman in the teal suit who was all over the news.

And yet, there in the waiting room, a young girl in a pink T-shirt and sweatpants recognized her. The girl had a patch over her eye and walked with a slight limp. She obviously had a weakness on one side of her body. Like Gabby, she must have been there because of a brain injury.

"I saw you on TV," the girl said. Gabby's appearance on the House floor was still being played in a steady loop on news programs.

Gabby smiled at the girl. "I try," she told her. "I will try."

The girl looked to be about nine years old, the same age as Christina-Taylor Green, who was lost on January 8. Gabby motioned for the girl to come closer, and they both took a couple of steps toward each other. Gabby gazed into the girl's face. "Beautiful!" she said, and with her left arm, she gave the girl a long hug.

The girl smiled up at her, looking thrilled. Then Gabby turned on her good left foot, took a full step with her braced right foot, and made her way slowly down the hall to the therapy room. Back to work.

CHAPTER TWENTY-THREE

Gabby's Voice

Over many nights, as this story became a book, Gabby and I read these chapters together, one at a time. She was fully engaged, weighing in on every page. She corrected imprecise anecdotes and added her memories to mine. Our hope was always that she would be able to write the final chapter in her own voice. —M.K.

* * *

Hope and faith. You have to have hope and faith.

Everything I do reminds me of that horrible day. Just rolling onto my side is hard. Hard to sleep at night. Reminds me of how badly I was hurt. It was hard but I'm alive.

Lot of people died. Six wonderful people. So many people hurt. Always connected to them.

Long ways to go. Grateful to survive. It's frustrating. Mentally hard. Hard work. I'm trying. Trying so hard to get better. Regain what I've lost. Want to speak better.

Trying to get back to work. Back to work for Arizona. Back to work for the American people. I love the people of my state. I'm so sorry I'm unable to work right now. My staff's been awesome. Been hard for them, too. They are working hard.

I want to thank all the doctors. Thank the nurses and therapists. It's been challenging. They are all special.

A whole lot of cards and letters. Thank you.

I appreciate the help of my mom and dad. Mark is an inspiration. I love them very much.

I will get stronger. I will return.

CHAPTER TWENTY-FOUR

The Journey Ahead

"I remember."

What do you remember, Gabby?

"I remember mittens, parked."

It was exactly one year from the day that Gabby and twelve others were shot and six innocent victims were murdered, and we are at the parking lot of the Safeway at the corner of Oracle and Ina in Tucson. Gabby didn't really want to return for the anniversary but I encouraged her to. I thought that there might be some sort of closure if she returned to the *very spot* that forever changed her life. We didn't tell anyone. Pia Carusone, Gabby's chief of staff, and I discussed whether it would be a good idea to let the media know. There would have been a lot of interest, and it would certainly have been a powerful moment on TV. But this had to be a private time for Gabby to reflect on the tragedy that had devastated so many lives that day.

Earlier that afternoon I had done a television interview remotely from Gabby's congressional office. After the interview the cameraman saw me jump into a car with Gabby. He didn't know that we were en route to the Safeway. We weren't aware that he had followed us until Gabby and I got out of the car in the Safeway parking lot. He appeared out of nowhere. He was respectful and didn't get too close, allowing her a little privacy. We walked around to the front of the store, and the crowd slowly grew as the shoppers recognized that familiar face and walk. We had a short conversation with the assistant store manager who had been there on January 8. Gabby took a close look at the rock garden memorial that Safeway had built at the site, and then she and I started to talk about where she had been, where the shooter had been, who was standing around her, and where she fell after the 9mm round pierced her skull. She was interested, sad and solemn. So was I. Gabby was taking it all in. She walked back and forth several times. She greeted the folks lining up around her and then she said to me, "I remember."

Most of us can't remember where we parked our car when we walk out of a store. It happens to me often. But here was Gabby, who has defied the odds, and one of the two things that she remembers from that day is where she parked. She pointed to the spot, and it was exactly one year later. Up until this day the last thing she remembered leading up to 10:10 Arizona Time on January 8, 2010, was learning of the death of her favorite waitress the night before.

The anniversary weekend was good for Gabby, good for me, and I think good for many of the remarkable people in the City of Tucson, Arizona. It was a chance for healing and closure and a moment to honor six special souls: Christina-Taylor Green, Dorwan Stoddard, Judge John Roll, Phyllis Schneck, Dorothy Morris, and Gabriel Zimmerman. Gabby had known Judge Roll for years, and Gabe was a cherished member of her staff. Gabby would never have the opportunity to meet Christina, Dorwan, Phyllis, and Dorothy.

Gabby was still in therapy six days per week, Sunday through Friday, though Sunday consisted of only one hour of music therapy. The therapy was working, and we had settled into a routine. That was why we were still living in Houston. Up at 7 A.M., out the door at 8 A.M., arrive at TIRR, and at 9 A.M., begin the sequence of physical, occupational, and speech therapy. This was followed by more speech therapy in the afternoon. The harder Gabby worked the better she got. But as we approached the anniversary it was starting to become apparent to her and to me that she wouldn't be returning to Congress. One afternoon shortly after New Year's, Gabby and I were sitting on the couch in our living room in Houston. She turned to me and simply said, "step down." It didn't take me more than a second to understand the meaning of those two words; Gabby intended to resign her seat in Congress.

We headed to Tucson for the anniversary knowing that this would be one of the last things she did as a Congresswoman with the constituents she loved so much. We arrived on Thursday afternoon, January 5, and spent much of the time with her staff and some of the families of the victims. Gabby had a short visit with Daniel Hernandez, the intern who had administered first aid and is credited with saving her life. Daniel is a big guy, and to see the two of them hug in Gabby's office was like watching a bear hug a bird.

One of the more difficult things Gabby did as we approached the anniversary was meet with the families of the victims. This is an emotional, draining experience for her. It is also a work in progress. During the Thanksgiving weekend just eleven months after the shooting, we scheduled a meeting with the Green family. Gabby was understandably nervous. John and Roxanna lost their smart and precious little girl on January 8 because she wanted to learn first-hand about democracy and meet Gabrielle Giffords. Christina never got to do that. She was shot through the chest and murdered just seconds before she was to be introduced to her congresswoman. Now Christina's parents and their son Dallas were meeting Gabby instead. It was an emotional encounter. Gabby and I expressed our grief for their loss. Christina was just the kind of kid Gabby loved to meet. She was smart, athletic, inquisitive, a force to be reckoned with. She was the star of her baseball team—no surprise, since baseball was in the Green family DNA. The meeting lasted an hour and we made a commitment to keep in touch. Gabby and I think of Christina often. It may be hard to imagine that you can miss someone you have never met. You can.

On the evening of January 8, 2012, we arrived at the University of Arizona, accompanied by more security than Gabby typically traveled with. While there were no known threats, this was one of those opportunities for another disturbed individual to violently and publicly strike out. So my tough-as-nails wife donned the bulletproof vest of perhaps the smallest member of the Tucson Police Department. With a scarf around her neck, Gabby was able to camouflage the vest. It was unfathomable to me that someone might try to harm Gabby again, but I didn't want to risk anything, and I really appreciated the extra measures taken by Gabby's Capitol Police detail, the Pima County Sheriff's Department, and the Tucson Police Department.

As Gabby took the stage in front of a crowd of thousands, I could tell that despite the sadness of the moment she felt buoyed by doing something that didn't involve either painful physical therapy or mind-jarring, frustrating speech therapy. She was once again U.S. Congresswoman Gabrielle Giffords and she was at work. That night on stage Gabby belted out the Pledge of Allegiance with few mistakes. I suspect that it might have seemed practiced, but the truth is that I had asked Gabby a few weeks earlier if she could recite it, and I needed only to get her started with the first word, "I." I had checked one more time the day before to see if she had suddenly forgotten but she was good to go. I can't say that I've ever been more thrilled to hear those words and reflect on what they stand for. I loved her so much.

The return to Houston was difficult. Gabby had endless therapy ahead, but the looming resignation took the hope out of it. Before she made the decision to resign, Gabby's goal was to get back to work this Congressional term. Now she felt she had nothing. It was hard emotionally for Gabby, but it was also a relief. Now Gabby could do this at her new pace.

Gabby and Pia and I wanted a face-to-face with Gabby's key staff and consultants to discuss the best way for her to resign, so everyone came to Houston. Her announcement had to be thought-out and planned because of her high profile and her position as a Democrat from a traditionally Republican district. She certainly couldn't just send a resignation letter to Speaker John Boehner. A few of Gabby's trusted advisors argued that Gabby should finish out the remaining ten months of her term and then retire. In this scenario there would be no special election and Gabby's congressional staff would remain in their jobs until January 2013. Gabby heard all sides of the issue and then made her decision. She was acutely aware that the people of District Eight had been without their congresswoman since three days after her term began. She had complete faith that Pia and her staff were doing a superb job. But only Gabby had been elected. She would resign as soon as we could figure out how to do it as smoothly as possible.

Every President since Woodrow Wilson has delivered the State of the Union address as a speech in front of both chambers of Congress, the President's Cabinet, the Supreme Court Justices, and the military leadership. Before Wilson, the State of the Union was delivered as a handwritten report from the president. Gabby arrived in Washington, D.C., on January 24, the day before the State of the Union, and I came in the next morning. I had been invited to sit in the president's box, and I was surprised and honored to see that I was seated between Dr. Jill Biden and the first lady (not necessarily the best place for me when the first lady would certainly be wearing heels and had about six inches on me in flats). I chatted with Dr. Biden briefly and with Laurene Powell (Steve Jobs's wife), who was sitting directly behind me. Gabby and Laurene are acquaintances, but I had never met her.

I heard a rumble in the crowd and assumed that the president and first lady had arrived. It was Gabby, and for what seemed like minutes everyone in the chamber gave her a standing ovation. Gabby was seated between Congressmen Raul Grijalva and Jeffrey Flake, who are both from Arizona. Though a Republican, Jeff Flake took on the primary responsibility of helping Gabby to her feet during the President's remarks. Applause during the state of the union is ritualistic and well planned. Members of the party in opposition to the president remain seated with their hands firmly planted in their laps when members of the president's party stand and clap. Jeff very graciously rose to help Gabby when Democrats stood to applaud, and he was the sole Republican on his feet on numerous occasions during President Obama's speech.

The next day was a bummer. Gabby would resign from Congress that morning. It was an emotional day. As we left the hotel for Capitol Hill, Gabby said she was "down in the dumps." Spouses are not permitted on the floor of the House of Representatives, so I proceeded up the long winding staircase to the gallery to watch this phase of Gabby's political career come to a close. As long as I've known Gabby she has held elected office. First in the Arizona Senate and then in Congress. For the first time in ten years, she would have no constituents, and she felt sad and unmoored. Gabby entered the chamber with Pia. The Speaker of the House, John Boehner, formally recognized the reason for this assembly—Gabby's resignation—and then he invited members to speak about their colleague. Eric Cantor, the Republican majority leader, gave an impassioned speech about Gabby. He also spoke glowingly about Pia, Gabby's chief of staff, who did a truly remarkable job for twelve uncertain months, handling every detail and guiding a congressional office in mourning over a direly injured boss. It occurred to me during Cantor's speech that if Pia were ever to run for office herself, it would certainly be as a Democrat, and she now had a great endorsement from the well-respected Republican majority leader, Eric Cantor, to use in a campaign ad.

Gabby's good friend Debbie Wasserman Schultz spoke eloquently. Holding back tears she said, "I am so proud of my friend, and it will always be one of the great treasures of my life to have met Gabby Giffords and to have served with her in this body." Then with Gabby standing beside her at the podium, before hundreds of members of the House, Debbie read Gabby's resignation letter:

"In 2001, strongly holding the belief that there is no higher calling than serving my country, I went from selling tires in my Tucson family business to being a freshman representative in the Arizona State House, and for ten years I served in the Arizona Legislature, in the United States Congress, and after marrying Mark as a proud military spouse, always, I fought for what I thought was right. But never did I question the character of those with whom I disagreed. Never did I let pass an opportunity to join hands with someone just because he or she held different ideals.

"In public service, I found a venue for my pursuit of a stronger America, by ensuring the safety and security of all Americans, by producing clean energy here at home instead of importing oil from abroad, and by honoring our brave men and women in uniform with the benefits that they earned. I found a way to care for others and in the past year I have found a value that is unbreakable even by the most vicious of attacks.

"The tragic January 8 shooting in Tucson took the lives of six beautiful Americans and wounded thirteen others, me included. Not a day goes by that I don't feel grief for the lives lost and so many others torn apart. Christina-Taylor Green, Dorothy Morris, John Roll, Phyllis Schneck, Dorwan Stoddard, and Gabe Zimmerman embodied the best of America. Each in their own way, they committed their lives to serving their families, community, and country and they died performing a basic but important act of citizenship that's at the heart of our greatness as a nation. They will always be remembered, always. They will be remembered always—by their country and by their Congress.

"I don't remember much from that terrible day but I have never forgotten my constituents, my colleagues, or the millions of Americans with whom I share great hopes for this nation—to all of them, thank you for your prayers, your cards, your well wishes, and your support. And even as I have worked to regain my speech, thank you for your faith and my ability to be your voice. The only way I ever served my district in Congress was by giving 100 percent. This past year that's what I have given to my recovery. Thank you for your patience. From my first steps and first words after being shot to my current physical and speech therapy, I have given all of myself to being able to walk back onto the House floor this year to represent Arizona's Eighth Congressional District.

"However, today I know that now is not the time. I have more work to do on my recovery before I can again serve in elected office. This past year my colleagues and staff have worked to make sure my constituents were represented in Congress, but if I can't return, my district deserves to elect a U.S. Representative who can give 100 percent to the job now. For that reason, I have submitted the attached letter of resignation to Arizona governor Jan Brewer. Amid all that was lost on January 8, there was also hope and faith. This past year it is what I have often clung to. Hope that our government can represent the best of a nation, not the worst. Faith that Americans working together in their communities and our Congress can succeed without qualification. Hope and faith that even as we are set back by tragedy or profound disagreement, in the end, we come together as Americans to set a course toward greatness. Every day I am working hard. I will recover and will return and we will work together again for Arizona and for all Americans."

Then Gabby walked up the stairs to Speaker Boehner to hand him her letter of resignation. She stumbled once. Noticeably emotional, the Speaker gave Gabby a kiss on the cheek and a hug good-bye. It was done.

Within minutes, the criticism began, from both sides of the aisle. Many of the Republican bloggers who had called for her resignation immediately reversed course and accused Gabby of wasting taxpayer dollars by forcing a special election. On the other side of the political spectrum were some Democrats whose sole focus was to ensure a congressional majority for their party. They were equally unhappy. Gabby's congressional district was a Republican-performing district. That means that more voters tended to vote for the Republican candidate than the Democrat. In the 2010 election cycle, Gabby held on to her congressional seat by 4,156 votes. Many believed that no Democrat could win now, and they took it out on Gabby. Then there was Vice President Joe Biden. On the morning of Gabby's announcement, I spoke to the vice president. I told him how there were Democratic colleagues of Gabby's who were unhappy with Gabby for putting her seat at risk, for likely turning it over to the Republican party. The vice president's response was loud and clear. He said, "Gabby needs to do the right thing for her but also for her constituents; all of them. You tell those folks to go to hell. And you can tell them I said so."

We visited Gabby's congressional office one last time early that afternoon, and then returned to the hotel. It was one of the lower points of Gabby's new life. Being elected to the U.S. House of Representatives is no small task. Gabby worked tirelessly in the Arizona House and Senate and then, when given the opportunity, she worked hard to represent Southern Arizona at the national level. Now it was over and those days were behind us. Part of her felt that she had let folks down, and that maybe if she had worked harder on her therapy she would have remained in office. As the person closest to her, I can certainly attest that no one could have worked harder than Gabby. She gave recovery her best as she had given service to Arizona her best, and I was proud of her. But it was not a happy day.

Raymond Edwin "Ray" Maybus is the former governor of Mississippi, former ambassador to Saudi Arabia, and current Secretary of the Navy. The afternoon that Gabby resigned from Congress he called me. I put him on speaker-phone and he told Gabby and me that he had decided to name a navy ship after the former representative from Arizona. The USS *Gabrielle Giffords* would be the tenth ship in a class of new vessels called a Littoral Combat Ship. LCS-10 would be a stealthy surface combat vessel designed to operate close to shore. The USS *Gabrielle Giffords* is scheduled to go into service in 2015 if her construction proceeds as planned. Roxanna Green, Christina-Taylor's mom, was invited to be the ship's sponsor. She will be actively involved with the ship's crew from the laying of the ship's keel until the vessel's retirement many decades from now. I welcomed Secretary Maybus's decision to name this ship after Gabby. Gabby served on the Armed Services Committee and her spirit of courage and resilience in the face of overwhelming obstacles resonates with the navy. At the time of her injury, and for all the years we've been married, Gabby was also the only military spouse serving in Congress. I've served on active duty for over twenty-five years in the United States Navy. The navy is tough, but so is Gabby, and I'm certain that sailors for the next four or five decades will be proud to serve aboard the USS *Gabrielle Giffords*.

Gabby often reflects on those killed and injured January 8, 2011. While she has the luxury of not remembering the bloodshed the day she was shot, she now understands how many people died. She often also reflects on her future and ours together as well. She looks forward to the day when her body catches up to her mind again, when the work of all the extraordinary people involved in her survival and recovery is over. She looks forward to her return to her old interests and commitments and to new ones. Gabby was born to be a public servant and I've served our nation in the U.S. Navy and at NASA for over twenty-five years. Our future certainly will involve service again. While we are not sure what form that will take, we do know that it is out there, somewhere. Only time will tell when and where, but we'll be back in the Arizona that we both love so much.

ACKNOWLEDGMENTS

Writing this book and telling our story were not easy for Gabby or for me. We each had difficulty reliving the shooting and the challenges that followed January 8.

This book would not have been possible without our families. Gabby's parents, Gloria and Spencer, left their home in Tucson for over seven months to be here with Gabby and me as she navigated the long and difficult road known as rehabilitation. They have supported us every step of the way and continue to do that today. My parents, Patricia and Richard, gave me the strength I needed to get through this tragedy. They've always reminded me that I could do or overcome anything. My brother and best friend, Scott, despite my being two hundred and fifty miles up in space, became a sounding board when I had decisions to make. Gabby's sister, Melissa, spent hours at her bedside at the University Medical Center. Our daughters, Claudia and Claire, were with us on January 8 and have been with us throughout this long ordeal. Raoul Erickson, who is like a brother to Gabby, made multiple trips to Houston just to make sure she was eating all of her peas. Raoul would do anything for Gabby.

We deeply appreciate everything that Suzy Gershman has done for us over the years. We met her when we hired her to be our wedding planner in 2007 and she became a friend, planning everything else ever since. We're not sure where this family would be without Suzy. Many, many thanks to Tilman and Paige Fertitta who are two of the most generous people in the world. Without their assistance this entire experience would have been far more difficult.

We could not have been better served by Gabby's staff. Pia Carusone, Gabby's chief of staff, is extraordinarily dedicated and loyal. She became a trusted partner and friend to me while getting her boss through this horrible ordeal. We could not have managed without her. Gabby's district director, Ron Barber, was injured as he stood by her side on January 8, yet continued to do his job while recovering in the ICU. I will never forget seeing Ron on a conference call with Gabby's staff from his ICU bed just days after being shot in the face and leg. That is the definition of service.

Rodd McLeod, Gabby's longtime campaign manager and friend, put his life and future on hold to make sure that Gabby's constituents were properly served while she and Ron Barber recovered. He held her district office together. We also need to thank Jen Cox who has been with Gabby from the beginning of her first congressional campaign and we hope and pray will never leave. Jen is the person Gabby trusts with the most personal details of her life. She is irreplaceable.

Pam Simon is the kind of employee who, you could say, would "take a bullet for her boss," and that is exactly what she did. Pam, we thank you for your service to Gabby and to this country. We also want to thank Dr. David Bowman, Nancy Bowman, Dr. David Beal, Anna Ballis, and Gabby's intern, Daniel Hernandez, who administered first aid to Gabby and the other victims. And thanks go out to Gabby's staff members Mark Kimble and Sara Humel Rajca, and her intern Alex Villec, who were at the Congress on Your Corner event on January 8 and were put in harm's way serving their country. I took much comfort in knowing that Gabby had a trusted spokesperson in C.J. Karamargin who worked tirelessly to speak on Gabby's behalf, when she couldn't, over these many months.

Thirteen people were shot on January 8 and survived. Gabby was honored that they came to participate in the democratic process that morning, and they remain in our thoughts and prayers. Besides Pam Simon and Ron Barber, they are: Bill Badger, Kenneth Dorushka, James Fuller, Randy Gardner, Suzi Hileman, George Morris, Mary Reed, Mavy Stoddard, James Tucker, and Kenneth Veeder. Gabby and I are relieved that they all seem to be recovering well.

All of us can only hope that if we're incapacitated, our team will rise to the occasion and press on with the mission. Gabby's Washington,

D.C., office did just that. Thank you to Lauren Alfred, Peter Ambler, Gavi Begtrup, Sean Coit, Jim Dennany, Emily Fritze, Ashley Nash-Hahn, Major Josh Koslov USAF, Larry Meinert, Elaine Ulrich and all of the interns for holding down the fort.

Nothing is more important to Gabby than serving her constituents. In Gabby's absence, her Arizona staff continued to work for the people of Arizona's 8th Congressional District. Thank you to Tom Alston, Dan Frey, Sean Goslar, Pam Harrington, Joni Jones, Amanda Sapir, Shay Saucedo, and Patty Valera. And thank you to Molly Allen, Jamie Gershberg, Linda Quinn, Elena Ruiz, Jessica Schultz, and Hayley Zachary, who have labored to make sure that Gabby is ready to run for reelection in 2012. Their effort, along with the help of Gabby's Finance Committee and Joan Kaye Cauthorn, has been critical to Gabby's political career. We thank them for their dedication. We'd also like to thank Andrew Floyd, Steve Gershman, and Gary Jones. Spouses of Gabby's supporters and staff, they have gone above and beyond for us.

We also need to thank those folks who rushed into the maelstrom to help in any possible way and continue to do so today. Thank you to Lynne Abbuhl, Liz Berry, Melissa Blaustein, Daniel Graver, Anne Hilby, Michael Hill, Maura Policelli, Danielle Raines, Melissa Rasowsky, Colin Reischl, Caryn Schenewerk, Brittni Storrs, and the dozens of other former staffers who descended on Tucson to assist Gabby and memorialize their friend Gabe.

We benefited from the expertise of Gabby's political team: Jennifer Bluestein, Jim Crounse, Peggy Egan, Anna Greenberg, Jason Ralston, and Dave Walker. In difficult times it is so important to get great advice from smart and trusted people.

When Gabby first decided to run for national office one of the first people she contacted was Michael McNulty. Michael, the son of former Congressman Jim McNulty, is Gabby's Campaign Chairman and a trusted advisor. He has been with her every step of the way. We thank him for that.

Gabby also wants to thank her business and political mentors. As a young CEO, Gabby reached out to Dorothy Finley, who was there for her, and has been ever since. The late Arizona State Senator Andy

ACKNOWLEDGMENTS

Nichols guided Gabby during her early career in state government, and Fred Duval helps her today.

On that tragic day, all of the victims were very fortunate to have a level-one trauma center and a great hospital in the University Medical Center (UMC). I took great comfort in knowing an experienced Navy trauma surgeon was managing Gabby's care in Tucson. Dr. Peter Rhee, Captain, U.S. Navy, was crucial to Gabby's survival. Go Navy! We would also like to thank Dr. Randy Friese, who first treated Gabby when she arrived in the emergency room and traveled with her to Houston after she was discharged. We deeply appreciate the incredible job done by Gabby's neurosurgeons Mike Lemole and Marty Weinand, who performed multiple surgical procedures on Gabby during her two-week stay at UMC. Gabby's nurses at the ICU were just amazing. These dedicated professionals are the unsung heroes of the medical community. Nursing staffers, including Tracy Culbert, Amanda Berner, and Joshua Coleman, spent two weeks caring for Gabby around the clock. They were impressive to watch. Gabby and the other victims benefited from the hands-on management of UMC CEO Kevin Burns, who paid close attention to every detail of their treatment. From the top administrators to the supportive folks who worked in the cafeteria or at the front desk, this was a very special group, perfect representatives of the caring citizens of the City of Tucson. We thank them for their tireless efforts.

As the events of January 8 unfolded, the Tucson Police and Fire Departments, Pima County Sheriff's Department, and the City of Tucson all quickly flew into action. We want to personally thank Tucson Police Chief Roberto Villaseñor, Assistant Chief John Leavitt, Tucson Fire Chief Patrick Kelly, Sheriff Clarence Dupnick, and Mayor Bob Walkup. We want to thank U.S. Marshall David Gonzales for the help he provided to Gabby's staff and to us, and we're also grateful to former U.S. Attorney Dennis Burke and his staff, who assisted the victims and their families and kept us informed about the criminal proceedings. We want to thank the woman who married us and comforted Gabby while she was in the ICU in Tucson and later in Houston: Rabbi Stephanie Aaron.

In Houston an equally talented and professional team of doctors and nurses handled Gabby's care. Her neurosurgeon, Dr. Dong Kim, became a great friend, advocate, and cheerleader for Gabby. He left no detail overlooked and, on May 18, 2011, performed what we expect to be her final neurosurgery with the assistance of Dr. Brian Oh. We thank them for their professionalism, optimism, and dedication to their patient. We also want to thank Dr. Imo Aisiku, who managed Gabby's care while she was in the ICU at Memorial Hermann hospital and frequently checked on her at TIRR. Doctors Gerard Francisco and Jacob Joseph saw Gabby every single day and managed her rehabilitation through the many months at TIRR Memorial Hermann. They did an outstanding job and were instrumental in her speedy recovery. They continue to follow her closely today and we thank them for that. As in Tucson, Gabby's nurses at TIRR were very, very special people. We appreciate all they did for her around the clock. Gabby immediately connected with her nurses Adrian Baines, Deanna Bennett, Darlene Clayton, Vivian Lim, Cynthia Madriz, Pam Martin, Aubrey Murray, Kristy Poteet, and Marcia Turner. We are forever grateful for what they did and continue to do for her, especially Kristy Poteet and Vivian Lim, who remained committed to Gabby's recovery after she left TIRR. We also want to thank nurses Lesia Coco, Theresa Gambrell, Lita Harris, Kay Keyes, and Leslie Lacy. Speech pathologists Angie Glenn and Kelley Warren spent hundreds of hours working with Gabby to retrieve her language skills and her ability to speak and to enable her to enter the chamber of the U.S. House of Representatives and communicate with her colleagues. Gabby has much more work to do, but they truly showed her the way. Gabby's physical therapists Lisa Hartmann, Dawn Phillips, and Nova Sbrusch, with the help of Willie Wilmore, worked so hard to get her up and moving again. Gabby's music therapist, Meagan Morrow, kept Gabby's brain lighting up with her voice, music, positive attitude, and great smile. We thank these formidably talented and dedicated therapists. We also want to thank Gabby's neuropsychologist, Jerome Caroselli, who earned our deep appreciation despite all of the testing that Gabby just hated. And thanks to Amber Gray, the TIRR social worker who spent as much time with the family as she did with Gabby. Dan Wolterman, the CEO of Memorial Hermann, did everything he could to make sure that the transition to his hospital was smooth. TIRR's compassionate CEO, Carl Josehart, made our experience at TIRR a positive one. He became a trusted counselor to Gabby, and to me. The TIRR outpatient facility at Kirby-Glen became Gabby's full-time workplace after her discharge from the hospital. She was fortunate to have a great staff there as well. We want to thank Sandra Lloyd, Amber Armstead, Jean-Marie Berliner, Kris Conley, Imelda De La Garza, Megan Ford, Dr. Cullen Gibbs, Regina Martheio, Laura Martin, and Melanie Molinaro. To everyone at TIRR, we appreciate all you did for us and our families. One of the biggest obstacles Gabby deals with is communication. It is getting better daily thanks to the continued hard work of her team of speech pathologists: Nancy Estabrooks, Diana Christiana, Indi Feustel, Traci Kurkowski, and Becky Saterbak. We also want to personally thank Michelle Beardmore at the U.S. Department of Labor and Sierrah McDonald and Theresa Pena at Maxim Healthcare Services for all of their assistance.

We also want to thank Gabby's colleagues in Congress, especially Kirsten Gillibrand, Adam Smith, and Debbie Wasserman Schultz, whose support continues to mean the world to us each and every day. It has been very helpful in her recovery to know that she is missed on Capitol Hill and that these friendships are something special. As Gabby continues to recuperate, it is reassuring to know that her team can turn to smart and effective members of Congress who can help make sure that the district's issues and needs are being met. We also want to thank Congressman David Schweikert. Though Gabby doesn't know him well, he has been a real friend to her in her time of need.

Gabby also received help from Congressman Ted Poe of Texas who, despite a difference in party and politics, was willing to help Gabby with an issue she cares deeply about—border security. He is a good friend. We also want to thank Gabby's friend and colleague, Congressman Jeff Flake, who drove from Phoenix on the day of the shooting so he could be of service. Thanks also to Nancy Pelosi and Democratic Whip Steny Hoyer for their genuine concern and thoughtfulness. John Lawrence, the chief-of-staff to Leader Pelosi, has been a trusted friend and advisor to both of us. We appreciate his friendship and support. We want to thank the officers of the Capitol Police security detail who have been with Gabby since the day she was injured. Senator Kay Bailey Hutchinson and her Houston office provided us with logistic and office help during Gabby's stay at TIRR. We are very grateful for all of Gabby's friends on Capitol Hill. We have received so many cards, letters, e-mails, and phone calls of encouragement. Gabby is really looking forward to getting back to work.

I also want to personally thank President Barack Obama and Admiral Mike Mullen, former Chairman of the Joint Chiefs, for calling frequently, checking on Gabby and me and offering their assistance during the weeks after Gabby was injured.

I could not have returned to my role as the commander of space shuttle *Endeavour*'s final flight without the support of so many people at NASA. To my crew members, Greg Johnson, Mike Fincke, Roberto Vittori, Drew Feustel, and Greg Chamitoff, thanks for having the confidence in me and standing by me when I returned to training after being away for over a month. Thanks for working hard and being a stellar team. We also want to thank their spouses: Cari Johnson, Renita Fincke, Valeria Vittori, Indi Feustel, and Chantal Caviness, who helped us in every way they could. To my Flight Directors Gary Horlacher, Derek Hassman, Richard Jones, and Tony Ceccaci, thanks for all of the hard work and support. This was an incredible team effort and your leadership was instrumental to the success of STS-134. I am grateful to C.J. Sturckow for selflessly filling in for me as mission commander during the early days after Gabby was injured. And to all of the folks who worked on space shuttle *Endeavour* and got it ready for its final flight, thank you for giving us an incredible spacecraft that got us safely to the International Space Station and back to Earth sixteen days later. I also appreciate the support of my flight surgeon and friend, Dr. Joe Dervay, NASA psychologist Dr. Walt Sipes, flight surgeon Rick Senter, and the flight medicine office led by Dr. J.D. Polk. I could not have completed this mission without your support. Thanks also to Beth Turner, Kelly Curtis, our STS-134 family escorts, and the astronaut family support office for all of the help they provided both in Houston and at the Kennedy Space Center in Florida. I also appreciate the help of NASA Administrator Charlie Bolden. Leadership begins at the top and it was nice to know that Gabby and I had a friend in Charlie. Thanks to my boss and astronaut classmate, Dr. Peggy Whitson, whose confidence in me during these trying times was greatly appreciated. And a special thanks goes out to my colleague Piers Sellers who immediately flew to Tucson on the day that Gabby was injured and stayed by my side to help in every way possible until the day I returned from space. He has a big heart and has been a great friend to both of us.

We are all forever grateful to our friends Amber and Steve Mostyn, who were so generous in assisting Gabby's parents while they were in Houston. We want to thank our friends Ron and Carmel Garan who provided help to Gabby's staff. I am personally indebted to Katherine Jacobsen for all of the help she provided me in taking over the management of Gabby's personal affairs. The paperwork alone would have been a nightmare without her.

This is the first book I have been involved with. It has been a great experience, though difficult at times. I'm thankful, every day, that we selected Jeff Zaslow to collaborate with us on this project. I really enjoyed the countless hours I spent discussing our story with Jeff, and the process of putting the words on paper. I've come to appreciate the time and effort needed to write a book. This certainly would not have been the same book with any other collaborator. I truly appreciate Jeff's passion and drive to help deliver something very special. We also thank Jeff's wife, Sherry Margolis; agent, Gary Morris; and researcher, Korey Tucker, for their helpful input on the manuscript.

Many thanks to our attorney Bob Barnett for his sound advice and guidance through this process. Nan Graham, our editor, and Susan Moldow, our publisher, at Scribner have been great to work with as well. They've been positive and encouraging but had just the right touch in propelling Jeff and us forward. We also are indebted to many others at Simon & Schuster, including: Brian Belfiglio, Elisa Shokoff, Paul Whitlatch, Roz Lippel, Rex Bonomelli, Daniel Burgess, Mia Crowley, Erich Hobbing, and CEO Carolyn Reidy. Great thanks to all of you for your help with this project.

We also want to thank Brad Holland, who has been taking care of Gabby's place and her new fish while she's been recovering in Houston. We value his friendship. Marc Winkelman has been a constant presence and makes Gabby happy with every visit or phone call. Then there are all of our friends who have touched our lives in many ways.

We could not name all of them here and I am certain I overlooked many I should have included. But you know who you are, and please know that we both appreciate your support and are forever grateful.

Finally, many thanks go out to Gabby's Cactus Roots. These are all of her supporters around the country, and we've come to consider them part of our family. They have sent tens of thousands of cards and letters and every one of them is special to Gabby and to me.

Thank you!

Gabby: A Story of Courage, Love, and Resilience

Gabrielle Giffords and Mark Kelly

Introduction

Congresswoman Gabrielle Giffords and astronaut Mark Kelly found in each other a steadfast commitment to public service, a deep curiosity about the world around them, and a shared passion for adventure. At their wedding in 2007, Robert Reich toasted "to a bride who moves at a velocity that exceeds that of anyone else in Washington, and to a groom who moves at a velocity that exceeds seventeen thousand miles per hour." On January 8, 2011, Gabby survived a horrific shooting that left six people dead and thirteen wounded at a Congress on Your Corner event in Tucson, Arizona. Her life and Mark's were changed forever.

Gabby: A Story of Courage, Love, and Resilience takes readers into the lives of this extraordinary couple—the influences that molded their passions in childhood, their professional triumphs, their family and friendships, and their marriage. Anchoring the book is the profoundly inspiring story of Gabby's recovery, a testament to enduring love, courage, and hope.

Topics & Questions for Discussion

1. Doctors, nurses, therapists, friends, colleagues, family—seemingly the whole nation—rallied to the cause of Gabby's recovery. Why do you think Gabby's recovery became a cause that brought different kinds of people together?

2. After witnessing the Tucson shootings and Gabby's medical progress through the filter of the media, what was it like to hear Mark and Gabby's side of the story? What surprised you?

3. Gabby loved the mission of her alma mater Scripps College, written by Ellen Browning Scripps, which stated that the school aimed to develop in students "the ability to think clearly and independently, and the ability to live confidently, courageously and hopefully" (p. 78). In what ways does Gabby exemplify this mission statement?

4. Mark writes that, at thirty, Gabby was finally prepared to run for elected office: "She was now the candidate Gabrielle Giffords and she was ready to serve" (p. 86). What do you think makes someone "ready to serve"? What life experiences and personal qualities seem to influence Gabby's identity as a politician?

5. How did Mark's training as an astronaut help him navigate Gabby's recovery process? What facets of Gabby's recovery were initially unfamiliar to Mark? Have you ever been placed in a caretaker position?

6. Mark says that being an astronaut is like picking one card out of a deck: "Imagine that I offered you a million dollars if you pick any of the fifty-two cards except the ace of spades . . . But the deal would be: If you pick the ace of spades, you'd lose your life" (p. 132). Would you risk your life for the opportunity to travel to space? Do you consider yourself a risk-taker? Reflect on the biggest risk you have ever taken in your personal life. What was the outcome?

7. Mark writes, "I know the magnitude of what it means to use destructive force against people . . . Much of it is beyond senseless,

like the gunman's rampage in Tucson. But even violence with a purpose—including my missions in the skies over Iraq—requires solemn reflection" (pp. 99–100). Do you agree with Mark's statement? Compare and contrast the violence of war with the Tuscon shooting.

8. Gabby's recovery is ongoing, but the progress she has made so far is nothing short of miraculous. Through media coverage of her experience, many of us learned for the first time about the incredibly slow and arduous work involved in overcoming brain trauma and the number of people involved—from surgeons to speech therapists to dedicated family. Do you know or know of people who have suffered this kind of injury? Do you have more appreciation of the medical and therapeutic communities having read this book?

9. Mark describes Gabby's discomfort with the increasingly violent rhetoric in politics in the years and months leading up to the shooting. In the 2010 race for Gabby's seat, Gabby's opponent Jesse Kelly invited supporters to pay fifty dollars to shoot an automatic M16, encouraged the shooters to "help remove Gabrielle Giffords from office," and promised to "Get on Target for Victory in November" (pp. 154–55). Sarah Palin's PAC website showed a map with a gun sight over Gabby's district, and Palin tweeted: "Don't Retreat, Instead—RELOAD!" (p. 153). What do you make of this rhetoric? Are statements like this harmless political bluster, or do you think they could have played a role in the Tucson shooting?

10. Reflect on the chapter of the book written in Gabby's own words. What one word or phrase do you think best describes Gabby?

Enhance Your Book Club

1. Gabby and Mark have dedicated their lives to public service. Honor their commitments with your book club by picking a worthy cause and volunteer together for an afternoon. For inspiration and direction, consider the following issues that Gabby and Mark

championed: environmentalism, supporting young women in politics, health care advocacy for war veterans, promoting science and exploration in education, immigration. If any other causes described in *Gabby* struck a chord with you and your book club, research how to get involved in your own community.

2. It's one thing to read about Gabrielle's progress in *Gabby*; it's another thing to see how far she's come. As Gabby wrote herself, "To understand something, you have to see it" (p. 158). Watch some of the online clips of Gabby and Mark's interview with Diane Sawyer on a special edition of *20/20* and discuss your impressions and observations afterward. What aspects of Gabby's recovery surprised you? What moments did you find particularly inspiring? How did the clips enhance your understanding of Gabby's recovery? You can watch the entire interview online here: abc.go.com/watch/2020/SH559026/VD55153303/gabby-giffords—mark-kelly-courage-and-hope.

3. As Gabby's doctors repeatedly explained to Mark, no two brain injuries are alike, and no two patients will recover in the same way. Visit the "Cognitive Skill of the Brain" section on the Brain Injury Association of Utah's website at www.biau.org/what/what_cognitive.html, where you'll find an interactive map of the human brain. Click on each section of the brain and read the descriptions with your book club members. Can you identify the areas in which Gabby was injured? How does this information enhance your understanding of the medical issues Gabby faced, and still faces, in her recovery?

ABOUT THE AUTHORS

A third-generation Arizonan, **Gabrielle Giffords** represented Arizona's 8th Congressional District in the U.S. House of Representatives from 2007 until 2012. She served on the House Armed Services Committee and was the ranking member of the Committee on Science, Space, and Technology's Subcommittee on Space and Aeronautics. A graduate of Scripps College, she has a master's degree from Cornell University. She was a Fulbright Scholar in Mexico and a fellow at Harvard University's John F. Kennedy School of Government.

Mark Kelly was a captain in the United States Navy when he commanded the final mission of space shuttle *Endeavour* in May 2011. A veteran of four space flights to the International Space Station, he is a graduate of the U.S. Merchant Marine Academy and holds a master's degree from the U.S. Naval Postgraduate School. As a naval aviator he flew thirty-nine combat missions in Operation Desert Storm in 1991.

Wall Street Journal columnist **Jeffrey Zaslow** was the coauthor, with Randy Pausch, of *The Last Lecture,* the #1 *New York Times* bestseller now translated into forty-eight languages. His other bestsellers include *The Girls from Ames,* and as coauthor, *Highest Duty,* with Captain Chesley "Sully" Sullenberger.